NUMBER 84

Yale French Studies

Boundaries: Writing & Drawing

Yale French Studies

Martine Reid, *Special editor for this issue*
Liliane Greene, *Managing editor*
Editorial board: Denis Hollier (Chair), Peter Brooks,
   Shoshana Felman, Françoise Jaouën, Christopher
   Miller, Kevin Newmark, Charles Porter, Dominique
   Thomas, Richard Watts
Staff: Noah Guynn
Editorial office: 82-90 Wall Street, Room 308.
Mailing address: 2504A-Yale Station, New Haven,
   Connecticut 06520.
Sales and subscription office:
   Yale University Press, 92A Yale Station
   New Haven, Connecticut 06520
   Published twice annually by Yale University Press

Designed by James J. Johnson and set in Trump
Medieval Roman by The Composing Room of
Michigan, Inc. Printed in the United States of America
by the Vail Ballou Press, Binghamton, N.Y.

ISSN 044-0078
ISBN for this issue 0-300-05836-5

MARTINE REID

Editor's Preface: Legible/Visible

From the field of literature has come the question of the relationship between the written text and its timid counterpart, problematical opposite, and unacknowledged twin: drawing.

We do not wish to renew yet again the debate on text and image, but rather to concentrate reflection here on a point which is both obvious and obscure, which leaves some indifferent and yet is a sore point for others: a sort of blind spot which literary discourse has long neglected because of its apparently unquestioned desire to ensure that its own specific identity remain intact. But that desire has, perhaps, prevented it from inquiring, as it should, into the nature of the boundaries that such an identity necessarily implies, the reasons for their existence, and to what extent they can be crossed.

An answer to this question, which others too have raised, has gradually been formulated: it is a many-faceted, polymorphous reply the sole aim of which is to open up the paradoxical limbo that is the theme of this collection to the innumerable questions posed.

Thus it is that, after various opening remarks, reference will be made to the gesture of writing itself, to typography and to the absence of color which is a feature common to both the printed word and to the graphic representation that accompanies it. More specific analyses will follow which discuss the point of convergence between writing and representation in Stendhal, Verlaine, and a few others, Proust, Valéry, and Artaud. Finally, a few solutions devised by contemporary artists to reconcile writing and drawing will be mentioned.

In the sixties, literary criticism traded in the term *literature* for those of *text* and *poetics*. The author, as Barthes stated and many

YFS 84, *Boundaries: Writing & Drawing*, ed. M. Reid, © 1994 by Yale University.

others repeated after him, was dead.[1] For its part, literature too, and the *Nouveau Roman* in particular, was moving in the same direction, refusing commonly accepted authority, (auto)biography, character and decor, realism and reference alike. (The early writings of Robbe-Grillet and Ricardou are excellent examples of this.) The result was a certain terrorism which boldly rejected Sainte-Beuve and, in his wake, a host of persnickety successors, while casting aside any notion of history (whether it be that of the text or that of the author) and resolutely deciding to pay attention only to the text itself. It seemed that from then on the text was doomed to speak only of itself, an independent material serving as an intermediary between the author—now to be completely ignored—and the reader, who was just beginning to attract attention: "the birth of the reader must be paid for by the death of the author," wrote Barthes (Barthes, 67).

With the reevaluation of the contribution made by the structuralists, the end of the seventies saw the confirmation of a precise evolution in at least two separate directions. First, the notion of the "text" was broadened considerably. Genette summed up the result of several years of hesitant fumbling, particularly with regard to lexical considerations, with the suggestion that to the concept of textuality should be added those of *transtextuality* (to include *intertextuality*), *metatextuality, paratextuality,* and *architextuality.* In other words, "everything which establishes an obvious or discreet relation [of the text] with other texts."[2] He thus reestablished, in particular where transtextuality and architextuality are concerned, the relevance of raising questions concerning history and chronology, and finally put an end to the notion of the Text in proud isolation.

It was then that textual genetics came into being. Louis Hay stated in a recapitulative article that "[t]he method of textual genetics has emerged from a mass of empirical studies devoted to authors' manuscripts. This research has gradually made it clear that, under certain conditions, such documents are apt to reestablish the genesis of the written works."[3] As the term itself suggests, textual genetics is the

---

1. Roland Barthes, "La Mort de l'auteur" [1968], reproduced in *Le Bruissement de la langue* (Paris: Seuil, 1984), 61–67.
2. Gérard Genette, *Introduction à l'architexte* (Paris: Seuil, 1979), 87–88. These reflections are further developed and illustrated in *Palimpsestes* (Paris: Seuil, 1982), and in *Seuils* (Paris: Seuil, 1986).
3. Louis Hay, " 'Le texte n'existe pas,' Réflexions sur la critique génétique," in *Poétique 62* (1985): 150. See also the remarks in defense of textual genetics made by Gérard Genette and Michel Contat in *Le Monde,* 17 November 1989.

study of beginnings, of that which is the prelude, the germ of the written work, of rough drafts, of what Jean Bellemin-Noël has termed the *pre-text*.[4] It consists of the dynamic reconstitution of the process of textual production, and of a reflection on the origin of this. Thus it is necessarily as heterogenous as the material that it is dealing with: "at times the trace of initial impulses, and the marks of distant memories in the form of jottings, notebooks, and diaries; at others, composed of preliminary documents such as projects, plans and scripts; or yet again, as the instruments of the work of composition itself such as sketches, early drafts and, in more general terms, rough copies [manuscripts], put one in touch with the polymorphous since the writing process goes beyond the linearity of the code and spills over into a variety of other spaces" (Louis Hay, 171).

Textual genetics reasserts the value of the active, fluid process that is the textual production of the writer "at work," the evolution of the writing towards its final form.[5] It does indeed take into account a history of the text, but it is the text's own specific history, that is, the chronology of its appearance in text form (and it may also seek to reveal the traces of the unconscious in this raw material).[6] And it goes still further: it watches out for signs of an energetic pen, or of a lazy one which hesitates, deletes, jots, scribbles, or draws. On this point, textual genetics is close to preoccupations of an aesthetic kind. It takes into account the figurative qualities of the writing, and the layout of letters and words on the page. It finds its complement in *grammatextuality*.[7]

That is not the only interest to be found in work which now calls for the use of the expression "the poetics of writing," as opposed to the "poetics of the text."[8] When faced with the manuscript itself, the critic, whatever his personal convictions concerning biography may be, can no longer ignore the question of the role of the author. Any attention granted to the pre-text "inevitably involves taking the writer

4. Cf. Jean Bellemin-Noël, *Le Texte et l'avant-texte* (Paris: Larousse, 1972) (on the editing of texts by Milosz).

5. Cf., for reference, *Flaubert à l'œuvre*, collection directed by R. Debray-Genette (Paris: Flammarion, 1980), and *Ecriture et génétique textuelle, Valéry à l'œuvre*, selection of texts chosen by Jean Levaillant (Lille: Presses Universitaires de Lille, 1982).

6. Cf. *Littérature* 53 (1983), on the unconscious in the pre-text.

7. Cf. Jean-Gérard Lapacherie, "De la grammatextualité," in *Poétique* 59 (1984), and also Jan Baetens, "Le Transcriptuaire," *Poétique* 73 (1988), 51–70.

8. Raymond Debray-Genette, "Génétique et poétique: esquisse d'une méthode," *Littérature* 28 (1977): 20. (The whole issue is devoted to the genesis of the text.)

into account."[9] The manuscript specifically refers back to the person who wrote it, and to his day-to-day existence. It bears the mark, the imprint, the signature of his work. The author is there, in the manuscript, keeping watch and affirming his presence: he cannot be ignored any longer.

That is, in a few lines, all that need be said here on the theoretical status of the text: the debate is now open both to questions of a more general nature (via the categories listed by Genette), and of a more specific kind (textual genetics), as well as from both synchronic and diachronic standpoints. After long being eclipsed, the author is making a comeback[10] and so is his history—biographies of authors are more and more numerous, and the interest in autobiography has even reached authors of the *Nouveau Roman*. We should note, incidentally, that this is indeed a strange situation: it seems to be the combined result of the increased prestige of History (leading in particular to a transfer of interest from literary figures to historians), of an increasingly asserted narcissism coupled with the immoderate taste for "real life" promoted by the media, and also of a certain theoretical stagnation which the research in textual genetics has arrived at just the right time to conceal.

We are all aware of the narrative history of the disjunction which, from the very beginning, heralds the relation between writing and drawing. Some distant source of "good sense" (with the Greeks doing their best, in particular by the invention of the phonetic alphabet, not to get things mixed up) decided on the division of sciences and techniques, a vast operation of *schize* (sharing, division), which should make it possible to settle any kind of dispute by first clearly defining differences.

During the Renaissance, all the "extravagances" of the manuscript are brought together under the common denominator of typography.[11] Parallel to this forced sobering of writing, perspective strives to assign a structure to the visual space—a veritable corset determined by geometry and the precise limits of representation. This moment of clarification of identities, which is also the moment in which writing seems to

9. Jean Bellemin-Noël, "En guise de post-face: l'essayage infini," *Littérature* 52 (1983): 123.

10. See Michel Contat's remarks on this point in "La Question de l'auteur," in *L'Auteur et son manuscrit*, ed. Michel Contat (Paris: P.U.F., 1991), 7–34.

11. This is what Antoine Compagnon has so aptly named "the immobilization of the text." Cf. *La Seconde main ou le travail de la citation* (Paris: Seuil, 1979), 233 ff.

diverge definitively from drawing, is paradoxically the one in which these two modes of representation are used together to "conceal," show, and confuse—since it is also during the Renaissance that the *cancellaresca*, those astounding pen games [*jeux de plume*], are invented. These too insist on giving letters a size which is derived from the anthropomorphic ideal canon used in painting.

Later on, there is no lack of responses to this arbitrary partition of practices. We are aware of the way in which Sterne and Mallarmé (to cite two of the best-known enterprises) play with [*jouent*] and challenge [*se jouent de*] literary space. The end of the nineteenth century sees the invention of the comic strip in which text and image work together on the semantic field. But the very status of this "ninth art," in principle reserved for children, bespeaks the condition of a poor relative of drawing with respect to writing.

The twentieth century, thanks to this thundering, blistering conflagration of representation, produces, after a few movements which pave the way for its diffusion, [12] surrealism, which upsets in the most spectacular way the old imperatives of differentiation. Writers give their readers something to look at; they begin with illustrations for reading matter and end up making of their texts books of images.[13] Painters provide reading matter (or pretend to do so), take signifying writing as material for representation, and illustrate poems and tales.

Some among them—Michaux from his position as writer or Dubuffet from his position as painter—work with the entire spectrum, from visible to legible. The painters grouped under the label "art brut" for their part defy the dual institutionalization of writing and painting, refusing, through the obliqueness of admirable discoveries, the *schize* of writing and picture.

Words were to appear in pictures, not to provide explanations, to add details, or to reinforce their realism as had been the case before (the letter in the hands of David's Marat), but rather to disturb it by forcibly introducing the signified (Miró's "Une étoile caresse le sein d'une

12. I am thinking of the work done under the auspices of *Art Nouveau*—noteworthy for its ingenious typographical innovations, but unfortunately endless.

13. It is important to remember here to what extent the marriage of text and image provoked the mistrust of certain writers, Flaubert, for instance, who consistently opposed the illustration of his novels: "A drawn woman," he writes, "looks like a woman, enough said. The idea of a woman is thereafter shut down, complete, and all the sentences in the world are useless; a written woman, on the other hand, makes one dream of a thousand other women," *Correspondance*, III, ed. Jean Bruneau (Paris: Gallimard, Pléiade, 1991), 222, 12 June 1862, to Ernest Duplan.

négresse"). Far from making things clearer by naming them, the presence of the legible was to be a source of confusion, decidedly complicating the vision of things by a mixing of categories.

But all this (in the end just a few things, and recent ones at that) cannot mask the weight of diverse cultural imperatives which are clearly understood, and this is the case with the assertion that one must not mix up the paint brushes [*s'emmêler les pinceaux*]. If there are a few exceptions, duly catalogued, they are precisely that, exceptions, and thus serve only to reinforce an unchanging division.

Since then, tautology has appeared as the surest means of preserving that order of things. What should one expect? That the writer should write, the painter paint, the reader read, that the spectator (now, there is a more ambiguous term—should one say the enthusiast, or the connoisseur?) should look on.[14] As far as writing and reading are concerned, where the "literate" eye is called upon to decipher a message in a given time, the question is one of legibility. Where painting and perceiving are concerned, and the movement of the eye over a painted surface (what kind of "literacy" is required for that operation?), visibility is the question. In all events, the basis of these practices is mimesis.

Writing is the reproduction of an established set of signs. That is how it remains in the domain of the legible. Illegible writing shows things to be what they are not. That is why it is "sanctioned" by whatever means possible (by various authorities, from school on). It is accused of trying to hide something, of being a disguise. It is "read" (by graphologists and others) as a gesture of refusal, as antisocial. It is at least an indication of the tenuous, fragile nature of this legibility of the most basic kind. It shows the legible to be a category that is forever under threat, forever in danger of disappearing, of becoming lost, *despite* appearances, in a paradoxical obscurity where writing can be seen and recognized, but can no longer be read. Illegible writing indicates in fact that the sign has been remorsefully eaten away by its own figurative nature, and that it does indeed take almost nothing at all for the figure to resort back to its status as a mere drawing.

14. Not to mention the fact that the writer may draw—this is true of a great number of Romantic writers—or the fact that the painter may write. But one has to keep busy. There is nevertheless one value judgment which immediately puts things in perspective by perpetuating a widely accepted idea: one cannot possibly draw *as well* as one writes, and vice versa. (The embarrassment caused by Fromentin or by Redon, who both hesitated between brush and pen, is an excellent example of this.)

As it follows the train of thought to which it gives body and move-ment, the writing process comes across as a work-form that is forever on the point of *drifting off course*. And it is there in the hazardous limbo between the legible and the visible that the illusory barrier be-tween one domain and another is erased. And graphic representation appears: it appears during the pauses and hesitations of the thought process, when the pen can be caught accomplishing other gestures: additions, scribbles, and the excessive embellishment of letters, the transformation of words, lines, and inkblots into heads, animals (reviv-ing some "mimological" effect),[15] or other, less creditable things—"the hand talks" says Dubuffet.[16] The visible returns and jostles with the legible: it is unpretentious, playful, useless, and it draws writing towards mocking, childish counterwriting.[17] "When I was young, says Colette, "I played with my writing and used my ignorance of art, as I did my lack of literary experience, to draw as I wrote. For example, if I stumbled on the word 'murmur' and hesitated about how to continue my sentence, I would add the tiny foot of a caterpillar to each of the even downstrokes of the letters. . . . I added the somewhat horselike head of the caterpillar to one end of the word and turned the final flourish into its tail. . . . Then, as well as the word 'murmur' I had the much prettier sign of the caterpillar. . . . Decorated as they were with insects and butterflies, I felt that my manuscripts were not 'serious enough.'"[18]

That is not the only way in which the figurative may reappear in writing to the extent of masking it completely for a moment. All manner of figurative practices emerge and tirelessly struggle against millenary divisions; and in the process, they inevitably reveal the para-doxical framework of an exercise in legibility. Thus writing may explic-itly give way to drawing, either accidentally (Valéry's "absences" in his notebooks)[19] or voluntarily. The "objects" represented then are

15. Cf. Gérard Genette, *Mimologiques* (Paris: Seuil, 1976), and in particular, "L'Ecri-ture en jeu," 329–49.

16. Jean Dubuffet, *L'Homme du commun à l'ouvrage* (Paris: Gallimard Folio, 1973), 34.

17. Cf. the remarks made by Serge Tisseron in this issue. On the "childish" charac-ter of Hugo's drawings (specifically linked to drawings by his own children), see also Pierre Georgel's remarks in "Portrait de l'artiste en griffonneur," in *Victor Hugo et les Images*, ed. Madeleine Blondel and Pierre Georgel (Dijon: Aux Amateurs de Livres, 1984), 74–138.

18. Colette, *L'Etoile Vesper* (Paris: Edition du milieu du monde, 1946), 180.

19. Cf. Serge Bourjea's remarks in this issue and "'Je viens absent de dessiner ceci . . . ,'" *Poétique* 73 (1988): 71–82.

numerous—they are often enigmatic insofar as they are not those usually considered suitable for the representation of knowledge or memory in the true sense. Jacques Leenhardt points out, with reference to Stendhal, that the writer is thus able to reintroduce sensation into the heart of the cognitive process by the inclusion in his text of a concept-image.[20]

From these objects which the mind uses to convey perception by more tangible means and to fix it in the evolution of memory or reasoning, to the self-portraits, illustrations, and images which reinforce the writing and choose to represent the subject graphically as if to reaffirm the dominance of the visible over the legible (that is the case of the drawings to be found in the correspondence of Musset, and Proust, or in Maupassant's little "comic strips"), the road is long and the practices extremely diverse—it would indeed be a good idea for them to be listed in detail—and this just up to the point of the pure and simple autonomy of the former and latter gestures. Thus the shadow of different types of visibility is projected, from the proximity or even the very interior of the writing itself (the word "murmur" turned into a caterpillar) to more distant areas. And that shadow is also, in graphic terms, a movement from darkness to light (from what is scarcely represented to what is perfectly recognizable). It would seem that the *forced* gesture of writing, and the obligation that it represents contain, in spite of everything, this tiny explosive force which may come to the surface at any time, whether or not it takes the trouble to justify its doing so: "drawing keeps coming back."[21]

In the days of technical reproducibility, the book (and behind it the editor and commercial imperatives) no longer shows any interest in the gestures which brought it into being. To begin with, there is (until the typewriter becomes common property) the copyist. His role is to *make a fair copy.* This expression implies a dual task: on the one hand, he is to ensure that the writing is as perfectly legible as possible, or has regained its initial legibility (what criteria will he use? what calligraphic norms will he adopt?); on the other hand, he is to remove all trace of the writing process (the copyist, naturally, does not reproduce the crossings-out, or the inkblots, scribbles, drawings,

---

20. Cf. Jacques Leenhardt, "See and Describe: On a Few Drawings by Stendhal," in this issue.

21. "Drawing keeps coming back," notes Derrida. "Does one ever stop drawing? Can one ever give it up?" *Mémoires d'aveugle* (Paris: Réunion des Musées nationaux, 1990), 44.

and mistakes in the manuscript he is copying: a copy is not a photo-copy). Forced legibility which may, at times, confuse signifier and sig-nified and harm semantic legibility: "My copyist," wrote Flaubert to Bonnenfant, "makes some superb mistakes, he writes 'garçon de glace' instead of "garçon de classe' and Adriatic 'légumes' instead of 'lagunes'; in other words, I'm going quite mad. . . . " (*Correspon-dance*, 611, 9 April 1856).[22]

Then there is the printing process, which ensures a maximum de-gree of legibility.[23] Curiously, when faced with the book as an object, the author no longer recognizes his own work. "The sight of my work [*Madame Bovary*] in print deadened my mind completely," noted Flaubert. "It seemed so flat. Everything looks so black. *I mean that textually.* That was a great disappointment—And it would take a quite dazzling success to drown the voice of my conscience crying out to me: 'It's a failure!'" (Flaubert, Letter to Louis Bouillet, 5 October 1856). And thus, once printed, Flaubert is no longer Flaubert in the eyes of Flaubert himself. And, worse still, its legibility has been lost. Every-thing is black, an ambiguous statement which evokes both the singular "color" of the printed character, and blindness. Flaubert now sees only blackness, just the blackness of the text, that is to say its total, and irreversible illegibility. It is a strange metamorphosis of the printed word that apparently condemns the writer to blindness (he no longer sees or recognizes his work) at the same time as it reveals his work to the public—and that certainly suggests to Flaubert some kind of phan-tasmatic reversal (the strangely "Oedipal" gesture of a father refusing to see the son he has engendered in his works).[24]

Valéry was to describe a very similar version of the same experience: "The writer's mind," he says, "gazes at itself in the mirror that the

22. Flaubert writes to Edma Roger des Genettes: "Madam, the copyist I engaged is Mme Dubois of 30, rue Saint Marc. I would advise your brother to fix the price before-hand, and to choose the type. The best type is that used for texts for the theater" (*Correspondance*, II, 626, Summer 1856[?]).

23. "The printed text," remarks Michel Thévoz, which is a paradigm of the ideol-ogy of representation, should ideally combine the metaphysical opposition that exists between the diaphanous signifier and the more consistent signified," *Détournement d'écriture* (Paris: Minuit, 1989), 16. The paradoxical significance of typography should, however, be recalled: the history of printer's type is proof of the desire to remain as close as possible to the style of handwriting (the invention of italics is in itself sufficient proof of this) while attempting to achieve maximum legibility. Cf. J. Peignot, *De L'écriture à la typographie* (Paris: Gallimard, 1967).

24. Is blindness the ultimate anchorage of the enterprise of writing (the blind Homer)?

printing-press provides for it. Then, if the paper and ink are well matched, if the face of the letter is attractive, the type-setting meticulous, the justification exquisitely proportioned, and the page well printed, the author is both embarrassed and proud. He sees himself covered with honors that he does not, perhaps, deserve. He thinks he can hear a voice that is clearer and louder than his own, an inexorably pure voice articulating his words and pronouncing them dangerously clearly, one by one. Everything that is weak, or bad, or arbitrary, or inelegant in which he has written speaks out too loudly and too clearly. Appearing in magnificent print is the mark of a judgment that is both precious and formidable (Peignot, *De L'Ecriture*, 88). The metaphor is that of a distorting mirror. The printed word here goes too far. The author can no longer recognize himself, or rather he can no longer recognize his own voice. Confusing the spoken with the written, Valéry affirms that the printed text gives words excessive clarity and force. The legible ("a far clearer, more precise voice") is now *too* legible. Such excess is perceived as a danger, and that danger is the danger of *detachment*. What the penstroke linked together, the printing press sets apart. The manuscript was a mirror of ink, an object both personal and personalized, but when it is transformed into print, that intimacy is shattered. By suggesting that the "real" (this is me) is to be found only in the manuscript, Valéry in his turn acknowledges the affective relationship which unites the author with his manuscript, and thus the curious threat represented by editor and publishing. That is how he refers to the essential ambivalence which lies behind the writing process: the proper (*my* writing) and property (my manuscripts) are sentenced, in order to justify their existence, to become public property at the cost of a mutilation which is felt to be not only dangerous, but painful.

The transformation from written to printed word is not merely to ensure the legibility—the dazzling legibility—of the text. This "forging process" (Peignot, 33) renews the age-old division and repeats the tautology. Unless it has a precise and significant pictorial dimension, a text is a text, that is to say that it exists to be read.

Take the example of Stendhal's *La Vie de Henry Brulard*. From the beginning, the author admits that his enterprise is scarcely legible; he plays along with that and even seems to make it the sine qua non of his writing—his writing is not legible, he sees it less and less distinctly (the lack of light in Rome in the middle of winter and his recent need to wear glasses). He does not see what he ought to write any more clearly (as he remembers his childhood and recalls a few memories, all sorts of problems arise; no solution is possible, but writing and identity, images and autobiography are mingled). Stendhal constructs the only object which could "correspond" to this near illegibility in fact and essence: a barely intelligible manuscript, decorated with "drawings" (from the simple line to the self-portrait), plans, topographical readings, and engravings. A curious mirror which intermingles questions of legibility and visibility in a masterly manner, and, in its way, also proves that the ultimate consequence of any attempt at self-representation is disfigurement.

Take the case of Victor Hugo. His writing is constantly accompanied by graphics. These vary from the negation of the writing, quite simply its elimination (one whole page is entirely covered with black ink), to illustrations and theater sketches, not to mention the endless and remarkably varied scribblings (each inkblot appears as an invitation to pictorial representation), caricatures, playlets, etc. Here, it is the work in its entirety which acquires an incredible graphic dimension, with "penwork" that the author himself showed great interest in, as can be seen from the care he took with his notebooks and albums.

Take the case of Antonin Artaud. He draws well and a lot and produced, among other things, admirable portraits and self-portraits. He never ceases to comment on his figurative practice. Actually he insists on it: "after a certain day in October 1939, I never wrote again without drawing at the same time."[25] The exchange mixture imposed between writing and drawing is not without the expression of a certain violence—as exemplified by *"sorts":* pieces of paper covered with writing, then violated, aggressed by diverse graphic processes (superimposed drawings, scribbles, and erasures executed in very vivid colors), and finally perforated, torn, and partly burned.

These examples (I have chosen three at random) have caused considerable trouble for editors—publications prove that we do not know what to do with this *visible* in the text (at best the division is confirmed: text on one side, drawings as "album leaves" on the other). Trouble also for the critic, who often hesitates between two standpoints: the one being a rejection (drawing as anecdote), the other as "oversemantisation" (at all costs making sense of the most insignifi-

25. Antonin Artaud, *Luna-Park* 5 (October 1979), cited by Paule Thévenin in Paule Thévenin and Jacques Derrida, *Antonin Artaud, Dessins et portraits* (Paris: Gallimard, 1986), 45. Several *"sorts"* are reproduced in this album (135–41).

cant figurative deviation). Defiance, error, anomaly—all drawings by writers are decidedly troublesome.

Every science, according to Michel Foucault, has its margins, and in those margins an immense and unavowable teratology is concealed.[26] Graphic representation is the teratology of literature and of the sciences of manuscript study which it has recently created. Thus, because of (or thanks to) the obstinate and obtuse presence of drawing in literature, there is a profusion of forms and figures, a multitude of monsters present in the literary field. "Defending the eye,"[27] they are just waiting for attention to be turned toward them.

—Translated by Nigel P. Turner

26. Michel Foucault, *L'Ordre du discours* (Paris: Gallimard, 1971), 35.
27. Jean-François Lyotard, *Discours, figure* (Paris: Klincksieck, 1985), 11.

YVES BONNEFOY

Overture: The Narrow Path toward the Whole[1]

What pulsing in that line that sometimes moves about in the dabs, beneath the highlights of a bit of color: the drawing!

That drawing that at first sight can seem *less* to one who has learned to love the magnificent altar pieces, or the transfiguration of matter in a Titian, a Vermeer, or the storms—lingering, or just about to burst forth—in a Delacroix, but that sometimes shows that it can be *as much* if not even *almost more*, in the next to nothing of a line that hesitates, that breaks off. As though the admission of inadequacy, when it shows itself at the peak of mastery, were the truth before which all others fade, but also an outpouring, a source.

Giacometti, who was also a great painter, used to say, "Drawing is all." From his earliest years, he had been a master of the artistic vision, thanks, in particular, to drawing, but eventually gave up the idea of this mastery, and then understood that he was at last a drawer, and later he never stopped searching, destroying, starting over—living its absolute in those few lines that were sometimes all but obliterated by his erasures, and he was still drawing "with just his eyes," his brother tells us, only a few hours before his death.

---

1. These notes on drawing are one part of a three-part essay called *Comme aller loin dans les pierres* published in 1992 by Jacques Clerc with lithographs by Henri Cartier Bresson.

YFS 84, *Boundaries: Writing & Drawing,* ed. M. Reid, © 1994 by Yale University.

II

Our experience with what is: on a whole first level, it is only our language. Our words draw from without the material with which they will build, arrange, and interpret things, and thus the world is put together, thus the universes that each civilization has dreamed of appear and disappear: sumptuous figures, rich in dimension and movement, but which are only the pages, gone as soon as turned, of a book one has little reason therefore to call reality.

Reality nonetheless survives, on that horizon in things that words can never reach, or in the space between them: much like the leaves above the walls of enclosed gardens. Let's say that the real is the tree one sees before our intellect tells us it's a tree; or the slow swelling of the cloud, that tightening, that tearing in the sand of its color that defy the power of words.

And poetry is what speech becomes when one has learned not to forget that there is a place, in many words, where, despite what has just been said of them, they make contact with what they cannot say.

III

In speech, poetry; and beneath the pencil, the drawing.

What is the person who draws doing if not, in the first place, encountering this level where language decides? If Michelangelo wants to understand the musculature of the ephebe, Degas the posture of the little ballet dancer, there must be a precision in their way of looking at things that is not unlike the precision of thought. The muscles, furthermore, have a name, and movement follows laws that are known.

And in this way the drawer can be "true," and afford truth to painters who find in their colors, their values, in their use of perspective that once was so important, in the figurative painting that only yesterday was still dominant, in their themes and allusions, the material to build an image of the world that will enchant their era. But the drawer possesses a power, a power he can feel, which is denied to these painters whose ambitions are so vast.

So narrow is his stroke, so surrounded by great empty shores!

And so easy then for him to feel intuitively that that white page is the unknowing which surpasses his ability to know, a light quite other than that sun which he has perhaps already placed on the right in his drawing, behind that cluster of trees. A light that is more than the simple physical sun, since it wells up from the depths of all things, since it is the radiance of that unity that words fragment.

After which he will surely be able to sense that drawing is less defining contours, finding their truth, than venturing into that whiteness and discovering there the precarity of all that has been acquired, the vanity of wants, and thus drawing near to that reality-unity that language robs us of. In this way, the drawing, the "great" drawing, will be poetry. "Pure" poetry, already modern, next to paintings which are works made up of narrative, sermon, science—and of course made rich as well by that poetry they sometimes gather from drawing, and which they intensify or dilute.

IV

Where the drawing of little merit is the one that seems weighted down by undiscarded "painting," great painting preserves, on all its levels, the bold stroke that erases, that renews the world.

But let us be careful: this stroke is no longer the line made by pencil or charcoal that color would enhance; it can be the purple stripe of the sunset in a Constable or a Hodler as much or even more than the line reduced to itself that the word "disegno" suggests in the Florentine tradition. The drawing in painting is the kernel of the invisible, not the quintessence, however supreme, of intelligible forms. Let us say, "This painting has no drawing," as we used to say of certain forms, "They have no life."

V

Why is the drawing so difficult in the West? Because of the Idea that dominates so many Platonic minds, and because also of the Christian notion of a Word that has produced the universe: proof, in both cases, that reality is identified with language. Our civilizations of the evening sun are born from this confinement of the mind in words, which allows the mind to run headlong into history without a handrail, at the risk of disaster. The Chinese painter, on the other hand, was totally a drawer, only painting the crab when it had become so close to him that he no longer needed to look at it, and in brush strokes that captured not its form but simply the gentle breathing of one crab among other crabs.

In the West, the drawing is obviously as rare, as unusual as poetry.

But squeezed between the high cliffs of conceptual thought, it manages to move along more frothy and clear, and even, because of this, to follow paths more varied than in the oriental washdrawing: unexpected paths that forge far ahead and that now pass peacefully beside us at the very moment and in the very place where we might have thought ourselves lost.

For instance a certain *Triumph of Galatea* by Poussin, as a sudden flow of light from a page turned in Friedlaender and Blunt. The spiral of the rhythms in Raphael rising up in the body of his own Galatea—in the chords of an earth made music—toward that invisible point which is in us the center of gravity that will help us to survive.

VI

Drawing, de-signifying:[2] breaking the seal, opening the envelope—but it remains sealed.

Painting, then: letting the world—all its shores, all its suns, all its ships gliding "in the gold and in the purple silk of water"[3]—be reflected in the windowpane.

—Translated by John T. Naughton

2. *Dessiner, dé-signer* in the French.
3. Bonnefoy is citing line eighteen of Baudelaire's "La Chevelure": "Où les vaisseaux, glissant dans l'or et dans la moire."

MICHEL BUTOR

Bricolage: An Interview with Michel Butor[1]

Martine Reid If I have been eager to interview you and to place this interview as the lead piece of a journal issue devoted to writing and drawing, to the readable and the visible, it is because it seems to me that among contemporary writers, you are the one of those who has most clearly striven to prove the double affirmation which you yourself have formulated: "Painting is also something we read . . . literature is also something we look at."[2] A similar remark opens a text which you published in 1969, *Les Mots dans la peinture*. On the subject of words which hold your attention in painting and of which you propose a list (title, signature, address, maxims, rebus, proverbs, various inscriptions in which words are reified), you write, "the presence of these words ruins . . . the retaining wall our teaching constructs in between literature and the arts."[3]

Michel Butor Yes. You know, this is even more clear in France than it is in the United States. Generally in the United States, art schools are part of the university. Any self-respecting university maintains an art museum. It is not true of France; art schools are considered as something completely exterior to university teaching. As a result, it is very difficult to build bridges between the disciplines. It's true for painting; it's also true for music. In the United States, conservatories are part of the university. All this goes to show to what extent there are walls in

---

1. The following interview was conducted at Michel Butor's home in Lucinges on 29 September 1992. I am deeply grateful for the generous gift of his time.

2. Michel Butor and Patrick Stefanetto, "Entretien," *Traitements de textes: Cartes et brouillons* (Gourdon: Dominique Bedou Editeur, 1985), 17.

3. Butor, *Les mots dans la peinture* (Geneva: Skira/Flammarion, 1969), 5.

YFS 84, *Boundaries: Writing & Drawing,* ed. M. Reid, © 1994 by Yale University.

France and in other European countries. Art, literature, and music are not departments inside a single institution; they are considered completely distinct institutions unto themselves.

M. R. From this point of view, we can assert right away that all of your works seek to undermine—systematically, stubbornly, playfully—compartmentalization, the division of techniques, but also the division of knowledge, of which we know the long and capricious history.

M. B. Certainly. My work is one of undermining [*travail de sape*]. I have always sought to build bridges across borders, be they the borders between the arts, or the borders between countries. For me, these two things are linked together. To build bridges across borders doesn't mean that these borders do not exist, that they have not been, and even now are not, justified. It is much too easy to say, "There are no more borders; anyone can do anything; etc." It's not true, and this isn't the question. The question is how to show that these borders which distinguish different fields, and rightly so, are not permanent and impermeable. We absolutely must understand that the borders between nations are not the same as they were one hundred years ago, that the borders between the activities of the mind and between the institutions which take charge of them are not the same either. Clearly there is considerable inertia; changing institutions is very difficult, even when actual practices have already evolved considerably. We have quite a hard time changing teaching; it's extraordinarily difficult to change such weighty institutions. In the same way, altering the borders between peoples presents extraordinary difficulties. I've always tried to show that first of all, borders are not constant, that the establishment of these borders was linked to a specific situation; and then as a corollary, that these borders could and should be crossed, even if to cross a border does not mean to abolish it. We can easily understand that there is a region in which people speak German and a region in which people speak French. We can draw the line between these two regions on a map. This is completely different from preventing the French from going to visit the Germans. Very often there are phenomena, movements, which cause borders to harden. As we know only too well, borders can become stifling and murderous. The dotted lines on the cartographer's map can be transformed into walls of flame . . .

M. R. You have published quite a lot on painting and painters. Regarding art criticism, and particularly a text of Vieira Da Silva, you said, "it is not truly art criticism; it is a text which comes out of viewed painting."[4]

4. Butor and Stefanetto, 17.

M. B. There are all kinds of possible connections between text and painting. The first of these connections is the text which speaks of painting. There can also be texts—and we have seen only too many these past few years—which state that one cannot talk about painting; but to say that one cannot talk about painting is itself to talk about painting. This is the first connection: a text about painting, an art history text for example, a critical text; in this case all forms are possible. All of these texts about painting obviously play an important role in terms of the way in which we look at painting. There are also texts in which there are passages of art criticism. For example there may be passages of art criticism in great novels, because the novelist uses pictorial references to render a description. In French literature, two examples immediately come to mind: Balzac and Proust. Then, there is a second connection between text and painting: a text next to a painting. As soon as a text is placed next to a painting, a new object is produced. Let's say that it is an object which has two parents, a parent-text and a parent-painting. This is what generally happens in an artist's book. Finally there is a third connection: a text which is located within a painting. It is the text within the painting which absolutely forces us to realize a fact, one which should be obvious, that writing is a visible thing. Writing is a way of making language visible. In an illustrated book, you are dealing with a fundamental plastic structure which is the rectangle of the double page, with, on the right for example, a rectangular plate, the reproduction of a painting, and on the left, a rectangle of text. All one has to do is to move away a bit to see that the rectangle of text is also a rectangle of drawing and color, that it is a *gray color*. Moreover, it is in just this way that the designers of art history books treat the text: there must be a pretty gray color. In this structure, the text already is presented as an image. In Western culture, especially in the nineteenth century (and we can begin to wonder why), the image-text was considered as something so different from the image in the ordinary sense of the word that it was deemed absolutely necessary to put borders between the two, that it was dangerous to bring these two elements together. As soon as text enters into the rectangle, I might call it the sacred rectangle of traditional Western painting, then, despite all the entreaties (academic as well as judicial, etc.), one cannot help but notice that writing is drawing, that writing is image. There, the text has a considerable influence not only on the way in which we perceive the painting (we interpret it of course), but also on the manner in which we profit from it, we look at it. It is a part of the painting; we can easily see that writing entails lines alongside other lines; the composition of the whole takes account of this. If it is the painter himself who has written the words, he manages the situation on his own. If it is a writer on the one hand and a painter on the other, problems of very intimate dialogue are born; and there the writer notices not only that he is speaking of painting, but that he is making painting, and not in the common metaphoric sense, but in the sense of Horace, *ut pictura poesis*, which is very important, but in a much more literal way.

M. R. Very early on, you began to consider, "la peinture comme trajet," painting as a journey, I am thinking particularly of the work of Jackson Pollock which haunts a text like *Mobile*. Is it because this type of painting calls for/recalls writing? In terms of hand movements at least . . .

M. B. Indeed, especially with Pollock, gesture recalls (with differences of course) the gesture of writing through a very important concept. In late nineteenth-century writing, as it is represented in painting, ink was used, a liquid pigment, which was not the case in painting. Pasty pigments were used in oil painting, or in certain instances liquid pigments such as watercolors, but this dried very quickly. . . . Pollock, on the other hand, uses a liquid paint which creates a kind of thread, and this is very close to handwriting. In this respect, we must remember that there has been an evolution in writing. Ancient writings are letter by letter, then, gradually, there are links between the letters. It is said that writing became more and more cursive. Subsequently, we find a distinction between words, which derives from the fact that a word is made practically from a single stroke, an extraordinarily complicated stroke, much more complicated than the movements of any figure skater, much more complicated than most strokes by painters on their surface. In very cursive writings, some words may be linked with each other. Pollock's painting recovers this ductility of writing. We might say that Pollock's art rediscovers a kind of elementary writing, but his stroke didn't take him as far as writing. He confronts the structures of this genre and then figurative structures, etc., all sorts of things, but from the perspective of writing, he remains in what I call infrawriting; he remains a scribbler. As part of the traditional writer's activities— assuming that he must write by hand—there is quite often an escape toward a kind of liberated stroke, and that is scribbling. To scribble is to take possession of a space. It is clear with Pollock that certain of his paintings are immense scribblings, which incidentally gives them a remarkable "childlike" quality. In a sense, we find ourselves, there, on the margins of writing. One might study the connections between actual writing and scribblings in manuscripts. There are areas of readable writing and then we have areas where the bad pupil starts to scribble. Writers are bad pupils at times. Thus there are scribblings in manuscripts, and between scribbling and writing, neat writing [*l'écriture au propre*] as we say, there are all kinds of marvellous phenomena, such as erasures, cut text, pasted text, etc., which take on often extraordinary plastic qualities. There are three steps: scribbling, the rough draft, and finally the actual text. We should quickly note a few things about the rough draft. There are phenomena of agitation involved, since the writer will correct himself; this heightens the kind of dance we find on the page and in the rough draft, especially with certain writers. We can see that these writers are not content with a sort of furrowing labor, line by line; no, the motion of the hand creates all kinds of detours and returns. To bring writing into painting, the painter will encounter different problems. With static lettering, in which each letter is considered a stable figure (which is what occurs in inscriptions and in the European Middle Ages for example), the painter who wants to put writing into his picture is confronted with stable figures which he paints without much difficulty. If writing becomes very cursive, this presents us with different problems. There are "cursive" painters; there are painters who use liquid pigments, who have long brush strokes (I am thinking of El Greco). Then the difficulty will be the reverse. This pictorial cursiveness displaces writerly cursiveness, which is usually readable. With El Greco, in the Evangelists series, we find all kinds of examples of unreadable writing, hypercursive writings . . .

M. R. Here we pick up on a series of things which you said in *Les Mots dans la peinture*, specifically that painting is in no way "pure vision." In the progression of these ideas, I would like to come back to your collaboration with painters; I am thinking especially of Christian Dotremont and Alechinsky. Why did you make this choice, to work as a writer in painting?

M. B. Christian Dotremont was originally a writer. He was the writer in the Cobra group. He became a painter gradually, starting with writing and developing certain aspects of writing. He is truly a painter of the written. I know several of his images which are not directly writing; I can think of a certain number of sketches; but for the most part, his works are logograms, writings which have been transformed in such a way that they are difficult to read. There is a translation into more readable writing on one side, and the search for a buried word is one of the essential elements of perception in these works. With all the members of the Cobra group, there is a certain cursiveness in gesture, in stroke; but it is certainly Alechinsky who has the clearest confrontation with writing.

M. R. You yourself from time to time have lent your writing to this kind of work.

M. B. Of course. I have done a certain number of books in which there is manuscript, then there are works in which I have written some text; and certain painters have taken manuscripts as material. Alechinsky used not only manuscripts in its conventional meaning, but also used *typescripts* [*tapuscrits*], in other words typed pages, with deletions, rough draft effects.

M. R. What interests me in this kind of procedure, since we are discussing the work of undermining, is the principle by which, the traditional *auctoritas* is destabilized. Who is the author? Jacques Derrida asserts somewhere, "Il faut être plusieurs pour écrire" [One must be several in order to write]. Is it the same thing here? One must be several to paint, or to write-paint?

M. B. The principle of the traditional *auctoritas*, but traditional only recently, is something which is questioned, and which is brought to life in a different way by all this kind of work. One must be several to write, and this in several different ways. The romantic idea that the work of art is individual expression is something which we must completely revise. This in no way prevents individuals from having a central importance in works of art, but the individual is only a link in an extremely complex chain. When we read someone's book, we never read the work of a single individual, if only because we hold a material object in our hands, an object which is the result of a complex of industrial and commercial process, and because that process—it cannot be said enough—informs the whole business. In order to be published, one must follow a certain number of rules, some written, some not. The writer is often quite insignificant compared to the object itself. In many publishing houses, the writer is only a prop to publicity. Also, the writer writes within the language [*langue*]. No writer has invented the language in which he writes. He transforms it; he introduces a style, new frequencies in vocabulary and syntactical relationships; but these always preexist him. One writes within a language as one writes within a literature, by transforming it. Thus what today's writer writes prevents the reading of other writers, living as well as dead. The reader does not have an infinite time for reading. If he sets aside a certain number of hours for one particular author, he cannot set it aside for another.

M. R. It seems to me that particularly in your work with painters (I am coming back to this subject), you are seeking to remain as close as possible to a situation which might be called "l'écriture a lieu" [writing takes place]. I like this term, since fortuitously it conjugates space (writing in situ) with time (its moment, its immediacy).

M. B. The space of writing: what does this mean? It means the space where a writer puts words to paper. It can be a painter's studio, or a printing house, or a study. Inside this study, there is a more restricted space which is the very medium of writing; in our culture it is paper, but doubtless not for long. In *L'Emploi du temps*, I think we can easily see the imbrication of places: the city which one does not leave; the character who always writes in his study; then there is the table and the page which he writes on. All this is the physical space of writing, but if we look at it a bit closer, all the cultural elements appear as necessarily implicated.

M. R. Once again, let's come back to you. How do you conceive of rough drafts and manuscripts? You spoke of this just a little while ago.

M. B. There are two separate things. There is the rough draft, the outline, etc., and then the manuscript. In working with painters, I have tried to use a certain number of the plastic elements of the manuscript. In these cases, the manuscripts are as neat as possible, even if from time to time certain erasures remain; but in any case, I make it as readable as I can. Before reaching the stage of the final manuscript, there are several steps. I think about the nineteenth-century writers who had their texts copied before entrusting them to an editor. Flaubert's definitive manuscripts are not written in Flaubert's hand. As far as my rough drafts are concerned, at the beginning I wrote by hand, but very quickly I began to work on a typewriter. With certain passages there was a manuscript version first, then a typed version. With a certain number of texts, I rewrote the pages, sometimes more than twenty times. If I had left everything in, there would be twenty different stages. I worked on my texts a great deal with a typewriter. Generally, once I had a typed version, I reread, corrected by hand, retyped, and then again, until my texts achieved a kind of stability, not that I found them perfect, but, weary, I stopped correcting them. There is a moment when I find everything equally poor. Then there is nothing else to do but to publish. Now I have finally entered the modern age; I use a Macintosh. This allows me to revise a great deal on the computer, yet all the same I still go through several versions since many errors remain. In my last years of teaching, I didn't have the time to do long-winded works. All my latest works were written in pieces; they are mosaics, quilts. When I retired, I imagined that I could recover my longwindedness, but for the time being this is not the case. For years, I've worked by bits and pieces; I write quite short texts. They can be used in their original form; thereafter they can be combined, integrated, etc. Most of the time, for these texts I do a first draft in a little notebook. These are my original rough drafts. It is the rough outline of writing with illuminations, scribbling, erasures. Afterwards I move on to the computer. If the text is an article or an essay, I don't need an original manuscript version. I need a manuscript version only for poetic texts. Generally I do poems upon request. I wrote a lot of poetry in my youth. I was a postsurrealist romantic, with a bit of automatic writing thrown in, a faucet you turn on and let run. But since then, when I've written poems, it has always been in response to a request. In that respect, I'm completely opposed to the poetic theory which I call postromantic and which still holds sway with most contemporary poets. My poetry is always occasional poetry. It is always requested by someone or something, a painter or a musician, or anyone else. If I accept, it's because I have the feeling that I can do something. There's always a moment in which I don't have any idea what I am going to do and then—notably if I am walking in the woods—suddenly there it is: a thread starts to appear and I pull on this thread. This is what happens when I work in notebooks . . . . During these walks, ideas come to me, and I feel the need to write them down. Before, this didn't happen; I had a pretty good memory and if ideas came to me, they stayed with me. Actually, I felt that my memory performed a necessary selection process. But now it works less well; that's why I carry notebooks . . .

M. R. With regard to rough drafts and manuscripts, I thought of words I've seen here and there, neologisms, such as "tapuscrits" [typescripts], "pictuscrits" [pictuscripts] . . . . What do you mean by these?

M. B. We lack the words we need to describe a certain number of objects which we nevertheless use constantly. Things don't happen in quite the same way when we write by hand and when we type; this is why we need other names. The word *tapuscrit* is obviously a burlesque neologism; it allows us to mock the neologisms of so many literary theoreticians who

create useless words, which, moreover, are quickly abandoned . . . .
Pictuscrit, I don't think I invented that word, which designates an object, a text in which there is painting, in which the pictorial appears. Furthermore, I have also used the word *ordinuscrit* [computoscript], because phenomena are so different when one works on the typewriter or on the computer that here as well a different word is essential.

M. R. I would like for you to speak of another practice, one which concerns correspondence, the habit which you have adopted of cutting up a postcard, pasting it together again, of adding to it as needed a piece of another card, of making a hole and putting a bit of string through it, then of sending this "product," along with a few words, to your addressee. What exactly is this transaction?

M. B. It comes from the fact that I correspond copiously. I'm not complaining, on the contrary. But to receive mail, one must also nourish the mail. Consequently, one must respond to letters which one receives. I respond as often as possible to the letters I receive, but now I can't always face up to it. I have used the postcard format so that I can write letters more easily; and by the way the format has become oversized. I was too cramped. The postcard is my excuse to write very brief texts, if you will. In any case, people who receive the card receive something personalized. I get by with brevity. I think I must have started to cut up cards about twenty or twenty-five years ago. In the beginning it was greeting cards, and then as usual new ideas came to me . . . . I continue on. I also have friends who help me, who make postcards so that I can cut them up, paste them together . . .

M. R. "Principle of redemption," that is what Lyotard calls this practice. You produce something else, a derived product, a "quasi-postcard."[5] Lyotard observes that the gesture is a curious one, notably because one comes to reconsider what is above all a touristic commonplace. Faced with all these disparate practices (from the novel, the nouveau roman, to the redemption of the postcard), how do you conceive of the work [l'œuvre]? Must we reexamine the concept?

M. B. Doubtless. If one questions the notion of *auctoritas*, then automatically the question comes to bear on the notion of *l'œuvre*. This doesn't mean that these notions, the work and its creator, cannot be useful at a certain level. But, as I said, the work never belongs to a single

5. Jean-François Lyotard, "Sites et récits de sites," in Butor, *Traitements de textes*, op. cit., 9–14.

creator. Whether he knows it or not, the author is part of an enormous collaboration, behind him, around him, on all sides. Collaborative works only prove that which exists in any artistic process. Thus the notion of the work of art must also be relativized. By my understanding, it is advisable to insist especially on the character of activity and operation, rather than that of the work of art.

M. R. The word which comes to mind when one thinks of these practices, of all these operations as you call them, is that of bricolage. Roland Barthes has cited the word to qualify *Mobile.* Does that still suit you: Michel Butor as Monsieur Bricolage?

M. B. Oh yes! In any case, I am not a *bricoleur* in the current sense of the term. I am a very poor man-about-the-house. I am a *bricoleur* only metaphorically. I am a *bricoleur* in the sense that one can define *bricolage* as a way of putting together elements which come from different areas. Roland Barthes spoke of bricolage in this sense when he discussed *Mobile.* The practice of collage, of cutting up, etc., all this is linked to that. But I would say that the notion of bricolage has two levels. First, there is the *bricoleur,* the one who knows how to make something. Most men are *bricoleurs.* To tinker about [*bricoler*], they use the tools which are furnished them by department store chains. This is the vulgar aspect of bricolage. The other level is the invention of material. This is what I would like to call the gathering of significant objects, the recovery of what has been eliminated, thrown out. This is very important for me. It is recycling. Each time there is a phenomenon of collage in twentieth-century painting, there is the phenomenon of recycling. I find some of this in my own work. This is the phenomenon of the quest for lost objects, for the disdained object to which we will give a new life and a new dignity; we will be forced to look at it in a different way. It is important for me, because today we move easily from the lost object, the object which has been thrown out, to the lost man, thrown out in the big cities; think of the United States in particular. Consequently, for me recycling always ends up as human recycling.

—Translated by Noah Guynn

I.

SERGE TISSERON

All Writing Is Drawing: The Spatial Development of the Manuscript

An author's manuscripts are recognized the same way writing is recognized, that is, through its stylistic hallmarks: stricken words, scholia written in the margins, scribblings, and quick memos like "must get some milk." Such annotations, which are in many ways similar to those studding the early draft of a comic strip, have done much to disabuse us of the illusion of a text immediately cast in its final material form. Another obstacle, however, has arisen: what sort of criteria are there to evaluate the work of the manuscript? Indeed, to what extent is the manuscript guided by the work in progress (in which case the completed work would then be the criterium by which successive drafts ought to be measured)? Or to what extent is the manuscript guided by other forces at work? If we admit that the writing process is not only the transposition of a text which existed originally in the writer's mind, then the role of the inscriptive gesture in the writing process has been generally and markedly underestimated, particularly by linguistics and semiology. I would like to develop such an approach here. The genesis of the text, as of any written mark (particularly that of drawing), must be considered from the viewpoint of the original spatial play which the hand stages. Neither the paradigm of the eye nor that of language allows us to grasp the meaning of "first draft" dynamics—the moment when its enunciation is born in distinction from what it enunciates. The paradigm of the hand, however, achieves such an understanding. Originally what is at stake in the hand is the very nature of the psychic investments which are bound up in it.

The importance given to hand gestures does not exclude the increasingly large share of textual creation which is performed by ma-

YFS 84, *Boundaries: Writing & Drawing*, ed. M. Reid, © 1994 by Yale University.

chines, starting with the home computer. In fact, the current techno-
logical evolution is drawing noticeably closer to the conditions
presiding over the manual creation of a manuscript. The computer has
gone beyond the limitations of the typewriter, which excludes the
possibility of many operations quickly and easily performed by the
hand, such as free usage of the full page and a variety of graphic marks.
The computer allows for words and sentences to be moved with a few
brief commands, for fragments to be stored, for multiple typographical
fonts to be used, and even for graphics to be introduced. Whereas the
earliest typewriter technology estranged the user from the process of
marking, the current developments tend towards a reconciliation with
it.

A. MANUAL PLEASURES

Although the necessary beginnings of the text, as well as the intention
of writing it, admittedly are initiated in the psychic system, the inscription process involves first and foremost the hand. The initial moment of writing, as of any marking, is when "something" (for what
does one call an original notion, an idea, an intuition, an inspiration?)
which has neither extension nor duration is given both—a spatial
existence (its marking) and a temporal existence (the time it takes for
the eye to run across it). While this moment may entail numerous
inscriptive instruments, ranging from a mere pencil to a computer, its
actual realization is impossible without involving the hand. This manual process has been overlooked by linguistic studies particularly
which are systematically interested in the end product of the manuscript. Yet the manuscript has its own requirements. For instance,
insofar as it takes far more time to inscribe writing than it does to
conceive it mentally, writing is often forced to create the whole project
and each of its components at the same time. Thus, an erasure can have
meaning with respect to the word or the sentence it eliminates, but
also as an element inscribed in a larger invisible network, the breathing
of the text as it were. Similarly, the fact that some sentences or parts of
sentences remain unfinished does not necessarily mean that the
thought underlying their inscription was lost at the same time. Indeed
nothing proves that thought travels along in complete signifying units.
A piece of a sentence provisionally left unfinished can act as witness to
the question proposed by the suspended ending, a question that under-
lies the paragraph in which it appears, even the text as a whole. Lastly,

the hand imposes the logic proper to the particular investments standing at its origin.

The Freudian theory of pleasure is based on the distinction between "pleasure of function" and "pleasure of organ." The former is said to involve the satisfaction of fulfilling a vital function, such as quenching one's thirst, satiating one's hunger, and acting on sexual tension. On the other hand, the latter is said to derive from the autoerotic satisfaction of a partial impulse: the excitation of one erogenous zone finds fulfillment in the very same spot where it occurs, with no direct relation to the fulfillment of a particular bodily function, even if it supports it.

Moreover, in Freud's perspective, the external world is perceived as a projection of one's own body. Consequently, according to him, the pleasure of manual activity can only be considered in reference to impulses sublimated after they have been invested in the body itself and bound to erogenous zones. In this perspective, manual pleasure adheres to the economic rule by which a sudden release of energy follows an accumulation phase experienced as painful. This release allows for the excitation to settle back down to its prior level. Manual pleasure is, under such conditions, related to various pleasure centers successively attached to various erogenous zones, oral, anal, and genital. Indeed, the hand can communicate pleasure to all of them by substituting for the primitive object of the impulse, such as when fingers enter the mouth to replace the breast or enter the anus to replace the tubular turd, or when they become a penis for the vagina, or when the hand becomes a vagina for the penis. Autoerotic satisfaction derives from the ability of hand to do onto oneself what the mother initially did for the infant. The various hand-related activities may then be said to derive from the various instances of sublimating their original impulses.

Some authors, however, question the status of the pleasure principle as the essential paradigm of psychoanalysis. They argue for a recognition of the "binding impulse" which parallels the sexual impulse and yet is independent from it. Although English psychoanalyst Bowlby (1978) gives the most cogent defense of this notion, it is Irme Hermann (1943) who should be credited for laying the foundations of the argument. According to him, along with the genito-sexual impulse, there exists a binding impulse (which Irme Hermann calls an "instinct") characterized by the desire to cling on to the mother's body. Unlike monkeys who can fulfill this instinct thanks to their powerful gripping lower limbs and the mother's thick fur, similar efforts to fulfill the same instinct remain frustrated among human babies. According to Irme Hermann, a sizable number of human achievements are intended to signify this essential frustration for which they substitute compensatory achievements. Such an approach no longer presents the world as a projection of the body itself but as a projection of the maternal body from which every human being is originally separated.

This lost dual unity then finds genital and nongenital substitutes. In the former, the child's hand replaces some parts of the maternal body or hand and supplies the pleasure which the mother initially gave to the child. Those parts are sought through contacts with the world, nature, groups, and institutions. According to this view, the hand is no longer regarded in relation to autoerotic pleasures but in relation to the special role it plays in attempting to reconstruct symbolically the lost dual entity. At times, its actions can be related to the epistemophilic impulse (the hand is then used to serve the desire for knowledge); at other times, it is used for the sexual impulse (in which it acts as an instrument of autoerotic fulfillment). However, it can be driven by its own needs, namely those concerning the end of the dual unity which has been irretrievably lost. Gesturing, as a motional force distinct from the original stage of impulses, is a critical means of breaking away from maternal symbiosis. Gesture plays just such a role in the young child's development including the model of processes which childhood implements, as well as in any creative activity which calls for it, particularly writing, although this is independent of the signifying constraints of grammatical and syntactical rules.

B. THE HAND, BLIND NET

The sign used in ancient Chinese civilization to designate the gesture of marking shows a hand tracing out the four corners of a square. It thus harks back to the gesture which initially partitioned off the unbound surface of the earth, establishing agricultural property and the birth of agrarian culture. Yet the origin of this gesture in a collective history is paralleled by an individual psychic history which belongs to each of us. This history places the gesture of marking into a double process of appropriating space: that of the physical, as well as psychic, distance separating the infant from the mother after birth, and that of the surface of the body itself. In my opinion this double process may account for the processes of working the manuscript, namely, the way it is treated by its creator, whether he or she is a writer or a graphic designer. Those processes find an origin, as well as their most delineated expression, in the first lines which a child draws on paper or any other marking surface, around the second year of his or her life. Thus the gesture itself, not the marks or the gaze, is what matters most.

A child's graphic activity goes through several phases which sharply distinguish it from the adult's graphic activity (Lurçat, 1964). When the child first begins to scribble, between the age of six and twelve months, he has not yet acquired visual control over his gestures, let alone the ability to draw. Visual control begins around the age of eighteen months: in such a case, it is control after-the-fact, since the eye follows the hand without yet guiding it. Only after the age of twenty-four months does the possibility of visual control over marking and gesture appear: the eye no longer follows the hand but guides it. Thus the earliest drawings are not guided by a visual exploration of space but by an exploration of movement. At its origin, graphic expression is blind. It is guided by muscular, tonic, and plastic sensations.

The earliest gestures which pertain to inscribing, however, are movements drawing away from the axis of the body, that is with the right hand extending away from the bodily axis, from the left to the right, and the left hand extending from the right to the left. These are the very gestures by which the baby is separated from the mother's body or from any other adult whose contact he may have sought. They are consequently a way for the child to stage the mother's coming and going—really her frequent absences—so as to tame and master the experience in the imaginary, as an early form of kinesic symbolization. The earliest markings, the inscriptions of those gestures, are a form of kinetic symbolization which guarantees the transfer from the kinetic realm, the realm of visual representation. The new graphic forms which the child produces clearly demonstrate the possibilities of recent neuromuscular growth. In the act of tracing, however, the child acts out more than its growing neuromuscular possibilities. The child creates a game and the practice of this game produces meaning. Moreover, the appearance of the child's first markings coincides with the development of newly acquired skills: walking (the simultaneous appearance of the first steps and the first markings has been pointed out by Prudhomme as early as 1947), sphincteral control, and language development. All those skills have something in common: they demonstrate an active control over separation anxiety and open the way to the child's independence. Thus, marking, precisely because it emerges at this time, has a privileged relation with the psychic process involved in the first separation, the separation of any human being from the mother or surrogate adult.

Considered in the context of separation processes, both actively or passively experienced by the child, the earliest markings are explained by Freud's famous *"fort-da game"* which he observed his grandson Ernst playing. The parallel between the two turns out to be particularly significant.

The child traces his first markings with a gesture he does not yet control, and it is only later that he visually discovers its production. In other words, with the *fort-da* game, the time of visual reunion follows a muscular action, whether it is throwing the spindle or drawing a mark. In both cases, the greater pleasure is bound to the second phase: the one which corresponds to the return of the spindle in one case and the discovery of a graphic concentration following the act of scribbling. What are, then, the psychic processes involved in those distinct moments?

In the time when he carries out the marking gesture, the child identifies himself with the departing mother; later, considering the outcome of his gesture, the child identifies with the trace which this movement leaves behind. Simultaneously, however, the child is free to be the one who also rejects the mother, as the trace which he sees becomes the mother separated from him. In this transaction, it is clear that what is at stake is the structural relationship rather than any of its representations, a structure which is organized around separation. The drawn mark is the first mode of image production in the individual's history, actually the first in the history of humanity. It stages the symmetrical separation process from beginning to end: the child passively separated from the mother who pushes him away from her, but also the child coming away from her by pushing *her* away. This whole scene is paralleled by the corresponding mental separation, even if verbal language cannot yet express it.

However, the role of tracing in creating the separation does not pertain only to the origination of the mark but also to the discovery of the trace. Every gap in drawing is also a bridge and vice versa. A trace simultaneously separates and binds the pieces of space which it delimits, much like the leaden line which separates and binds the stained-glass pieces on a latticed window. The trace is the reified symbol of separation. Hence, the choice of drawing over other forms of expression is particularly suited to the visual and mental exploration of the space which *simultaneously separates and binds* the mother to the child. Moreover, the possibility of transforming a separating gap (across three-dimensional space) into a bridging space (across the two-dimensional page) is a property characteristic of drawing. Tracing is the privileged way of turning the pluridimensional experience of muscular and tactile activity into a two-dimensional experience controlled by the eye; only in this way is the separation gradually accepted and symbolized. Repeating the gesture reinforces the psychic posture of the depressive position (Melanie Klein, 1968) which has already been inscribed through the dynamic relation with the world from the age of six and a half months. Although graphic activity gives greater strength and stability to the introjections at work in the relations to the mother or the surrogate adult, it is not in a position to replace those relations. Each type of investments at play in graphic activity requires that the corresponding psychic phenomena already be constituted. Graphic activity only occurs and develops once the relation between mother and child already has been internalized. Only then can drawing help the child settle his relation to the mother into a psychic, rather than physical, space and into a different duration, that of his own history.

Finally, when playing the drawing game, the child is not alone. Not only does he treat those early inscriptions as though they were real live imprints (he talks to them, names them, etc.) but he also develops a deep and original relationship with the page. With his or her every gesture, the page answers back as his mother would, and even better than she since it does so in a religiously exact manner (*au doigt et à l'œil*). The child changes his hand movement and the paper returns the changes back to the child's eyes, like an "ideal mother," as it were. Yet is the page able to gain the child's trust (without this initial contact of trust there would be no "inscriptive game")? It can only come from the child itself. Thus the child trusts the page with the internalized mother which inhabits him. Through his or her gesture, the child secures her echoing answer that is the processes involved in the mother's primary introjection and the internalized mother-child relation. At the same time, such echoing guarantees him that he is held within the maternal psychic system, which his own developing psychic system cannot forego.

The child's earliest graphic activity thus constitutes a place where the processes of the early mother-child relation are reproduced and stabilized. It represents a first containing structure for the child, while movements serve the process of early symbolization. Words appear later in gesture. Indeed, just as in the *fort-da* game, the child may add onomatopoeia to the marks he traces. Acting first as a "magic word," this word brings together the body, the gesture, and the affect in the same movement, just like the trace on the paper. Only later, when those connections have receded somewhat, or even are discontinued, can the act of naming occur. The child names the contents of his drawing after the fact. This, however, does not involve the processes of tracing per se but other, later, forms of symbolization.

THE WRITER AT GRIPS WITH HIS OR HER TRACES

c1. Tracing, Separation and Attachment: The Dual Space of Writing

Just as the child draws outward, pulling the trace away from himself, the adult draws outward and pushes away what he writes. In writing as in drawing, the "thrown-out" gesture conjures up a trace, a line. This "line," which seems tied to his movement, is used by the inscriber to pull back the thought that has been cast out in the act of inscription. Even better than the spindle tied to a string in the game described by Freud, arm and hand assisted by the pencil allow for a movement of casting and retrieving, of separating and binding. This back-and-forth motion, this tossing and retrieving, gives new life to the processes symbolizing the separation of mother and child and contributes to the constitution a mental framework capable of containing thoughts. The hand's drawing gesture is an essential movement by which thought learns how to think itself through. At first it darts out like an unruly horse, which is later led back and tamed, bound to the line which the hand holds fast upon the paper. Only once this prior condition has been fulfilled can the production of meaning occur, with the ebb and flow of thought as it gets on and gets waylaid, multiplies, fades, and backs away.

However, the inscriber, the subject of all this throwing and pulling also becomes its object. He is not only the one who casts out his mark—his thought—across the paper; he is also cast out by it, thus at the risk of losing his identity. The movement by which the author disinvests himself from the self and transfers it to the text turns the text into the primitive mother to whom the child tries to stand closer as she represents for him the spring of life. The feelings of being "played out," "beat," or "undone" which the writer experiences after

intense efforts come from this motion of ebb and flow, from this casting and retrieving; he or she willing assumes the position of a swimmer, washed away from the boat by a wave while trying to hold on,
pulling on the towline of writing just to remain afloat. Such is the trial
of writing. Whereas the one who refuses to relinquish thought to it
may continue to believe that he is still tightly secured to his thinking,
the one who ventures into this trial agrees to lose, if only temporarily.
Writing severs his moorings, casts him away like a swimmer trying to
pull his way back to the ship with a rope while waves drag him away
from his goal. As soon as we start tracing, only the trace guides us, what
we call in its sophisticated form, "the thread of writing" (*le fil de
l'écriture*). It is the only tie connecting the lone swimmer who has
agreed to dive into the unknown, trying to reach the hypothetical
target at the end of the way, not knowing whether he will ever succeed
or whether the stakes are worth the effort, not knowing whether the
thread leads to a treasure trove or a wreckage—no matter. The creator
is the one who agrees to venture forth with no certainty and follow this
thread unwinding ahead of him like Ariadne's thread, and falling behind him like a spider's web. The anxiety of the blank page may just be
the anxiety that there is no thread to pull or follow, the apprehension of
being left behind, with no *link* to anyone or without even the first half
of the thread.

From this perspective, the act of creating a manuscript—with all
its scribbling, its crossed-out words, and sometimes its memos—has
the same function for the writer as it does for the cartoonist. Such
work is the means whereby the creator tries to escape the fate of inexorable distance opened by the tracing gesture and simultaneously
opened and closed by the trace. Whereas the parallel between reading
a text and reading a drawing remains largely unresolved, the fact that
writing and drawing follow the same creative logic at the time of
tracing is a matter beyond doubt. Modelled after the child's early tracings, the inscriptive processes are always of a sensory, emotional and
motional sort. They are also involved in the symbolization of a containing form potentially capable of receiving the thought contents.
Without the early symbolization of "casting-out" and "pulling-up"
establishing the inscriptive gesture, the process of instilling meaning
in the trace, either drawn or written would be impossible, particularly
the production of meaning which revolves around the mirroring function of the trace and the various representations of the body itself.
The sensory and motive processes at stake in the inscriptive gesture

precede all its other processes and accompany them through each of their phases as a necessary condition.

c2. Traces and Proper Bodies

Once the child leaves the womb, he experiences a far more diverse and violent group of stimulations than before. The digestive system awakens the erogenous zones around the mouth and the anus, while at the same time it brings along a group of other stimulations, those of smooth internal muscles, and sensations of hunger and satiety. Also the exchanges with the surrogate mother and with the primary maternal environment (involving people, cultural habits, climatic constraints, etc.), work to focus investments onto other areas of the body proper. Once invested with the contacts to the primary maternal environment, those areas become the object of an autoerotic stimulation in which the hand "plays" the part of the Mother and the Child, stimulating other parts of the body, based on the model of the initial stimulations coming from the early surroundings.

One of the first tasks of the new-born child's psychic system is to gather those scattered areas of sensory focalizations by ascribing each part of his body, which has been felt and invested in and for itself, to a single group. A subsequent task involves bringing each part of the group which has been thus constituted to a specific function. In other words, the child will have to give meaning to the part. Throughout the task, the child is helped along by his environment which is instrumental in totalizing the various areas of the body and giving meaning to the sensations experienced by the newborn: for instance, a mother covering up her child because he is cold teaches him how to recognize as a feeling of coldness what had been only an undifferentiated, uneasy sensation, disconnected from any particular cause. The child's hands, however, play a critical role in this achievement. Exploring his own body, grabbing and touching his various body parts, the child throws hitherto missing bridges across the scattered sensory centers which correspond to more loosely innervated areas of the body, or parts which have just been neglected by the mother's hands. The child's hands glide over the body, exploring its limits, bringing together the scattered parts and then, more daringly, slowly replace the adult's hands in bringing the pleasure which the child originally received from them.

Thus, the hand reaches out to take hold of space and of the world. In some respects, the initial building of the text is similar to the initial process of gathering, by means of the hand, the sensations which are for now scattered across the body. For instance, the writer first jots down his ideas on different parts of the page. Or else he divides up— often by means of a color index—groups of words recalling thoughts, sensations, and feelings into separate blocks. And even when writing starts out on a seemingly organized thread, oftentimes during the process, the writer feels the need to break off writing to scribble down ideas and thoughts which spring up with no apparent, or at least immediate, connection to the object of his work and without his yet knowing their use and position in the overall construction.

In any case, do we not speak of "the body of the work"? An artist's various intuitions and perceptions are assembled together on the page in much the same way as the various cutaneous, muscular and aural sensations are progressively integrated into coherent units. In both cases, the gathering involves a movement from the depth up to the surface. The innermost body is held out on the surface periphery of the psychic system while inner sensations are pulled out of the deep onto the body's surface (internal perceptions, particularly pain, are perceived as being surface pain precisely because they are projected onto the surface of the body). Similarly the writer's various intuitions, stimulations, perceptions, and thoughts are projected onto the surface of the page. The work is, however, not a static surrogate to the artist's skin (its mere projection onto the surface of the page) insofar as it does not reproduce the sensory points characterizing the skin. Nonetheless, the work is a dynamic surrogate insofar as the processes regrouping the work into a continuous whole parallel those smoothing over the surface of the bodily shell: each sensation is first inscribed and precisely identified for its own sake; those inscriptions are then connected together; finally the process of their connection brings out channels of meaning which receive favored status as starting-points for subsequent developments.

My hypothesis is that each of those three moments, which are building blocks in the creation of the psyche, corresponds to a group of specific practices in the creation of the text.

Out of those three, the first moment would correspond to the inscriptive rhythm (fast, slow, even, or erratic) and to the manner of writing (smooth, hurried, or erratic, riotous even) whose patterns reproduce those of the various types of physical and psychical stimulation. At this time, the muscular and cutaneous aspects of writing would operate as a way of symbolizing, by means of the hand, unfocused bodily sensations which are not yet identified into representations. Parallel to the exploration of scattered centers of thought and representation there exists the corresponding use of different pages marked by just a few words, scribblings in the margins and the corners of the text, puzzling scholia (designed to avoid losing the particular thread of writing the writer is following at the time, and the corresponding train of thought occurring then), ellipses designed to point out that thought is still to follow a logical development which is eclipsed for the moment, while something requires the author's undivided attention elsewhere, etc.

The time when the originally scattered sensory centers are connected together on the surface of the body and in its depth could correspond, in the manuscript's arrows, to the paragraphs postponed or displaced, to the developments which are added in the margins or between the lines to bind two separately identified fragments which are still far apart.

At last, in a third development, and in the same way as the child first grasps the imaginary whole of the body upon perceiving himself in the mirror before he realizes its perceptive unity, it is possible that the writer anticipates the imaginary whole of his text, created after the image of his own body as a whole. The outline of his work—or fragments of drafts corresponding to various parts of the project—fulfill, even if they remain incomplete, the function of anticipating fantasmatically the projected totality.

The writer at work thus reinforces, confirms, and objectifies his own mental framework and his psychical relation to the primitive mother, and he or she does so independently of the work contents, solely by virtue of the processes involved in creating a text. The spatial lay-out of the text on a two-dimensional flat support enables various series of supplementary investments to come into play: the release of threatening stimuli and representations; the connection of those stimuli to a gesture leaving a trace, (that is the earliest form of symbolization which substitutes the mere kinetic release for the possibility of its representation); the constitution of a thought content through the metaphoric ability for the white page to take it in and contain its traces; the exploration of the gap separating the child from his mother which the trace seeks to fill in through its hallmark movement of binding and breaking away, of coming and going, of throwing away and grabbing back. Only then can the signifying process of the text occur, according to the grammatical and syntactical rules of the language being used.

These steps do not occur in succession but simultaneously. The process of turning thoughts into forms requires the possibility of a containing form in which the creator's thought can be cast and then retrieved. Such mechanism requires the possibility for the containing form to be invested both as: a) a metaphor of the mother's body, which is everyone's primal container, psychically as well as physically (the realm of bonding investments); and as b) a metaphor of one's own body (the realm of narcissistic and sexual investments).

These various functions of writing explain why seemingly useless and interfering activities take place under the creator's pen, parallel to the process of producing meaning itself. These occurrences are the necessary moments when the support of writing and the act of writing are reinvested so as to allow for a renewed production of meaning. Such activities as the author's darkening certain letters in his text and introducing repetitive graphic patterns or scribblings, are not only procedures of waiting for inspiration or ways for the mind to find some distraction. They are ways of investing the page as a metaphor for the container of thoughts. In other words, they are a way for the scriptor to make sure the page and his gesture are fulfilling their roles, and that the process of bringing meaning upon thought may enjoy further the support of the more archaic production of meaning which is represented by the investment of the page as a metaphoric container of one's own body and the mother's body. In this respect, anxiety before the white page may just be an anxiety about a lack of a container to receive the contents. It is not the white page that is used to contain the text, but rather the outlined page which is already inscribed, be it by a trace, a word, or a drawing. The habit of drawing or writing, calligraphied words in the margins corresponds to processes of appropriating space. And the advice about writing just anything—as long as you get something written!—in order to trigger off the writing process can be understood as the necessity of creating a first container even if later it must submit to considerable modifications. Contents and container are created in mutual reference throughout the text. In fact, linguistic models are often ruffled in the earliest drafts and, here again, the writing guidelines advocating disregard of syntax and grammar rest on good intuition.

Thus, the inscriptive process is above all the hand exploring a given space and organizing it according to its own possibilities. The process of the inscriptive movement first transforms physical stimulus into image and into representation; it then gathers those representations into a whole and hierarchizes them in order to connect them to a single purpose which will provide the cornerstone of the whole: sensation in the poem, illusion in the novelistic story, idea in the essay.

SELECT BIBLIOGRAPHY

Anzieu, Didier. *Le Corps de l'œuvre*. Paris: Gallimard, 1981.
Bowlby, John. *Attachment and Loss*, vol. 1. New York: Basic Books, 1982.
Freud, Sigmund. *Three Essays on the Theory of Sexuality*. New York: Basic Books, 1962.
Klein, Melanie. *Envy and Gratitude and Other Works*. New York: Delacorte Press, 1975.
———. *Essais de psychanalyse*. Paris: Payot, 1968.
Lurçat, François. "Rôle de l'axe du corps dans le départ du mouvement." *Psychologie Française* 6:4, 1961.
———. "Genèse du contrôle dans l'activité graphique." *Journal de Psychologie* 2, 1964.
Harris, Margaret. *A la découverte des bébés et des jeunes enfants*. Paris: Clancier-Guénaud, 1983.
Hermann, I. *L'Instinct filial*. Paris: Denoël, 1972.
Tisseron, Serge. "Le Dessein du dessin," in D. Anzieu and Coll., *Art et fantasmes*, Paris: Champ Vallon, 1981.
———. "Préalables à une recherche psychanalytique sur le trait." *Psychanalyse à l'université* 2:42, 1986.
———. *Tintin chez le psychanalyste*. Paris: Aubier-Archimbaud, 1985.
———. *Psychanalyse de la bande dessinée*. Paris: PUF, 1987.
Wallon, Henri. *De l'acte à la pensée*. Paris: Champs Flammarion, 1970.
Winnicott, Donald Woods. "Objets transitionnels et phénomènes transitionnels," in *De la pédiatrie à la psychanalyse*, Paris: P.B.P., 1969.
———. *Playing and Reality*. New York: Basic Books, 1971.

GEORGES ROQUE

Writing/Drawing/Color

> I want young people starting out in painting today to observe what is being done by handwriting instructors; these men start out by teaching the form of letters which the Ancients called "elements," and then they teach the syllables and finally the composition of words. May our own painting students follow this rule in order to learn how to paint . . .
> —Alberti, *Treatise on Painting*

> When I write the word "wine" in ink, the ink does not play the main role; rather, it allows for the durable inscription of the *idea* of wine. Thus ink functions to guarantee us of a permanent supply of wine.
> —Paul Klee, *Theory of Modern Art*

Instead of adopting a head-on approach to the relationship between writing and drawing—an approach which would inevitably include the all too commonplace etymological consideration of *graphein*—I will introduce a third term, color, in an effort to analyze the intersecting, triangular relations of writing, drawing, and color. Such an approach seems particularly appropriate since the drawing/color relationship is also a well-known pairing, with a historical significance all its own. By introducing a third term into these dualistic relations (color with respect to drawing/writing and writing with respect to drawing/color), I hope to expose and perhaps challenge the arbitrariness and artificiality of such binary divisions and regroupings (text and image, painting and . . .).

Let's start with a first configuration—a banal one which initially might seem a bit obvious. Generally speaking, drawing and writing alike appear to involve the exclusion of color. When one thinks about drawing, one thinks about black pencil, charcoal, stump, graphite— not colors.[1] Colored pencils always strike one as somewhat childish

---

1. The case of watercolor and pastel is doubtless somewhat unusual; if art historians tend to associate them with the art of drawing, the fact remains that they scarcely look like drawing; in many cases, the common ground is much more the supporting material—paper—than the drawing itself.

YFS 84, *Boundaries: Writing & Drawing,* ed. M. Reid, © 1994 by Yale University.

(but why?), just as a box of water colors always seems somewhat puer-
ile, and both lack the seriousness, and obviously the blackness, of
drawing. And so drawing is done, preferably, in black, in black on
white—just like writing. Whence the common ground between the
two media: the exclusion of color.

Like drawing, writing—at least printed writing—favors black and
seems to exclude color. (But what of writing done by hand? Don't
people write in blue, at least as often as they write in black? When I was
a student, the ball-point pen was forbidden—it was said to corrupt
youngsters' impressionable handwriting—and the ink pen was required, blue more often than black. As for the color red, it was reserved
solely for the teacher's corrections. One underlines in red, one "highlights" in yellow, but one writes in blue or in black. The latter two are
not, however, interchangeable. For all official correspondence, French
etiquette requires that one write by hand—the typewriter and the
computer being too "impersonal"—and in such instances, black ink is
a must. I am not certain why it is impolite to write in blue, but I myself
have internalized this rule, and feel compelled to use black for a considerable portion of my correspondence).

Am I losing myself in specious considerations? I do not know, trying as I am to understand this colorless kinship between writing and
drawing. After all, one does not tend to write with colored pencils and
use a variety of colors, unless one is trying to venture into the domain
of art and to give writing a *plastic* dimension that it does not usually
have. As for drawing with colored pencils, it must be understood that
such activity does not even qualify as drawing. Rather, it is an enterprise that almost negates drawing as such: "I know it's drawing, but
come on!"

One writes, like one draws, in black on white. *"C'est écrit noir sur
blanc"—Robert* [It's all there in black and white], as the expression
goes, designating something that is clearly visible, undeniable. There
is thus a certain visibility or clarity of the written word, and drawing
shares these qualities. Indeed, in terms of clarity, the contrast created
by black letters on a white page or background is optimal. Chevreul
studies this issue in his famous treatise: *De la loi du contraste simul-
tané des couleurs* (1839), in which he evaluates different possible combinations of colored printer's ink and paper. As one might expect, he
concludes that the standard combination of black ink on white paper is
the most satisfying one, in terms of both readability and ease on the
eyes (and in determining these things he makes a distinction between

reading for short periods of time and reading for long periods of time).[2] The preference for black on white established by Chevreul finds further justification in a property which he attributes to color, and which is the most interesting of his findings: "a property possessed in variable degrees by colours,-viz.: that of leaving upon the organ which has perceived them during a certain time the impression of their respective complementaries." Such an impression, however, can only confuse things and make reading uncomfortable: "It is clear that the more durable this impression is, [all] other things being equal, the less the organ will be disposed to receive distinctly new impressions, for there must necessarily be superpositions of different images, as in the mixed contrast, which, not being coincident, will tend to render the actual effect less marked than it might otherwise be," (Chevreul, §519, 126).

Thus, Chevreul presents as harmful to printed writing the very property which plays a central role in any work involving color—and it is with this observation in mind that a whole generation of painters will invoke Chevreul's law. As we have seen, the demand for clarity or immediate legibility, which color contradicts or compromises, is a trait which drawing and writing have in common. Clarity must, however, be understood in two senses: the clarity of drawing and writing which are readily distinguishable from their background, and the clarity of a lucidly expressed thought.

Now if there is one aspect of drawing upon which critics and artists are constantly insisting, it is that drawing allows for the clear expression of thought. This conception is, moreover, shared by those who defend color against drawing: Roger de Piles, for instance, states that "l'on appelle dessin la pensée d'un tableau"[3] ["drawing is the *thought* of a painting"], and explains that "[le dessin] représente la pensée de tout l'ouvrage avec les lumières et les ombres, et quelquefois avec les couleurs mêmes, et pour lors il n'est pas regardé comme une des par-

---

2. "Contrast of tone is the most favourable condition for distinct vision, if we consider White and Black as the two extremes of a scale comprehending the gradation from normal Grey: in fact, Black letters upon a White ground present the maximum of contrast of tone, and the reading is done in a perfectly distinct manner, without fatigue, by diffused daylight, affording the proof of what I advance." M.-E. Chevreul, *The Principles of Harmony and Contrast of Colors and Their Applications to the Arts*, ed. Faber Birren, newly revised edition (Westchester, PA: Schiffer Publishing, 1987), §6, 125. In our contemporary terminology, Chevreul's "contrast of tone" would actually be "contrast of lightness" [*contraste de clarté*].

3. Roger de Piles, *Cours de peinture par principes* (1708) (Nîmes: Editions Jacqueline Chambon, 1990), 150.

ties de la peinture, mais comme l'idée du tableau que le peintre mé-
dite," (de Piles, 79) [drawing "represents the thought upon which the
work as a whole is based, with its light and its shadows, and sometimes
with its very colors. For that reason, drawing is not held to be one of the
painting's components, but rather the idea of the painting that the
artist has in his mind."] Obviously, this statement assumes that drawing provides not only the sketch of a painting, but also the painting's
very essence; that drawing—not color—gives painting its great, forceful, over-arching lines. One might even go so far as to say that drawing,
according to this definition, encompasses all aspects of a painting,
including its color.

A drawing done in black, with its clear vision of the "idea of a
painting" also relies on the complicity between the idea and the hand
and between the hand and its tracings. Such a notion also reinforces or
overdetermines the relationship between drawing and writing, as if
there were some kind of correspondence between the hand and the
mind, or, as de Piles writes, between "le caractère de la main" [the
hand's character] and "le caractère de l'esprit" [the mind's character]:

> On connaît de qui est un Tableau comme vous connaissez de qui est
> une Lettre que vous recevez d'une personne qui vous a déjà écrit
> plusieurs fois. Et il y a deux choses qui font connaître ces sortes de
> lettres, le caractère de la main, et celui de l'esprit.—Il est vrai,
> interrompit Damon, que sans ouvrir une lettre, l'on juge souvent de
> qui elle est par le dessus.—C'est justement comme vous jugez des
> Tableaux, dit Pamphilie.[4]

> You know who has done a Painting just as you know who has
> written a Letter you receive from someone who has already written
> to you several times. And there are two things that enable you to
> know or to recognize such letters: the character of the hand, and that
> of the mind.—It is true, interrupted Damon, that without opening a
> letter, one often determines who sent it by the outside.—That is
> exactly how one judges Paintings, said Pamphile.

And de Piles adds that the hand's character "n'est autre chose qu'une
habitude toute singulière que chacun prend de former ses lettres, et le
caractère de l'esprit est le style du discours, et le tour que l'on donne à
ses pensées" [is simply a unique and individualized habit that dictates
how people form their letters, and the mind's character is the discur-

---

4. Roger de Piles, *Première Conversation* (1676), cited by Bernard Teyssèdre, *Roger de Piles et les débats sur le coloris au siècle de Louis XIV* (Paris: Bibliothèque des Arts, 1957), n. 3, 250.

sive style, the turn of a phrase that people use in expressing their thoughts.]

There is thus a sort of truth of the hand, which never lies and which reveals the state of mind of the person who is writing or tracing[5]—a truth of the hand which drawing and writing have in common. This privileged relationship between drawing and the hand helps to explain the frequency with which the medium is compared to writing. Matisse, for example, speaks of the exhausting work he does in order to let himself be penetrated by his model's essence or character, by the model's human expressiveness and by "all that can only be expressed by drawing." Only after making such an effort is he able to take up the pen with some measure of confidence: "J'ai alors le sentiment évident" [I now get the distinct feeling], "he continues."

> que mon émotion s'exprime par le moyen de l'écriture plastique. Aussitôt que mon trait ému a modelé la lumière de ma feuille blanche, sans en enlever sa qualité de blancheur attendrissante, je ne puis plus rien lui ajouter, ni rien en reprendre. La page est écrite; aucune correction n'est possible.[6]

> that my emotion expresses itself by means of a plastic writing. As soon as the zealous stroke of my pen has shaped the light of my white page, without taking away the latter's tender whiteness, there is nothing more I can add or take away. The page has been written; no further correction is possible.

And so we have a toned down analogy with writing, if we take into consideration, as Matisse invites us to do, the whiteness of the background (which has become [a] common place), and the unwillingness to repent ("the page has been written"). There thus emerges a sort of ethics of drawing, which forbids the use of an eraser, and which re-

---

5. This idea resurfaces in the writings of Jean Dubuffet, *L'Homme du commun à l'ouvrage* (Paris: Gallimard, 1973), 36–37: "Respecter les impulsions, les spontanéités ancestrales de la main humaine quand elle trace ses signes. Par exemple une certaine verticalité légèrement penchée qui est de l'écriture et de tout tracé humain perpétré avec application, en tirant un peu de langue . . . Plus la main de l'artiste sera dans tout l'ouvrage apparente et plus émouvante, plus humain, plus parlant il sera. Fuir tous les modes mécaniques et impersonnels. Les typographies et calligraphies les plus appliquées ont moins d'attrait que quelques mots manuscrits mais tracés sans intentions par une main loyale. On doit sentir l'homme et les faiblesses et les maladresses de l'homme dans tous les détails du tableau . . . Ainsi dans l'écriture manuscrite la barre d'un *t*, le point d'un *i*, se trouvent déportés, le troisième jambage d'un *m* porte la marque d'un mouvement d'impatience ou de lassitude."

6. Henri Matisse, *Ecrits et propos sur l'art*, ed. D. Fourcade (Paris: Hermann, 1972), 160.

quires drawing to show everything without dissimulation, without cheating, without trickery. This notion recalls Ingres's famous, oft-quoted assertion that "le dessin est la probité de l'art" [drawing is the probity of art].

This ethical dimension places drawing and writing in opposition to color, which is conceived of as unstable, immoral, and deceptive. For instance, it seems significant that when the author of an art anthology introduces the subject of color, he defines it in contrast to its age-old rival: " 'Le dessin est la probité de l'art.' La couleur en est le charme et la séduction—une personne sage doit s'en méfier, comme d'une sirène"[7] [Drawing is the probity of art. Color is art's charm and its seduction—a siren of whom the prudent person should beware]. In the face of color's seductiveness, a concept to which we will return, the probity of drawing is affirmed, as is the probity of writing and of all that they both reveal.[8] Thus, a certain truth of the pen stroke would stand to reinforce the analogy between writing and drawing.

The truth of the pen stroke that manifests itself in drawing has long been construed as fidelity to the idea which drawing aims to express— as if there were a perfect equivalence between drawing and the idea, established by the intermediary of the hand. In addition to its fidelity, obediance, and honesty, good drawing must possess one other characteristic, common to all good servants: discretion. It is in reference to this characteristic, in fact, that Rodin proposes yet another analogy between drawing and writing, and particularly literary style:

> Il en est du dessin en art comme du style en littérature. Le style qui se manière, qui se guinde pour se faire remarquer, est mauvais. Il n'y a de bon style que celui qui se fait oublier pour concentrer sur le sujet traité, sur l'émotion rendue toute l'attention du lecteur. L'artiste qui fait parade de son dessin, l'écrivain qui veut attirer la louange sur son style ressemblent à des soldats qui se pavaneraient sous leur uniforme, mais refuseraient d'aller à la bataille, ou bien à des cultivateurs qui fourbiraient constamment le soc de leur charrue pour le faire briller, au lieu de l'enfoncer dans la terre. Le dessin, le style vraiment beaux sont ceux qu'on ne pense même pas à louer, tant on est pris par l'intérêt de ce qu'ils expriment.[9]

7. Henri Guerlin, *L'Art enseigné par les maîtres: la couleur* (Paris: Henri Laurens, n.d.), 1.

8. Cf. several of the contributions to the volume: *The Hand and the Trace: Some Issues in Handwriting, Visible Language* 2, vol. 19 (Spring 1990).

9. Auguste Rodin, *L'Art. Entretiens réunis par Paul Gsell* (Paris: Gallimard, 1967), 78.

The same principle holds true for drawing in art and for style in literature. Style that bears the marks of affectation, that puts on airs in order to call attention to itself, is bad. Style can only be good insofar as it allows itself to be forgotten so that the reader will focus on the work's subject matter and emotional content. The artist who shows off with his drawing and the writer who seeks praise for his style, are like soldiers who would parade around in their uniform, but refuse to go into battle; they are like farmers who constantly polish their plow to make it shine brilliantly, instead of digging it into the ground. Truly beautiful drawing and style are those which one does not even think to praise, so taken is one by what they express.

It would be banal to repeat the saying that style is above all a "poinçon servant à écrire [an engraver's point for writing]—and therefore an instrument common to drawing and writing—were it not for Rodin's agricultural metaphor that absolutely insists on such a comparison, with his emphasis on the plow's shiny brilliance (do we not speak of a writer's "brilliant" style?). As for the military metaphor, it says exactly what it means: drawing and style alike are soldiers who should serve their army rather than "parade around." In clear contradistinction to drawing, however, color is a bad soldier that does parade around, showing off instead of being content to serve, seeking to show its own brilliance. Color, in other words, tends to express itself.[10]

Perhaps now we are beginning to sense the reason for the longtime complicity between drawing and writing: both efface themselves for the sake of that which they seek to express, whereas color resists being reduced to such a function. In this light, the artists' and critics' frequent analogies between drawing and writing can be seen to derive from a desire to emphasize drawing's *instrumental* function: drawing as an instrument of the hand whose tracings are governed by the dictates of the idea, drawing as a faithful and trustworthy intermediary. It is as if drawing, like writing, has to be as discreet as possible, in order to convey meaning effectively. The signifier should be transparent, so that it in no way detract from the signified.

This notion finds confirmation in the theories developed by Charles Blanc in the second third of the nineteenth century, particularly in his eloquently titled book, *Grammaire des arts du dessin* (1867). The analogy with alphabetical writing, and its attendant

10. Such is not, however, Rodin's position—which is in fact a rare one for his time, since he places color on the same level as drawing. At the end of the above-cited statement, he adds: "de même pour la couleur" [the same holds true for color].

"grammatical" rules, becomes even more explicit in the introduction to Blanc's subsequent work, the *Grammaire des arts décoratifs.*[11] Blanc's position is important and symptomatic because it figures a whole classical tradition at the very moment when this tradition, which subordinated color to drawing, was being challenged by the Romantics, the Orientalists, and then the Impressionists, all of whom assign a central role to color. Charles Blanc's work thus constitutes a turning point of sorts, and it is for this reason that his conception of the relationship between color and drawing deserves examination (such examination appears all the more important, in fact, when we realize that his thought influenced a considerable number of painters).[12] "Tout dessin," Blanc explains

> est l'expression d'une pensée ou d'un sentiment, et par cela même il est chargé de nous faire voir quelque chose de supérieur à la vérité apparente, lorsque celle-ci ne révèle aucun sentiment, aucune pensée. Mais quelle est cette vérité supérieure? Elle est tantôt le caractère de l'objet dessiné, tantôt le caractère du dessinateur, et, dans le grand art, elle est justement ce qu'on appelle le style.[13]

> All drawing is the expression of a thought or a feeling, and as such, its role is to show us something superior to the apparent truth, which often reveals no thought and no feeling. But what is this superior truth? Sometimes it is the character of the drawn objet, sometimes the character of the person drawing. In great art, moreover, this superior truth is what we call style.

According to Blanc, this definition of drawing gives us a clear indication of its origins: "Le dessin est un projet de l'esprit, comme l'indique si bien l'orthographe de nos pères qui écrivaient *dessein*" (Blanc, ibid.) [Drawing is a design, plan or project of the mind, as we can see in the spelling of our forefathers who wrote *dessein*] This goes back to the Renaissance conception of drawing as *idea* (the famous *designo*) which we find in the writings of Vasari: "This design is nothing but a visual

11. Charles Blanc, *Grammaire des arts décoratifs*, 2nd edition (Paris: 1992), III. "Just as the twenty-five letters of the alphabet have been, and will continue to be, sufficient for the formation of words necessary to express all human thought, so too a few elements susceptible to multiple combinations have been, and will continue to be, sufficient for the creation of an infinite number of ornaments."
12. I have already discussed other aspects of Charles Blanc's views on color. Cf., my "Portrait de la couleur en femme fatale," *Art & Fact* (Université de Liège) 10: (1991), 4ff.; and "Couleur et sacrifice," *Athanor* 2 (1991), *Arte e sacrificio*, 55 ff.
13. Charles Blanc, *Grammaire des arts du dessin*, 1st edition 1867 (Paris: Henri Laurens, n.d. <1880>), 531.

expression and clarification of that concept which one has in the intellect, and that which one imagines in the mind and builds up in the idea."[14] In *The Idea in Painting, Sculpture, and Architecture*, Zuccari makes this definition of drawing even more precise by elaborating on the notion of an "inner design" (*designo interno*), which he too identifies with the idea.[15]

If Charles Blanc's conception of drawing thus remains marked by Renaissance and classical thought,[16] we might nevertheless think that such a view has had its day, and that it is no longer considered valid. However, this is not the case. We can find this very same notion, for instance, in Matisse's writings: "Dessiner, c'est préciser une idée. Le dessin est la précision de la pensée. Par le dessin les sentiments et l'âme du peintre passent sans difficulté dans l'esprit du spectateur" (Matisse, n. 8, 162). [To draw is to give a precise rendering of an idea. Drawing is the precision of thought. Drawing transmits the painter's feelings and soul directly into the viewer's mind]. Even more recently, conceptual art has once again attempted to radicalize this conception of drawing as the expression of an idea—a concept which has profoundly influenced contemporary drawing and which constitutes two of its great trends.[17]

But one point is striking in this formulation of the relationship between drawing and writing. For in the above-cited text ("Drawing is a design, plan or project of the mind, as we can see in the spelling of our forefathers who wrote *dessein*"), Charles Blanc legitimates this conception of drawing by referring not to the Renaissance, but to *etymol-*

14. Giorgio Vasari, Proemio of the second edition of *Le Vite* . . . , 1568, cited by Erwin Panofsky, *Idea: A Concept in Art Theory* (New York/London: Harper & Row, 1968), 62.

15. As Panofsky notes, "On Zuccari's terminology it should be remarked that, although . . . he heavily reproached Vasari for using the term 'idea' in the sense of 'imaginative ability' instead of in the sense of 'imaginative content,' he himself uses the term *designo* (= idea) in exactly the same double significance; he designated the process as well as the object of the act of 'designing' as designo," op. cit., n. 30, 227.

16. In Blanc's view, drawing encompasses architecture, sculpture, and painting (whereas color is only necessary to painting): "drawing is so essential to each of these three arts that they are properly termed the arts of drawing," op. cit., 21. Blanc thus stays faithful to Vasari, for whom drawing is "the father of our three arts," an idea taken up by Le Brun who annexes architecture to the Academy, and who commissions this inscription for the Institute's pediment: "Ecole de dessin." On Blanc's classical tastes, cf., M. F. Zimmermann, *Les Mondes de Seurat: son œuvre et les débats artistiques de son temps* (Anvers/Paris: Fonds Mercator/Albin Michel, 1991), 28ff.

17. Cf., Daniel Dezeuze, "Eléments de réponse à la question: pourquoi le dessin?" in *Le Dessin pourquoi?, Actes du colloque de l'Ecole d'art de Marseille*, published by the Ecole d'art de Marseille-Luminy, 1991, 39–40.

ogy. It is difficult not to see in this reference a collusion between drawing and writing, especially since the author makes a similar attempt at etymological legitimation in the introduction to his book:

> Le mot *dessin* a deux significations. Dessiner un objet, c'est le représenter avec des traits, des clairs et des ombres. Dessiner un tableau, un édifice, un groupe, c'est y exprimer sa pensée. Voilà pourquoi nos pères écrivaient *dessein* et cette orthographe intelligente disait clairement que tout dessin est un projet de l'esprit.[18]

> The word *drawing* has two meanings. To draw an object is to represent it with pen-strokes, patches of light and shadow. To draw a scene, a building, a group is to express one's thought through these objects. That is why our forefathers wrote *dessein*, and this intelligent spelling made it clear that all drawing is a design, plan, or project of the mind.

More interestingly still, Zuccari too invokes this "intelligent spelling" in order to justify the Italian *designo* (a term which lies at the origin of the French *dessein*/dessin): for him, etymology justifies the proposition that drawing is a sign of divine ressemblance: "*designo = segno di dio in noi*" (cited by Panofsky, 88) [designo = the sign of God in us]. Without getting into the etymological justification for a link between drawing and the idea, let us simply accept that this argument can help us to understand why color is excluded from such a project; ideas, thoughts, or concepts would seem to be more "naturally" linked to drawing than to color. And this characteristic would seem to bring writing and drawing even closer together, both of them being charged with the expression of thought. To return to Charles Blanc, we find a neat formulation of the problem in these terms: "Je suppose que le peintre étende sur sa toile le ton juste de la chair humaine: ce ton ne nous donnera point l'idée de l'homme, tandis qu'il nous suffira des plus grossiers contours pour nous rappeler cette idée" (Blanc, op. cit., 22) [Suppose that the artist paints his canvas using the very color of human flesh: this color will not give us the idea of a man, unless we have the crudest of contours to remind us of this idea]. Color, unlike drawing, is

---

18. Charles Blanc, *Grammaire des arts du dessin*, op. cit., 22–23. According to Bloch and von Wartburg's *Dictionnaire étymologique de la langue française*, the terms *dessin* [drawing] and *dessein* [design, plan, project], based on the model of the Italian *designo*, have only had their modern meanings since the end of the eighteenth century. Before then, *dessein* was more commonly used than *dessin* for both meanings.

patently incapable of expressing an idea. To develop this hypothesis further, Blanc proceeds to give the example of the black man, whom he presents in black and white: "Tous les nègres sont noirs, comment les distinguer autrement que par la proportion de leur membres, la hauteur de leur taille ou les lignes de leurs démarche?" (ibid.) [All black men are black: how can you tell them apart if not by the proportion of their limbs, by their height, by the lines of their stride?]. From this he concludes that "la nature s'est donc servie du dessin pour définir les objets, de la couleur pour les nuancer" [nature relies on drawing to define objects, and on color to nuance them].

And so we keep coming back to drawing's power to express an idea—a power which color does not possess. It is hardly surprising, in this context, that Charles Blanc condemns color for not submitting to an instrumental role, and that he exhorts it to remain a slave to drawing.

> Le coloriste passionné, avons-nous dit, invente sa forme pour sa couleur: rien n'est plus vrai. Tout, chez lui, est subordonné à l'éclat de la teinte. Non seulement le dessin fléchit, doit fléchir, mais la composition est commandée, gênée, violentée, par la couleur. Pour aménager ici une teinte violette qui surexcitera telle draperie jaune, il faudra ménager à cette teinte un espace, inventer un accessoire, peut-être inutile. [Blanc, op.cit., 573]

> The enthusiastic colorist, we have said, invents forms for his colors: nothing could be more true. The colorist subordinates everything to the radiance of tints and hues. Color not only requires drawing's submission; it also commands, compromises, and does violence to composition itself. In order to accommodate a violet hue which will offset some yellow drapery or other, it is often necessary to create a space for this hue, or invent an unnecessary accessory for it.

The odd tone adopted by Blanc in this passage can be explained, at least in part, by his historical context: the age of Orientalism and of an ever-increasing emphasis on the importance of color. According to Blanc, color is a force which must be reined in, for "en poursuivant avec passion le triomphe de la couleur, le peintre court le risque de sacrifier l'action au spectacle" [if the painter passionately strives for the triumph of color, he runs the risk of sacrificing action to spectacle.] And here, of course, we are back to the parade evoked by Rodin.

Based on these arguments, we might propose the following hypothesis for the second half of the nineteenth century, if not earlier: the instrumental function of drawing, and its potential autonomy, must be safeguarded against the threat posed by color. Furthermore, it is in an effort to reinforce this instrumentality, to which both drawing and writing ostensibly can be reduced, that the analogy between the two media develops. Whence Blanc's recourse to literature, this time in an almost pathetic peroration:

> De même que les littératures inclinent à leur décadence quand les images l'emportent sur les idées, de même l'art se matérialise et décline infailliblement lorsque l'esprit qui dessine est vaincu par la sensation qui colore; lorsqu'en un mot l'orchestre, au lieu d'accompagner le chant, devient à lui seul le poème. [Blanc, 573]

> Just as literature moves toward decadence when images take precedence over ideas, so must art inevitably begin to decline once the mind that draws is conquered by the sensation that colors; once the orchestra, instead of accompanying the song, itself becomes the poem.

Such considerations undoubtedly shed some light on the exact nature of color's "immorality," which consists both in a refusal to submit to discipline and to drawing, and in a willful attempt to be seductive on its own terms. For color is faulted with becoming a sign of nothing other than itself, whereas drawing remains the sign of something else (be it an object, a thought, or anything else that moves the artist). Whence the ubiquitous allusions to and analogies with writing, which is held to be another instrumental mode of thought, obediently submitting to that which it expresses.

This provisional conclusion might rightly be deemed a bit flat and uninspired, if its only thrust were to affirm that drawing and writing are both signs. It might even be accused of neglecting Damisch's famous advice that the question of writing and of the sign be dissociated in any study of the relations between painting and writing.[19] To nuance things somewhat, however, the important point to be made here is that a certain conception of painting which prevailed in the West ever since the Renaissance, depended, if not on the exclusion of color, at least on its vassalization or enslavement. In other words, it was necessary to reduce color's potential autonomy, its refusal to become a sign, a vehicle or an intermediary for other meanings, from the moment that

19. Hubert Damisch, lecture given at the round table on "La Peinture et l'écriture des signes," reprinted in *La Sociologie de l'art et sa vocation interdisciplinaire: l'œuvre et l'influence de Pierre Francastel* (Paris: Denoël/Gonthier, 1976), 198.

it breaks free of drawing and is no longer padding, illumination. It is of course on these grounds, and on these grounds alone, that the analogy with writing is put into place—it functions to reinforce the role of drawing.

Such would have been the lot of color: not to be unique and rare, but to be subordinate or subject to drawing. To set things straight once and for all, Charles Blanc puts it bluntly, summing up an entire tradition: "Non, la couleur n'est pas plus rare que le dessin, mais elle joue dans l'art le rôle féminin, le rôle du sentiment; soumise au dessin comme le sentiment doit être soumis à la raison, elle y ajoute du charme, de l'expression et de la grâce" (Blanc, 23) [No, color is no more unique or rare than drawing, but the former plays the feminine role in art, the role of feeling; subject to drawing just as feeling should be subject to reason, color brings to the marriage its share of charm, expressiveness, and grace].

In keeping with an age-old division which is still widely accepted and of which we are not even entirely conscious, color is relegated to the realm of emotion, sentiment—a position which makes it all the more incapable of expressing an idea. According to the tradition which Blanc both summarizes and exacerbates, color is feminine.[20] The immorality of color is thus also the immorality attributed to woman, and the same gender coding applies to its wiles, its persuasiveness, its deceptiveness. In its relation to drawing, color is a mere *ornament*— superfluous, but also necessary, added to drawing as a type of supplement.

All of these traits, however, are also those which, as Derrida has shown in the *Grammatology* and subsequent works, characterize writing in its relation to speech (*la parole*). Such a realization necessarily brings about a shifting of alliances, if it is indeed true that color shares common ground with writing! How is it possible, from this moment on, to insist upon a "complicity" between drawing and writing, aimed at keeping color in line? Perhaps at this point it is necessary to introduce a fourth term, speech (la parole), in order to obtain an equivalence which would look like this: color is to drawing as writing is to speech. Let's see if this new formula stands up to analysis.

Indeed, it is by no means difficult to show that color, in its relationship to drawing, acts as a supplement, an ornament, something which is added, and which plays the contradictory role of being simul-

---

20. Cf. my "Portrait de la couleur en femme fatale," in loc. cit.

taneously superfluous and necessary. The idea of color as make-up, for example, dovetails quite nicely with Derridean analyses of writing.[21] Besides, make-up, like color, is one of the definitions of the *pharmakon*.[22] In most cases, then, color functions to appear alongside and in opposition to drawing, like a supplement—it serves rather to color in the outlines traced by drawing, or else to *enhance* them. Obviously enough, this last term is of tremendous interest to us here. Drawing does not exclude color, but demands its subjection or subjugation; color is forced to remain, in keeping with Ingres's orders, the lady-in-waiting, the one in charge of costumes and makeup. In the form of wash or watercolor, for example, color is clearly present, but as a type of embellishment or enhancement. To enhance is to bring out, to bring up, to sublate [*relever*], "fard qui rehausse l'éclat du teint," *Robert* [make-up that enhances one's skin-tone]. It is of course in a similar way that writing constitutes the sublation [la relève] of speech.

Furthermore, the privilege which speech enjoys as presence-to-itself, and compared to which writing appears secondary or supplementary, recalls the privilege accorded to drawing as an apt expression of the idea, as the truth of the idea. This parallel is particularly fitting given the fact that the voice has always enjoyed a special relationship with the idea. All one has to do is think of Charles Le Brun, presiding over the Academy as its master, or rather as its "dictator," (L. Venturi). When called upon to pronounce his verdict on the relationship between drawing and color, he plays skillfully on the polysemy of the word "design" (*dessein*), insisting upon that "intelligent spelling" which Charles Blanc will later invoke once again:

> On doit savoir qu'il y a deux sortes de desseins, l'un qui est
> intellectuel ou théorique, et l'autre pratique. Que le premier dépend
> purement de l'imagination, qu'il s'exprime par des paroles et se
> répand dans toutes les productions de l'Esprit. Que le dessein
> pratique est produit par l'intellectuel et dépend par conséquent de
> l'imagination et de la main, il peut aussi s'exprimer par des paroles.
> C'est ce dernier qui avec un crayon donne la forme et la proportion et
> qui imite toutes les choses visibles, jusqu'à exprimer les passions de
> l'âme, sans qu'il ait besoin pour cela de la Couleur, si ce n'est pour
> représenter la rougeur et la pâleur.[23]

21. For more on this topic, cf. the study of make-up proposed by Jean-Claude Lebensztejn, "A Beauty Parlour," Traverses #7, *Le Maquillage* (February 1977): 74 ff.
22. Cf. Jacques Derrida, "La Pharmacie de Platon," *La Dissémination* (Paris: Editions de Minuit, 1972).
23. Charles Le Brun, address to the Academy, 1672, cited by Bernard Teyssèdre, *Roger de Piles et les débats sur le coloris au siècle de Louis XIV*, op. cit., n. 1, 178.

It is important to realize that there are two types of design, one which is intellectual or theoretical, and one which is practical. That the first one depends purely on the imagination, that it is expressed in speech and that it is manifest in all productions of the Mind. That the practical design is produced by the intellectual one and consequently depends on the imagination and on the hand. That the latter type of design too can be expressed in speech. It is this second type which, with the help of a pencil, produces form and proportion, and which imitates all visible things, to the point of expressing the very passions of the soul, without needing color to do any of this, except for the representation of redness and pallor.

This defense of drawing contains a good number of the ideas we have already encountered. First of all, the semantic play on the *word* "design" establishes a connection between drawing and design while endowing it, by means of a theory/practice opposition, with considerable breadth and legitimacy. Given Le Brun's intellectualization of drawing, it is clear that the medium indeed depends on the hand, but also on the imagination—just like design. From this it is possible to conclude that drawing and design alike are prone to being expressed in speech, with the latter functioning as the transparent instrument of the expression of thought. But it is clearly assured by the legitimation which states that drawing can take pride in its ability to imitate all visible things, without recourse to color; the latter, an ornament or supplement, added to drawing without necessity, is nevertheless indispensable for the representation of redness.[24] Thus, Le Brun's text sums up much of the thought we have already examined, but with a twist—the difference being its introduction of speech as the privileged expression of design and, consequently, of drawing. Whence the new parallel we have proposed in the form of an equivalence: color is to drawing as writing is to speech.

As a starting hypothesis, then, we might say that speech and drawing alike hold certain privileges: that of the expression of thought, of clarity, of black on white. And, just as writing is considered, in its relation to speech, the "instrument of an instrument,"[25] so color, in its subordination to drawing, is also conceived of as the instrument of an instrument.

---

24. This concession to color has enjoyed tremendous favor ever since Philostrates; most notably, it appears in the writings of Diderot and Charles Blanc. I have discussed this issue in my "Portrait de la couleur en femme fatale," in loc. cit.

25. Roland Barthes, "Sémiographie d'André Masson," *L'Obvie et l'obtus: essais critiques* III (Paris: Editions du Seuil, 1982), 144.

As soon as it is formulated, however, this attractive symmetry calls forth an objection, for it is not certain that speech is an instrument, since metaphysicians have—to go quickly here—thought of speech as the "natural" expression of thought. Drawing, on the other hand, may be constantly defined as the expression of thought, as the accurate expression of the idea, but it also remains an instrumental expression, a trace. Le Brun's "practical design," even if it can be expressed aloud in speech, nevertheless essentially depends on the *hand*.

Thus, emboldened by this development, and leaving the question of speech aside, we can now approach writing/drawing/color relations from a different angle. Up until now, indeed, we have insisted on drawing's complicity with writing, aimed at keeping color in line, subservient. But having taken into account all the traits which unite color and writing—supplement, ornament, seduction—in opposition to the probity of drawing, we find ourselves obliged to reexamine our initial outline, or at least to *nuance* it. The analogy between drawing and writing, in all the examples we have given, has always relied on the link between drawing and imitation, between drawing and the expression of the idea, and so has sought to establish its legitimacy by means of a certain conception of "instrumental" writing. It is not without interest, however, to note that historically, it is on the very same metaphysical basis that drawing has been promoted, as a supposedly clear expression of the idea, whereas color (like writing) has been consistently reduced to the ambiguous status of the supplement.

Drawing's alleged superiority to color is not, however, necessarily based on imitation, for if one were to take into account this criterion alone, one could reverse the entire argument, as Roger de Piles does in this unequivocal statement: "Le peintre qui est un parfait imitateur de la nature, pourvu de l'habitude d'un excellent dessin, comme nous le supposons, doit donc considérer la couleur comme son objet principal, puisqu'il ne regarde cette même nature que comme imitable, qu'elle ne lui est imitable que parce qu'elle est visible, et qu'elle n'est visible que parce qu'elle est coloriée" (de Piles, 145) [The painter, who imitates nature perfectly and is, we assume, endowed with excellent drawing skills, must therefore take color as his principal object, since he only looks at nature as something he can imitate, since he can only imitate it insofar as it is visible, and since it is only visible insofar as it is colored].

What, then, is the basis for drawing's privileged status, if it is true that color imitates better than drawing? Perhaps a little detour into semiotics will prove helpful here. In order to transpose the color/ drawing debate, we might say that drawing as signifier directly refers or corresponds to the signified (idea, concept), whereas color's plasticity takes precedence over its iconic dimension. But when we formulate things in this way, the source of the dissymmetry becomes immediately apparent: the plastic dimension of drawing is erased for the sole benefit of its iconic dimension.[26] For drawing, like color, also possesses a plan of expression. In the classical drawing/color debate, however, the two elements are not on equal footing: drawing is not the elementary stroke or trait which constitutes its "plan of expression," as the semioticians would say, but is almost always conceived of as representational drawing, whereas color is rightly conceived of in terms of its "plan of expression" alone. From this point on, it is not difficult to show that color, deprived of its "plan of content," is incapable of expressing a signified—a task which drawing accomplishes all the more easily since it has already been posited as a vehicle for content.

The fact that drawing is made up of *strokes* [traits] [27] suggests another relation to writing, a relation which would also include color, since color too is composed of elementary strokes or traits. And so there emerges, beyond the tired old opposition between drawing and color, another relationship which connect writing to both drawing and color.

In this sense, the "grammar of drawing" is a deceptive notion, for as soon as it posits drawing as the mere expression of an idea, confining it to the level of content alone, and thus neglecting the medium's constitutive traits or strokes. It is not without importance to note, however, that around 1880 other grammars come into being which act as kind of a crucible for "abstraction," as do certain grammars of the trait or stroke, which do not deal with drawing, as well as grammars of color. Bourgoin's *Grammaire élémentaire de l'ornement*, for instance, defines the elementary traits or strokes of the "graphic alphabet," and then proceeds to study its "rules of conjugation," by considering "les figures de l'alphabet <graphique> non plus comme des signes ou des figurations graphiques destinées à écrire les formes comme les lettres écrivent les mots, mais bien comme des figures ou des objects distincts

26. For further elaboration of this distinction, cf. Groupe *M, Traité du signe visuel: pour une rhétorique de l'image* (Paris: Editions du Seuil, 1992), 113 ff.

27. The author is playing on the double meaning of the French word "trait," which means both "stroke" (as in penstroke) and "trait" (as in character trait).—Translator's note.

existant en propre et par eux-mêmes"[28] [the figures of the 'graphic' alphabet no longer as signs of graphic figurations, designed to write forms as letters write words, but rather as distinct figures, objects which exist in and of themselves]. And what is true for drawing also holds true for color. A grammar of color is therefore possible, if it is based on the model of drawing's elementary traits: "As by the deflection of *a point in space* may be generated all the elementary figures and forms of geometrical and constructive science, so from a like deflection of *a spot in place* may be generated all the elementary and compound hues of colors; the science which is called Chromatics."[29]

Thus, if it is true that color is not drawing's *other*, relegated to the realm of emotion, beyond language, or, as we might say today, associated with [libidinal] drives, are we not justified in thinking that color has won its "autonomy" only with the help of a "science of painting," a chromatics, or rather a *grammar*, which breaks color down into alphabet, syntax and conjugations, in order to establish the rules of its *harmony?*[30]

And so the mediation of writing has taught us, at the very least, to relativize the opposition between drawing and color, to emphasize the fact that they are both susceptible to "grammatical" analysis, to a break-down into elementary traits or strokes, which have a notable impact on the development of nonfiguration, both in the decorative arts and in chromatics.

We can find confirmation of this if we take a look at the current situation of the arts. The "eternal conflict," as Matisse called it, between drawing and color appears to be waning—although not disappearing altogether[31]—in that color on the one hand, and drawing on the other, have both liberated themselves from the once-dominant instrumental-representational function, in order to stand on their own and assert their independent value. Henceforth, any examination of

28. Jules Bourgoin, *Grammaire élémentaire de l'ornement* (Paris: Delgrave, 1880), 33.

29. George Field, *A Grammar of coloring Applied to Decorative Painting and the Arts*, new edition (London: Lockwood & Co., 1875), 2.

30. In France, cf. also E. Guichard, *La Grammaire de la couleur* (Paris: H. Cagnon, 1882).

31. There nevertheless remains, beyond the age-old conflict, a lasting trait which is surely one of the main reasons for the conflict, and that is that color tends to parade around, in opposition to drawing. As Titus-Carmel noted: "Tempérer l'éclat de la couleur par le travail de la mine de plomb, la laisser seulement filtrer à travers les mailles de ce filet de hachures grises qui en éteint les feux," taken from his "Notes d'ateliers (1973–74)," in *Le Dessin pourquoi?*, op. cit., 15.

drawing and writing must no longer posit each medium as an instrument, but rather as a *trace* (or, to put it another way, no longer as a plan of content, but rather as a plan of expression). It is significant, in this context, that Barthes was only able to address the question of drawing by resorting to the idea that the essence of writing is unreadability.[32] It thus seems necessary to abandon the idea of writing's instrumentality, so that writing can appear as a trace and so that another connection between writing and drawing can emerge.

Whence the different stakes that surface beyond the instrumental function. Whence also the rediscovery of the value and virtue of drawing as stroke. As Daniel Dezeuze notes, after referring to the work of Derrida and Barthes: "Il y a donc une sorte de procès en défense de l'écriture qui est aussi la défense du dessin" (Dezeuze, 42) [There is thus a sort of trial, a defense of writing which is also a defense of drawing].

The importance that is henceforth attached to the stroke or trait in drawing, and likewise to the spot or patch in color, leads us, in conclusion, to reconsider the element that served as our point of departure: the black/white opposition which we identified as the common ground between writing and drawing, and which seemed to involve an exclusion of color. On this point, too, we must now be more prudent, more subtle. For this construct is based on the idea of black as noncolor—an idea which we must call into question. Just as the black trace acquires a certain legitimacy [*its lettres de noblesse*] when it is freed from a purely instrumental or representational function, so black as a color can affirm itself and triumph. It does so in the work of Matisse, for example—Matisse whose talent, as Renoir once told him, resides solely in his use of the color black (Matisse, *Ecrits et propos*, 202). Soulages also rehabilitates black, even more brilliantly than Matisse. Even for a painter like Albert Ayme, who does not use black, but sticks to different combinations of the three primary colors, the work of color and its dynamism, are clearly conceived of as moving from white to black—like writing, which is an important part of his art.[33] From this we might move off in another direction, turning our

32. Cf. for example one of his remarks at the round table "La Peinture et l'écriture des signes," in *La Sociologie de l'art et sa vocation interdisciplinaire*, op. cit., 191, and *L'Obvie et l'obtus*, op. cit., 144.

33. Cf. the catalogue, *Albert Ayme: Rétrospective 1960–1992* (Paris: Ecole nationale supérieure des Beaux-Arts, 1992). I raised this issue in my contribution to the catalogue, "Notes sur la partition des couleurs," 52–54.

attention to the importance of writing for 'color' painters like Van Gogh or Delacroix, in whose work color indeed seems to go hand in hand with writing.[34] In the final analysis, then, the antimony between color and drawing no longer seems so pronounced, thanks to their common links to writing. Henceforth other configurations may be emerging . . .

—Translated by Caroline Weber

34. Jean-Pierre Guillerm gives a synthetic view of the links between the work of color and the work of writing in Delacroix's art, in his essay "Blanc/Noir," *Des Mots et des couleurs/2*, ed. J.-P. Guillerm (Lille: Presses Universitaires de Lille, 1986), 7 ff. Cf., also his book: *Couleurs de noir. Le Journal de Delacroix* (Lille: Presses Universitaires de Lille, 1990).

JEAN-GÉRARD LAPACHERIE

Typographic Characters:
Tension between Text and Drawing

First, accounts by writers.

In the 1930s, Queneau studied the works of writers whom nine-teenth-century psychiatrists had proclaimed "fous littéraires" [liter-ary madmen]. Their alleged madness showed in "the excessive use of inverted quotation marks, commas, ellipses, upper case letters, and hyphens, etc."[1] This diagnosis rests on prejudices related to punc-tuation, written signs, and the literary text. The misuse of typography is so widespread that one would have to qualify as "mad" almost all nineteenth- and twentieth-century writers. Queneau quotes a sci-ence fiction novel by Defontenay, *Histoire merveilleuse de l'un des mondes de l'espace* (1854), in which words are separated by big blanks drawing attention to the strangeness of the "outer space" universe described. He also quotes "typographic poetry" which uses "the very fabric of printing a *matter* as a source both of reveries and sugges-tions"; for example *Un Coup de dés jamais n'abolira le hasard*, "in which typography itself (becomes) a poetic element"; or *Calligrames*, which revives the poetic genre of "figurative verse," (*Délire typogra-phique*, 286).

Leiris establishes a parallel between songs and typographic artifice: "Sentences saturated with music acquire a special luster which sepa-rates them from common language and hallows them with prestigious isolation."[2] Typographic devices (italic type, large print, footnotes, asterisks, blanks) produce an identical effect. They are "lures for the

---

1. Raymond Queneau, "Délire typographique," in *Bâtons, chiffres et lettres* (Paris: Gallimard), 285.
2. Michel Leiris, *Biffures* (Paris: Gallimard, 1982), 18.

YFS 84, *Boundaries: Writing & Drawing*, ed. M. Reid, © 1994 by Yale University.

eye and the mind" (*Biffures,* 18) which "allow written words to loom—from the invisibility of the page—with their denser, more active chemical substances, so that they are at the very birth" (ibid., 19). A page is meant to be read. It is not meant to be looked at. Printed words on a page are barely noticeable. As soon as reading begins, our perception of typography ends. Typographic artifices force the reader to look at the text. They make it visible as a thing and as a thing endowed with an existence of its own.

Typographic characters are signs which are "of a particular design or style useful for the composition or printing of texts."[3] They are signs in the ancient sense of the word "aliquid stat pro alique" [one thing which stands for another]. They lack autonomy, since they represent letters of the alphabet, thus corresponding to the phonetic uses of the language. They are, first, meant to be read and to represent discourse. Such is their function—the reason for their being drawn, engraved, and melted into the metal.

But these signs are not transparent as is a pane of glass which the eye crosses without noticing in order to grasp external objects. In other words, they are not mere referential signs, nor empty ones, different in this respect from the symbol of the alphabet whether phonetic or not, devoid of any intrinsic meaning. Characters are indeed drawings, sometimes beautiful unto themselves. Great artists have drawn them: Bodoni, Auriol, Garamond, Alde Manuce, Albert Dürer, Leonard de Vinci, Geoffroy Tory, etc. . . . The roman letters of Tory are "of an inimitable purity of form and unsurpassed elegance."[4] As drawings, these characters are composed of a graphic signifier (the drawing itself, the lines, the tracing) and of an iconic signification specific to this drawing.[5] Of "mechanical" characters, with thick, rectangular serifs, typographers say they "indicate an origin, that of a time of victorious mechanization, the rise of industry and bourgeois democracy"[6] and they speak of them as "stable," "persuasive," "convincing," "industrial," "mechanical," (Lindekens, 32).

Over the years, and especially after 1830, tens of thousands of typographic characters were created. They differ in design, height, and type

---

3. *Petit Larousse en couleurs* (Paris: Larousse, 1989).

4. Francis Thibaudeau, *La Lettre d'imprimerie* (Paris: Au Bureau de l'Edition, 1921).

5. René Lindekens, *Essai de sémiotique visuelle* (Paris: Klincksieck, 1976).

6. John Dreyfus and François Richaudeau, Article "mécanes," *La Chose imprimée* (Paris: Retz-CEPL, 1976).

thickness: thickness of lines which determines a gradation, from white to light gray and deep black. These types are so varied that typographers classify them in distinct rubrics, defined by formal properties, the way literary critics, confronted with the infinite variety of the works they study, classify these into genres. There exist several classifications. Placing his reliance on the shape of serifs (rectangular, triangular, filiform, absence of a serif), Thibaudeau (1860–1925) distinguishes four classes. From the styles and the dates at which the characters were created, Vox (1894–1974) distinguishes nine, to which he adds Gothic letters and roman forms.

Typographic characters are marks, in the sense given the word by Peirce and Eco:[7] that is to say, signs which are contiguous to their object. Characters are superposed on letters; they cover them up without making them disappear; they are spatially close to them and complete them with meaning. Black type thickness is the mark of a title; italics, marks of double meaning or irony, etc. . . . .

At the same time, signs and drawings, representing letters and endowed with a signified independent of their representation respond to purposes at opposite poles from one another: reading and contemplation; a substitution for units of language and the transmission of iconic significations foreign to language.

The rules governing visual perception, however, are such that reading a text and looking at it are mutually exclusive. It is impossible to read a text in a sustained fashion and at the same time look at the printed characters. "The attention given the one (readability) excludes the attention given the other (visibility)."[8] There is then an embryonic, "latent" if you will, conflict between characters considered as signs representing units of language and these same characters which are also drawings endowed with a proper and autonomous meaning; between a text to be read and a text to be looked at; between reading and looking.

Some writers, besides Valéry, Queneau, or Leiris, became aware that typography (characters and page setting) had a dual if not contradictory, at least conflicting mode of existence. Reverdy among others: "While some (i.e., the dadaists) practiced typographic arrangements whose plastic forms introduce a foreign element into literature, and

---

7. Charles Peirce, *Ecrits sur le signe* (Paris: Le Seuil, 1978); Umberto Eco, *Sémiotique et philosophie du langage* (Paris: PUF, 1988).
8. Paul Valéry, "Les Deux vertus d'un livre," *Œuvres complètes* (Paris: Gallimard, La Pléiade, 1957–1960), vol. 2, 1246.

thereby creating a deplorable difficulty in reading, I created an arrangement whose purely literary *raison d'être* was the novelty of rhythms, a
clearer indication for reading. . . . "[9] According to Reverdy, the conflict
opposes on the one hand "plastic layout" (this adjective refers to image, drawing, plastic arts—to which typography also belongs) and, on
the other hand, "literary arrangement" (this adjective refers to signs,
words, language); or again "difficulty of reading" and "clearer indications for reading"; looking and reading; visibility and readability; characters as drawings and characters as signs.

In the history of the "Western" text, this conflict breaks out on
several occasions: in Restif de la Bretonne; in the 1830s–1840s, during
the "Romantic" typographic revolution; at the end of the nineteenth
century and the beginning of the twentieth century, in "modern style"
typography (pages are less texts to be read than they are "complicated
puzzles, "real drawings" [Thibaudeau, op. cit.]); in the works of dada,
futurist, and surrealist poets.

It is the different aspects of this conflict which I analyze in this
article: the suppression of typographic harmony; the refusal of "congeniality" [*congénialité*]; typographic "ready-mades"; after which I will
explain why typography is unrecognized, neglected, or judged to be
insignificant.

II

Typographic harmony is the result of using characters of the same
design, height, and type thickness.

From the beginning of the sixteenth century, Geoffroy Tory imposes the following convention in a treatise on typography he wrote
and printed in 1529: *Champ fleury*.[10]

Geoffroy Tory shares with the humanists of his day the ambition of
giving literary dignity to the French language, and typography as well
since a literary language demands a typography in its image. He designs roman types, taking the human body, with its perfect forms and
proportions, as a model. "Our Attic letters (i.e., "roman type") are so
well proportioned to nature that they agree in measure and proportion
with the human body" (ibid.). They are perfectly set: arranged "into

9. Pierre Reverdy, *Nord-Sud, Self-Defense et autres écrits sur l'art* (1917–1926)
(Paris: Flammarion, 1975).
10. Geoffroy Tory, *Champ fleury*, reprinted (The Hague: Mouton, 1970).

tablets or in visible places, so that each letter can be seen and read in a straight line, in frontally and in good order," (ibid.). They are not inverted or crooked as was often the case. The width of spaces between letters and between lines is standardized; between letters, the width is that of an *i*; between lines, the height of an *i*. Tory also prohibits mixing characters of different height, design, and type thickness. He never juxtaposes small and large print, Gothic letters and roman type— which was a common practice in the sixteenth century because of the shortage of types of the same family in printing cases.

From Tory on, the printed text was standardized. Little by little it took on the uniform aspect to which we are accustomed and which, in fact, has allowed printed texts to be read silently, quickly, and unambiguously.

On second thought, the so-called convention of typographic harmony cannot be, in spite of its name, in harmony with the printed text. Indeed, there are no uniform texts. The contents (themes, ideas, articulation, characters, etc . . .) vary constantly, especially in works which do not belong to fixed genres or to genres with constraining rules, such as tragedy or epic poems. In order to grasp their content and represent them, one would have to use characters with different designs, height, and print thickness, adapted to the discursive and stylistic variations of the texts.

Restif de la Bretonne, who was a typographer and printed his own books, is undoubtedly the first to have understood the ambiguities of typographic conformity: "His system was to use in the same volume characters of different sizes which he varied according to the presumed importance of a particular period."[11]

In *Monsieur Nicolas*,[12] an autobiographical novel, he varies the characters in height, and this in function of the style he adopts. Thus, passionate or important passages, in which the destiny of the hero is at stake and which are written in an exalted and lofty style, are printed in pica ["*cicéro*"]: rather large characters, "from eleven to twelve points depending on the printing presses."[13] Passages in which the author observes the mores of his contemporaries and which are written in medium style are printed in brevier: average height characters. Finally,

---

11. Gérard de Nerval, *Les Illuminés* (Paris: Garnier, 1959), 149–50.
12. Restif de la Bretonne, *Monsieur Nicolas ou le coeur humain dévoilé* (Paris, 1796 and 1797), 17 volumes.
13. Emile Littré, *Dictionnaire de la langue française* (Paris: Hachette and Gallimard, 1970).

realist passages, which stage characters of lowly condition (shepherds, workers, servants) and which are written in a lower style, with numerous meticulous details, are printed in "small roman type": a character smaller than the brevier or eight-point type.

During the second half of the eighteenth century, the old theory of three styles is still alive. It postulates a hierarchy of genres and styles, from the most elevated (tragedy, epic, noble style) to the lowest, ridiculous and despised (novel, comic story, low style, realism).[14] Restif de la Bretonne transposes this theory to typography. In so doing, he substitutes mimetic necessity to harmonic convention. In its graphic and visual forms, the printed text represents its stylistic fluctuations.

Or further, again in *Monsieur Nicolas*, he prints the same word in capital letters in the middle of lower case letters, violating the convention of typographic harmony. He represents phonic facts mimetically, such as the assumed duration of certain syllables. A syllable that the typographer would have stressed (or accented), if he had said it aloud, is set in capital letters, even if it is in the middle of a word. A short syllable, or supposed to be so, or an unaccented one, is printed in tiny lower case letters.

Thus he establishes a synaesthetic relationship between phonic sensations which are perceived by the ear and visually perceived graphic sensations. The spoken text is rendered visible.

At the beginning of the twentieth century, the question of typographic harmony is raised once again. Marinetti and Apollinaire, among others, insist that it be done away with: Marinetti in *Imagination sans fil et les mots en liberté*,[15] Apollinaire in *L'Antitradition futuriste*, (ibid., 119). And in some of their works they abolish it: Marinetti in *Les Mots en liberté* and Apollinaire in certain *Caligrammes* poems.

The arguments put forth by Marinetti to justify the suppression of typographic consistency come under the same mimetic logic as that of Restif de la Bretonne, even if they are different in practice: "My (typographic) revolution is also directed against what is called typographic consistency, which is contrary to the ebb and flow of style unfurled on the page," (ibid., 146). In order to represent these fluctuations, he recommends using on the same page "three or four different colors of ink and twenty different characters if necessary," (ibid.). Marinetti applies

14. Erich Auerbach, *Mimesis* (Paris: Gallimard, 1977).
15. Giovanni Lista, *Futuristie* (Lausanne: L'Age d'Homme, 1973).

himself to grasping the most diverse noises of the outside world, from the most violent to the slightest, and which differ from one another according to acoustic properties: intensity, stridency, pitch, rapidity. He represents them not as they are (which is impossible except by recording the poem instead of printing it), but synaesthetically, by miming the world's noises with graphic and visual equivalents: type thickness, design, height, and disposition of characters. Block letters, big, thick, and black are reserved for the representation of "violent" auditory sensations; italics, fine, leaning characters which seem to be traced by hand, are for rapid sensations.

Marinetti, and to a lesser degree Apollinaire, thus choose mimesis at the expense of typographic agreement, especially in "instantaneous" poems where thicknesses, designs, and heights allow for the expression of the lyricism of matter exalted by Marinetti when he grasps cacophonous noises (exploding shells, sputtering arms, machines, motors, etc . . .) and shows them *hic et nunc* on the page.

The question of typographic consistency is again raised, although in terms different from those of Marinetti, in *Paradis*[16] by Philippe Sollers.

But even if typographic consistency standardizes printed texts, they are never totally uniform. Capitals A, B, or E, among others, do not have the same design as their corresponding lower cases: a, b, e. . . . From a semiological point of view, punctuation marks, underlining, numbers, blanks (and other typographic devices) are very different from letters and stand at the opposite pole from the alphabet. They do not replace any unit of language. They have no value (in the sense that they do not stand for a unit), but they signal a meaning, a rupture, a hierarchy, an analysis. As a result, a printed text which retains punctuation marks, blanks, upper cases, etc . . . , cannot be uniform because it is made up of heterogeneous signs.[17]

Such is not the case for *Paradis*. There are neither capitals, nor indented lines, nor paragraphs, nor punctuation marks. Sollers replaces " , . ; : ? " by the words "comma," "period," "semi-colon," "colon," "question mark," so that, except for blanks between words, the text of *Paradis* is uniform. Such an enterprise belongs to the "deconstruction" of the "Western text," as it was constituted by printing

16. Philippe Sollers, *Paradis* (Paris: Le Seuil, 1978).

17. Cf. my article, "Poly-, hétéro-, exo-graphies," in *Poétique* 84 (Paris: Le Seuil, 1990).

and silent reading. *Paradis* is in italic type without paragraphs or indented lines. If it is read silently and only with the eyes, it is incomprehensible. On the other hand, if read aloud, meaning comes through. *Paradis* is meant to be read (orally), not looked at. In deconstructing the forms of the written text, Sollers renews ties with the medieval forms of texts which are meaningful only if they are spoken.

III

Congeniality is the agreement between characters (their "signified") and the meaning of the printed text.

"Each character really does have its own expression. One can use it in accordance with the meaning of the text, or rather, to achieve an ironic or humorous contrast. In either case, it should be respected."[18]

Congeniality was forced upon great typographers such as Jan Tschichold, Massin, Faucheux; but for many its necessity was not felt: "All too often, alas!, typographers use characters as if they were a neutral material," (ibid.) all the more because editing habits (a single paste-up for books published within the same collection, etc . . .) make congeniality impossible.

It was more an artistic exigency than a (semiological) convention: in which it doubtless differed from typographic consistency, consistency which has standardized texts and has undoubtedly contributed to this fast and unimpeded reading. On the other hand, congeniality, by making type and text converge, reinforces the meaning of texts.

Congeniality being what it is, it is not surprising that it should be consciously repudiated in dada texts, insofar as dada poets had as their avowed objective, in the years from 1917 to 1921, the abolition of meaning and the end of literature.

On the cover page of number 12 of *391*, a brief text signed by Picabia is inscribed within a black frame. It is presented to the eye as a death notice since in "urban" works or standard printing works, obituary notices are set in that manner. In point of fact, congeniality is made impossible, playfully but consciously refused.

The type of *Une Nuit d'échecs gras* by Tzara[19] has every possible

18. Wilhelm Ovink, "Psychologie des caractères," *La Chose imprimée*, op. cit.
19. Francis Picabia, *391*, 14 (Paris: Le Terrain vague, 1920).

design, height, and thickness. In the "manuscript paste-up" of that page, Tzara specified: "print in all possible characters."[20] These variations do not adhere to any rule other than the fantasy and the arbitrariness of the author. Printing conventions are rejected: typographic consistency, the distinction between urban works and individual works. The same goes for the requirements of congeniality. It is an "advertising for the sale of dada publications" (391, 14). Contents are fairly uniform: titles of works, proper names, prices. As a result, the type used should have been the same had Tzara tried to ally graphic forms with the meaning of the text. As it is, all available signs in the cases are used: roman type, italics, types with or without serif, "typographic artifice," etc. . . . Typographers have transformed the nature of conventional marks: signs contiguous to their object and which complement their meaning. By refusing congeniality, Tzara "desindicialise" typography. He takes away its conventional significations. What is important is not the codified meaning of typography, or even the text to be printed, but the type in itself, as a form, its design, thickness, height, pure graphic signifiers, with which Tzara plays like other poets play with the sounds of language.

The thickness of characters has a codified meaning. An important word, titles, subtitles are printed in darker type than the rest of the text, which points either to the importance given the words or to status as titles. In *Une Nuit d'échecs gras*, the type's thickness varies without justification of this variation: white, lightfaced, semi-bold-faced, bold-faced, black. The title "CANNIBALE," "391" are in black type; "Vente de publications dada" [dada publications for sale] in bold-face; "Page composée par Tristan Tzara" [page composed by Tristan Tzara] in semi-bold; "Vagin mystique" [mystical Vagina] is lightfaced; not to mention within each of these type thicknesses other variations that only a typographer could perceive: quarter-bold, semi-bold, three quarters-bold, bold, extra-bold . . .

Tzara uses all characters. They are there, on the page, shown for themselves. Their use, governed by none of the typographic conventions, obeys only Tzara's fantasy, who plays and laughs at ("HIHIHIHIHI") these conventions, refusing them meaning and thereby emphasizing the materiality of the texts. A text is above all made up of letters, of ink, of blanks, of dashes. Without that, there would be no "literature," nor

20. Cf. Michel Sanouillet, *391* (Paris: Le Terrain vague, 1961).

poetry. These letters, precisely, are never looked at, since, upon read-ing, signs are abolished and reading and looking are mutually exclu-sive. Tzara shows up materiality (ink, designs, devices) for what it is in itself: self-evident, meaningless. It is the domain of absolute arbitrari-ness; a text which is made to be seen is independent of what is read.

From number 12 on, the type used in *391* changes constantly; varia-tions unlike what we see in *Monsieur Nicolas* or *Les Mots en liberté*, these variations have no relationship with the texts.

In #12, page 4, one of Picabia's poems is published. The title is not made up of words but of seven punctuation marks which are there for themselves, not for the meanings they carry in a sentence. They are arranged at the top, above the poem; they are separated from the text by a line, as is the adjoining poem on the same poem on the same page, signed by Ribemont-Dessaignes ("Un Prompt Tu" [A Prompt You]), printed in an elevated type body and black thickness. They are juxta-posed and follow one another, without relation to the text. They are an exclamation mark, placed upside down beneath the written line, a period, a dash, an exclamation mark, a colon, a comma, ellipses: "¡.—!:, . . . "
Congeniality is impossible since there is no text.

A "poem" by Man Ray, published in *391*, #17, in June 1924, illus-trates this preeminence of typography over text. This "poem" is not made up of words, nor letters, but of thick black dashes, of variable length, each one of which is supposed to stand for a word. It is arranged the way poems usually are: with a title (made up of three dashes) and seventeen lines of unequal length, which are divided into four groups or stanzas: a tercet, two quintils, a quatrain. It retains the visual and graphic appearance of a "poem": that is to say an arrangement in lines of unequal length and in stanzas. By reducing the "poem" to black dashes, Man Ray expresses his defiance of words as the dada poets did. With derision he reminds us of this truth, that poetry, which today has hardly any existence except written and printed, is laid out on the page in a codified, specific, visual, and immediately recognizable manner.

IV

Beginning in 1914, Marcel Duchamp exhibited manufactured objects in the middle of paintings (first a bottle-rack). He thus gives it the ridiculous status of work of art.

In the 1920s, poets insert "ready-mades" into their works. Breton for example collects at least one in *Clair de Terre:*[21] "PSTT," a list of all the Bretons in the phone book. Other ready-mades have a problematic status. They are *ILE* and *MEMOIRES D'UN EXTRAIT DES ACTIONS DE CHEMINS.* Of all the poems in the collection, they are the only ones not to have titles. *"ILE"* and *"MEMOIRES D'UN EXTRAIT DES ACTIONS DE CHEMINS.",* as they are referred to above, are not titles, but the unabridged text one can read on the page. Thus, *"ILE"* amounts to the single word *"ILE"*—although it is perhaps something other than a "word": simply three letters or the last three letters of a word, the beginning of which might not have been printed. Similarly, the poem referred to as *"MEMOIRES D'UN EXTRAIT DES ACTIONS DE CHEMINS.",* is a bit longer than the one before it, since it is composed of eight words that do not make up a sentence (although they are followed by a period) and may not belong to the same sentence.

These "poems" can be distinguished from the other poems in the collection by their typography. They are printed in very big black type. *MEMOIRES* is laid out in four lines as follows:

MEMOIRES D'UN
EXTRAIT DES
ACTIONS DE
CHEMINS.

The lines are of the same length and occupy the width of the page. Certainly, the last two lines have fewer letters than the first two; but they are printed in larger sizes of type which, in any case, regularly increase from beginning to end.

The three letters of *ILE* are arranged horizontally, but in the direction of the height of the page. *I, L, E* are in huge type body, more than four centimeters in height and width, so that between the three of them, they occupy a good third of the page. Furthermore they are characters which Thibaudeau classifies as "caractères de fantaisie" [fancy type]. The characteristic of this type is that it is never used to print a text to be read in a sustained fashion, much less a literary text. They are related to urban work and, since they are designed to call the attention of passersby, they are sometimes used for posters or advertisements. They are shaded characters in relief, which can be seen by an effect of perspective, in three dimensions: height, width, and thickness. They are also luminous type. Inside the letter, in the enormous

---

21. André Breton, *Paris* (Gallimard, Collection "Poésie," 1924).

ink blot drawn on the paper, appear in white the contours of the letters *I, L, E.* Finally, the first letter, *I,* has been placed upside down. This can be seen by the shadow it casts which stands out in the background or on the left, while the shadows are thrown in front of the other characters.

These two "texts" have been described. It is now a matter of interpreting them.

PSST, the list of Bretons in the phone book, is a "ready-made," either verbal or literary, which obeys the "rules" laid down by Marcel Duchamp. A "ready-made" is a manufactured object—a bottle-rack, a street urinal, etc . . . , produced in a factory and sold as a utilitarian object. It is "non-art" which is exhibited in the middle of paintings. Marcel Duchamp, it would seem, prompts spectators to reexamine critically the almost religious conception they have of art; and also, since it was the time of derision, his intent is to criticize art itself, by showing that perhaps it may not deserve to be revered.

Characters are manufactured objects: metal blocks, produced in foundries. For *ILE,* Breton chose thick types (*mécanes*), with a heavy design, big serifs, which have something industrial in their outline, and are used, in theory, only for ordinary works, so-called works of labor.

ILE and *MEMOIRES D'UN EXTRAIT DES ACTIONS DE CHE-MINS.* are two typographic "ready-mades." The emphasis is placed not on the text (there isn't one), but on the very types themselves which are made visible. By integrating them into a collection of poems, Breton prompts us to look at them, to contemplate them for themselves, as objects—or traces of objects—having a surface area, a form, lines, a substance full of ink. In these two pages, as in *Une Nuit d'échecs gras* by Tzara, the type is devoid of any signification, since it is unconnected with a text or its contents. They are no longer signs of anything. They are there as material objects, or substance.

V

Typography is misunderstood.

The plot of the novel *El Ard* [The Earth] by Abderramane Charkaoui takes place in rural Egypt in the 1930s.[22] It is also a "modern" text: page 6 numbers eighteen indented lines and sixteen ellipses. The En-

---

22. Abderramane Charkaoui, *El Ard* (Cairo: Dar El Cha'ab, 1954).

glish translation[23] reduces the indented lines to eleven and the ellipses to one. In the Arab text, the typography creates a visual rhythm. The English version leaves out these effects. The stress falls only on the realistic and rustic significations of the novel.

In the same way, the first editions of *Sarrazine* by Honoré de Balzac include many hyphens, ellipses, indented lines. They were printed at a time when French typography was very inventive. In subsequent editions, printed during Balzac's lifetime (including the one used by Roland Barthes for his commentary of *Sarrazine* in *S/Z*), everything easygoing, new, "modern" (hyphens, ellipses, indented lines) is left out, and the text is a massive, heavy, and austere compact block.

Typography is not dependent on language but on the graphic arts. Literature is the privileged domain of the word. Within it, graphic questions occupy only a marginal space. Moreover, our conception of the author—a "unique" individual, whose presence vouches for the text, the only authority capable of taking responsibility for it—prevents taking typography into account since it assumes there is not *one* single author, but *two:* the author of the text and that of the book; the novelist and the typographer (or the person in charge of printing, the artistic director, or the designer), who has chosen the characters, has guided the writer's choices. That is why in *Litanie d'eau* by Butor or *Conversation-Sinfonietta* by Tardieu, there is, next to the writer's name, the name of the typographer (Faucheux and Massin) who participated in the creation of the work, its coauthor. Like a film, but to a lesser degree, the printed literary work becomes "collective": the work of several authors which goes counter to the romantic myth of the genius, creator of a universe, in the image of God.

To speak of typography requires precise technical and historical knowledge.

Consider dada typography from 1917 to 1920. Literary critics proclaim it "innovative," "free," "full of daring," "revolutionary." "It subverts traditional codes." It is "a page-setting and a typography which are revolutionary for the time."[24] In the above quoted judgments, the emphasis is placed on the ruptures created by those typographical marks. But these opinions are not founded on any systematic study of typography from 1830 to 1917. Furthermore, typographic tradition, which dada is supposed to "revolutionize," is implicitly as-

23. Abderramane Charkaoui, *The Egyptian Earth* (London: Heinemann, 1962).
24. *Mélusine,* 4: "Le Livre surréaliste" (Paris: L'Age d'Homme, 1982), 25.

sumed to be academic, conservative, and rigid. What does it consist of exactly?

The great era of typography is the nineteenth century, "century of complete freedom," according to Thibaudeau (op. cit.). Beginning in 1830, printers, graphic artists, inventors of type diversify characters. This is an essential point, for the type of any given text acquires signification only from the time typographers have hundreds of different type fonts at their disposal to print the text. Innovations also have to do with page-setting, line-setting, illustrations, covers, title pages, printed advertisements, catalogues of printed books, and posters for department stores.

In fact, the boldness hastily attributed to dada poets and writers were the deed of "romantic" typographers. The first "typographic revolutions" concern the title pages of books. There, typographic conventions are done away with, a century before Marinetti and Apollinaire. The characters used have a design, a height, and a type thickness which are different in every one of the lines of the title. "Typographic cacophony is at its height! Titles have become veritable specimens of characters where all the genres alternate and blend into one another: it is miscellany elevated to a principle" (ibid., 364). These innovations go counter to the prevailing notion: "the condition of unity of style of the assembled elements, syntax of universal typographic language must be realized" (ibid., preface, xix).

Sometime in the nineteenth century books become a commodity and, as a result, they have market value and not just use value. They are sold in the windows of bookshops. Circulation increases; prices go down; hard covers are replaced by paperbacks. The cover and the title page attract the attention of customers; they become advertising images.

Compared with real "revolutions" through which the typographers of 1830–1900 revolutionize the art of the book, its organization, its typography, strictly speaking, Tzara and Picabia hardly innovate at all. The blending of body types, the suppression of typographic consistency, the refusal of congeniality are practiced as early as 1830, and this in a generalized fashion. Yet, even if Tzara and Picabia do not create a new typography, they move the "typographic cacophony" from the title page or from posters, where it had been confined, to the text itself, which had generally been preserved from it. In dada texts, variations in type do not obey any rule other than the arbitrariness of the authors and are not justified by any semiotic or aesthetic necessity. For dada poets, it is more a matter of denying the significations of typography than of creating new ones and using characters, not as semantic complements to the text, but as pure forms.

Other innovations took place in the nineteenth century, well before the dada typographic revolution. They first took place in advertising print. Thus it is with devices "jeté de texte" or "jeté de groupe" [haphazard arrangements]. This page setting was invented by a great typographer, Motteroz, in 1889. In a printer's catalogue, instead of arranging the words of titles symmetrically on either side of the central axis, he "throws" them on the page, without any justification either in relation to the margins, or in relation to the center. Thus the name given this device: "As he had done for the trade of new publications and Christmas gift books, Motteroz innovates, for the current library catalogues, some original arrangements, for example, which would lead to the liberation from the secular justification of the title with the central axis" (ibid.). This haphazard set-up is that of *Un Coup de dés jamais n'abolira le hasard* by Mallarmé, published for the first time in 1897. A great many lines of this poem are printed neither flush left, nor flush right—which goes without saying for verse that ends when its internal number has been exhausted—nor centered, as titles generally are. These lines, sometimes made up of a single word ("que" [that], "étale" [spread], for example in the second page of the poem), are aligned neither on the margins, nor on the vertical axis. They are thrown on the page, as Motteroz did with library catalogues and as dice can be tossed—cast—on a gambling table.

—Translated by Anna Lehmann

II.

JACQUES LEENHARDT

See and Describe: On a Few Drawings by Stendhal

These few reflections which I should like to put forward on the theme of *Bild und Text im Werk von Stendhal*, choosing the German title in preference to the French *Texte et Image* for the antecedence which it confers on the visual over the written, will not take the path—however interesting—of an analysis of the passage from the *thing seen* to the *thing written*. It will not be a question of *Ut pictura poesis*, nor of *ekphrasis*, but rather of the gesture of the writer, rare enough to be noticed, which consists of not respecting the separation of genres, and of placing sketches right in the middle of his text.

One could, however, first try to weaken this contradiction by simply calling to mind that the graphics of *Vie de Henry Brulard* or of *Le Voyage d'un touriste* are never anything but written forms on written forms, of which Stendhal reminds us, in his particular way, in *Le Voyage en France* where we find a lone "drawing"—that is to say a lone break in typographical continuity. In fact, it is not, properly speaking, a drawing, since what we have are letters forming a rebus, which was used—we are told—as a sign for a restaurant of the village of Les Échelles, and which reads:

A long sous *P,* G grand a petit.[1]   : Allons souper, j'ai grand appétit.

: *Allons souper, j'ai grand appétit'.*

/ G .

1. Stendhal, *Voyages en France*, texts edited, prefaced, and annotated by Victor del Litto (Paris: Gallimard, La Pléiade, 1992), *Voyage en France*, 422.

YFS 84, *Boundaries: Writing & Drawing*, ed. M. Reid, © 1994 by Yale University.

Without leaving the graphic order, Stendhal nevertheless breaks something which has become, over the course of centuries of technical improvements, more and more untouchable: typographical continuity. The presence of a rebus without a drawing in *Le Voyage en France*[2] should therefore make us attentive to the fact that it is typographic continuity which is first broken, even if more and more one sees a more radical opposition is taking shape between the way a sketch is perceived, and the way writing is perceived.

Let us call to mind an obvious fact: reading and seeing are not opposed to one another from the angle of perception. On the other hand, different *modalities* are put to work, which the *habitus* of the reader has crystallized little by little, to the extent that one is always tempted to oppose a civilization of the written to a civilization of the visual, as if they called on different senses.

It remains a fact that Stendhal innovates in the literary order with the appearance of his drawings—graphics—sketches, whatever name they are given. It will also doubtless be necessary to distinguish these terms, as I will show below.

It is perhaps important to call to mind here that the inclusion of drawings—or of the nontypographic—into the flow of the text, if traditional in the sciences or philosophy, rarely appears in literature. It occurs, with Stendhal, precisely at the moment when the techniques of mechanical reproduction are on the point of revolutionizing books and the press, and therefore reading. This chronological coincidence is strongly underlined by Stendhal in a few reflections he delivers on the question of techniques. At the same moment that he is innovating in literature by these breaks in typographical continuity, Stendhal notes in his *Journal de Paris*, that the perceptible visual universe, drawing and painting, are, at the moment in history in which he writes, borne along by a deadly logic: that of mechanical reproduction. I am deliberately using terms that bring to mind the famous article of Walter Benjamin: "*Das Kunstwerk im Zeitalter seiner technischen Reproduzierbarkeit,*"[3] for Stendhal had evidently felt, a century before Benjamin, the consequences, brought about by the technical revolution, which

---

2. I recall that in *Vie de Henry Brulard* one finds, for example, another rebus, whose principle is different, since typography and drawing are combined, the famous little rat (Lancette les tuera).

3. Cf. Walter Benjamin, "Das Kunstwerk im Zeitalter seiner technischen Reproduzierbarkeit," in *Illuminationen* (Frankfurt: Shurkamp Verlag, 1955), 148–84.

permitted the rise of industries making mechanically reproduced images.

> On vient d'inventer, il y a deux mois, un canon à vapeur qui lancera à une lieue de distance vingt boulets par minute. Nous triomphons dans les arts mécaniques, dans la lithographie, dans le diorama. Mais tous les cœurs sont froids, mais la passion sous toutes ses formes ne se trouve plus nulle part.[4]

> Just two months ago a steam cannon was invented which will shoot twenty cannon balls a minute for the distance of one league. We are triumphing in the mechanical arts, in lithography, in diorama. But all hearts are cold; passion in all its forms is no longer anywhere to be found.

The semantic shift created by Stendhal's sentence, passing from the steam cannon to lithography, alluding at the same time to the recent invention of steam printing presses, emphasizes the appearance of a new phenomenon: the mechanical reproduction of images (lithography). The progress in mechanization, from then on, was to affect and transform the pictorial image. This mechanization tears away at the image's specific capacity to *touch* visually, to make life itself perceptible, *present and extinguished* in the painting, this life, this "passion," this "heart" as he says, which one can, I believe, rightfully put side by side with what Benjamin will call the *aura*.

Thus comes into view, in the presence of elements heterogeneous to typography in Stendhal's texts (text signifying here the set writing + sketch), in this weaving of two visual orders addressing two different aspects of our sensibility, the will to bring out a rich opposition, founded nevertheless on one ambivalent medium (the mechanized image). The Stendhalian "text" thus finds itself the carrier of the trace of a perceptive difference whose richness—thanks to contemporary mechanization—he can still try to show, at the very moment of its announced abolition.

The presence of graphics—sketches—drawings, breaking typographical continuity, perhaps serves to awaken, to address a dimension of our sensibility on its way to entering into the big sleep of mechanical reproducibility.

This leads us to a contemporary whose name remains attached to the invention of the cartoon, Rodolphe Toeppfer. Not so much for his

---

4. *Journal de Paris*, in *Du romantisme dans les arts* (Paris: Hermann, 1960), 139.

claim to fame which this son of an honest romantic painter from Geneva owes to his albums on *Monsieur Cryptogame* and other virulent charges against the decadent romanticism of the bourgeois and tourists, but precisely for this critique of the *tourist* illustrated by the *Voyages en zigzag*, among others. Whence the question, which I should like to link to our theme: why, despite the negative connotations that the word "tourist" already had at the time, did Stendhal keep this term in the title of his *Mémoires d'un touriste?* The tourist is bookish. He travels Baedeker in hand, with his head full of quotes and commonplaces, the expression "commonplaces" taking on special flavor in view of the tourist's obligatory stops. The tourist only sees what books point out to him. Stendhal, who orders him "ouvrez les yeux, cachez les livres" [open your eyes, hide the books], is not far from thinking that one does *not see* if one does not see *for oneself.* Sensation flees when experience is not the result of an availability and of an aptitude particular to the sensing subject. The conditioned reflexes provoked by bookish knowledge in which tourists steep themselves are nothing but show: Del Litto quotes the pretty text by Nisard on this subject:

> For a travel guide traveller, for a *tourist*, all of whose oohs and aahs have been written down in advance, such a word is blasphemy, I know, but I speak my mind. The impressions of the tourist are fabricated at the inn, before departure. He knows by books and by the hearsay of tourists of his ilk, what is a mountain, a waterfall, a lake; he knows what to think and say about them; he has the formula. He knows where to show horror, surprise, melancholy; he keeps a supply in his suitcase. Having arrived in front of the mountain, his guidebook in hand, you will hear him say: "That's it!" In front of the waterfall: "It's just as Murray says!" In front of the lake: "He hasn't misled me!" What good is it to make such an effort to see something that you knew already? [V. del Litto, *Voyages en France,* op. cit., xxxvii.]

Thus returns the question of why Stendhal, on whom these negative connotations could not be lost, insists nevertheless on using the term "tourist." Historians will provide an answer. For my part, I should only like to suggest that his sketches belong to a strategy of revalorization of the notion. There are doubtless none in *Les Mémoires d'un touriste.* But, before and after, that is to say in the margins of this work, one does find sketches.

Everything happens as if the sketch were supposed to break the attention captured by books, typographic attention, one might say, which distances from the true power of seeing and feeling. During a voyage, attention is more pertinent than knowledge. Attention is an awakening, by the irruption of the sketch into the textual chain, and the writer has perhaps sought to maintain this awakened state, sollicit once again the imagination of the reader inclined to let itself be carried along by the written discursive flow.

But let us look at some of these drawings-sketches-graphics in order to ascertain what specifically it is that they generate at the very heart of writing. I shall quickly cite only a few examples. The first, appearing early in Stendhal's work (I do not aim here to write a history of the types of sketches), dates from 8 November 1805 and describes a visit by Stendhal to the Prés de Montfuront (fig. 1).

A summary description of this sketch enables one to pick out different types of marks.

First one finds analogical signs, drawings of trees sufficiently precise for one to distinguish different species, a waterway whose ebb and flow is made perceptible by undulating lines. Perhaps one can even distinguish shadows, or at least some horizontal strokes at the foot of a tree which represent the ground.

Then Stendhal situates, in this space rendered true-to-life, some elements which the drawing would perhaps not have permitted to identify with precision. Capital letters refer to captions accompanying the sketch.

Furthermore, one notices the indications concerning the path taken by the traveller: Journey out, Journey back, Marseille. These signs are sometimes redundant, like the inscription "eau courante" [running water] reduplicating the already noted undulation. A traffic is thus established between the drawing producing the illusion of real space, the graphic situating the elements in relation to each other, the captions which solve ambiguities or imprecisions, and the words, such as "PRÉS," (situated on the same level as the grassy surface which it designates.

Finally, a number of these captions do more than give information: they engage the reader in an actual story. Thus:

> C.—Grande petite rivière dont les bords sont délicieux, tout couverts de peupliers très grands et très rapprochés, comme dans tout le reste du contour du champ; l'eau court assez, elle peut avoir 12 pieds de largeur et un demi-pied de profondeur; l'ouverture en a peut-être trois fois autant.

A. Small channel. B. *Ibid*, 5 feet wide, 3 feet wide and 2 feet of very limpid and swift-running water. —G. Large small river whose edges are delicious, all covered with very tall poplars very close together, as along the rest of the field's edges; the water runs rather quickly, it can attain 12 feet in width and half a foot in depth; the opening is perhaps three times as deep. —D. House long and low to the ground. —H. Apple tree (small) under which we had lunch. —M. Small door opening onto a field in which there is a mill. —φ. I leave her up to P.

H.—Pommier (petit) sous lequel nous avons déjeuné.

J. Je la quitte jusqu'à P. [Stendhal, *Voyages en France*, op. cit., Annexes, 793.]

The landscape ceases to exist in itself; it becomes the theater of actions in which the traveller is inscribed physically and narratively.

Let us take a second example: the visit to the *Jardin de Buffon à Montbard* [Garden of Buffon in Montbard] which Stendhal relates in 1811. Here it is no longer a question of a drawing, nor does the term "sketch" perfectly describe all the particularities of what in fact appears here as a *graphic*, or simply as a *map*.

The relation to the accompanying text also changes profoundly in comparison with the one which accompanies the drawing of the Prés de Montfuront. There numerous captions developed into a description, perhaps they were even like the little goose of a novel or a play. Here, nothing of the sort. No captions, except for the indication "Village of Montbard, 3,000 souls" and the letter A which indicates Buffon's study. The essential is inserted into the text, which reduces the autonomy of the drawing (fig. 2).

> The countryside began to change, finally we arrived at Montbard. We found the portrait of Buffon in the home of our hostess. A girl led us to Buffon's aged gardener. This wizened old fellow, sinewy and clear-speaking, gave us a tour of seven or eight terraces thirty feet wide at most.
> We came to E, a platform in the form of a trapezoid:
> From this platform one has a very wide view over the line MM which, unfortunately, is formed by sparsely wooded and seemingly barren hills. As in the garden, nothing in this view suggests sensuality. I shared this reflection with M. Lecchi who answered: "Therefore nothing can attract one here but the desire to do homage to a great man."
> For an Italian, sensuality is such an integral part of the idea of a beautiful garden. Buffon's garden does not cover enough ground; but it does tend to inspire an idea of strength and magnificence. Nothing voluptuous in all these walls and all these stairways; on the contrary, something hard and dry.
> CCC are these excessively narrow terraces; E the Esplanade, which has a wide view from each of its three sides. L is a terrace gate which led us by an underground staircase to the Esplanade F planted with [*a blank space*] (these trees with pretty bark, which line the beautiful boulevard in Rouen next to the hospital). Finally we went up one

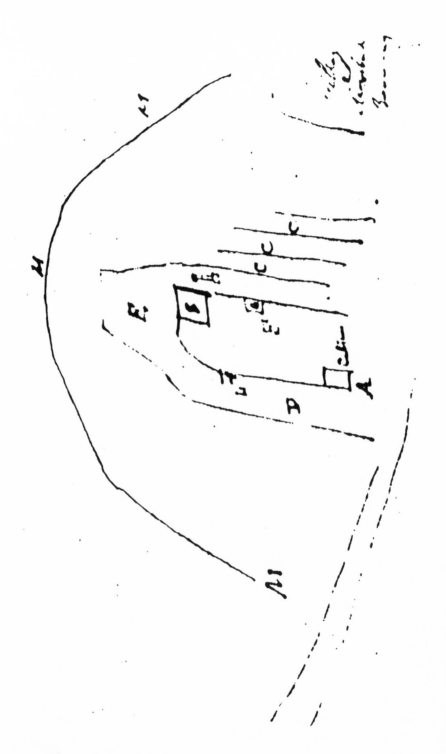

hundred thirty-eight steps inside the tower B, what remains of a castle of the dukes of Burgundy, given to Buffon by the King, and which had occupied the entire surface of the Esplanade. The windows of this tower, with walls five feet thick, and each with a recessed bench, are indeed Gothic.

All these details are from the dry and nervous gardener. He told us that in the family "we have titles which prove that this tower was built more than nine hundred years ago." That would place it around the year 900. This man stayed with Buffon for seventeen years. He saw Jean-Jacques kneel at the threshold of A, the study, where Buffon was working in silence. He would arrive at five o'clock, five-fifteen at the latest; he was brought bread and a carafe of water at eleven. He took his breakfast, came down at precisely one o'clock to have lunch, said nothing to his guests, went back up, worked until five o'clock, at which time they would come for him, and he relaxed chatting with his guests. His gardeners took care to sweep the leaves from his path.

"There were six of us then, said the old man; at five o'clock, the manservant came in and replaced the candles."

They assured me several times that Buffon only worked by candlelight.

"We stayed away from his pavilion when we knew he was there." There was a double door; the windows gave onto the countryside, across terrace D; they are twenty-five or thirty feet above ground. Next to this terrace passes the road from Paris.

Buffon would come in May and leave in September. His landholdings near Montbard brought him around forty thousand francs.

I was moved, I should have liked to stay longer. This severity in work *is a* lesson for *myself.** I should have liked to collect my thoughts and feel the majesty and strength which these gardens exude. My travelling companions, in a hurry, did not permit me this. [Ibid., 812–13]

The text which accompanies, or is accompanied by, the map is the object of a curious reversal. At first nothing seems able to arouse the interest of the traveller. The hills are dull, the forest thinly wooded. The garden has nothing which elicits the sensuality that a tourist full of memories of Italy expects. The terraces are too narrow, and the castle destroyed. Everything is set for a disappointment, and the tourist, with his bookish expectations, is taken over by boredom. Perhaps, by its sketchiness, the map which we see is the trace of this boredom.

*In English in the text.—Translator's note.

The narrative nevertheless brings about a transition, from the natural world, scant and poorly laid out, which surrounds Buffon's residence, to the naturalist himself. The entire discourse on the garden in fact shifts at the moment when the piety of Rousseau, kneeling at the door of cabinet A, where Buffon was working in silence, is evoked. The intercessor, himself a high priest of nature, awakens feelings of which Stendhal is not aware at the moment he describes the site—through the contemplation of the strength of character and work of the naturalist. It is not surprising that this reversal occurs precisely in reference to the only captioned element of the map, Buffon's study.

At this point, the moral portrait has come to give meaning to the garden of its master and organizer, opening up a new register for the comprehension of the graphic. The rising at dawn, the asceticism and frugality, the withdrawal within the self, even when surrounded by guests at the noon meal, all point to a rigor which the six gardeners strive to translate into the order of the garden: "His gardeners took care to sweep the leaves from his path."

The aesthetic of sensuality leading to likely disappointment is thus subordinated to an ethic of work and order. In its dryness, pure geometry, and pure image of mastery, the graphic paradoxically pays homage to a spiritual virtue—here opposed to sensation—, to the pure form of a spirit of order, classicism, and self-mastery.

If the graphic of the "Prés de Montfuront" opened into a country idyll with fruit pie and thrushes in aspic, that of Montbard, where no analogic sign appears (neither mountain, nor tree, only the lines of the map are readable), accompanies the reader into a new experience of ethical emotion.

"I was moved, I should have liked to stay longer." Stendhal assumes a role close to that of Rousseau: the veneration of Buffon's strength of character, as it is expressed by the very form of the garden. Shortly before, this form was cramped and without charm. Henceforth, the traveller reads another dimension there: "I should have liked to collect my thoughts and feel the majestic strength which these gardens exude."

The graphic of Montbard, by its technical qualities, by the accent put on form and sign, is perhaps an element which has played a role in the very elaboration of the text. One could imagine that, after having conceived it as an image of dryness and of disappointed "Italian" expectations, Stendhal himself read something else there: a rigor worthy of a new commentary. This would introduce us to the idea of an active role, no longer informative and servile, for the graphics and sketches proposed by the author.

Let us take yet another example. It is a sign-drawing-diagram-sketch (it is too early to decide which) whose functional ambivalence is great and whose presence there leads us to the question of Stendhal's aim. It is a very flattened triangle, like a pediment; it comes up in a sentence which has already designated it as such: "Above each triangle-shaped window . . . beautiful empty space" (ibid., *Voyages dans le Midi de la France*, 665).

But why draw a triangle after having mentioned it? This page is surprising, on the one hand, by the overabundance of redundant signs produced by the text, duplicating the image, although there is, admittedly, a change of register. The page also, and inversely, surprises by the *lacunae* which it reveals. Let us read the whole passage:

> I am going to sound like a bad Frenchman, but since I have chosen the hard way of preferring truth to reputation, I must say that I have not seen anything which has so much *style* for a long time, and which speaks so to the noble parts of the soul. A house covered with forty-franc pieces attached by nails would not have style in my eyes, but in the eyes of provincial shopkeepers, it would speak a very eloquent language. Well, an enormous building is very much like a house covered with forty-franc pieces; the house says: "It cost a lot of money to make me."
>
> Thus, I am such an enemy of my fatherland and such a bad Frenchman, that the little palace of Irun gives me much more pleasure than the grand theater of Bordeaux. This palace has five porticos with rounded vaults supported by four pillars; above, a beautiful balcony reigns, with wide and ornate architecture; it is held up by [*a blank*] of stone representing ends of beams. Above each triangle-shaped window (I lack the exact words, so occupied I am with sensation). Above the windows, beautiful empty space; the [*an illegible word*] and the large-cut stones, well lined up and of a rich yellow color, bordering on black. The façade ends with a beautiful cornice, very accentuated, whose different parts are set off strongly. [Ibid., 664–65]

The argument thus develops as follows:

1. I am a bad Frenchman (twice), preferring Irun to Bordeaux because Irun has style and Bordeaux was bought with gold alone.

2. The balcony of the palace is held up by . . . (a blank space) of stone which portrays ends of beams.

3. I lack the words, so occupied am I with sensation.

The missing word is doubtless *corbeaux*, these corbels which hold up the balcony and portray, as is the tradition since the Middle Ages, the ends of beams.

I should like to suggest that the lapse of memory, this slip which is all the more interesting since we know Stendhal's competence in architectural matters, has a close relationship with the triangle's walk-on part in the very heart of the text.

The word which Stendhal lacks at the moment he describes the balcony of the Palace of Irun, *corbeaux*, enters into phonetic resonance with *bordeaux*, the object of which he ought to speak with a warmth he cannot muster. It is as if *bordeaux* concealed *corbeaux* at the end of an interplay of phonetic slips whose sequence is enriched by the apologue on the taste of the shopkeepers whom a house "covered with forty-franc pieces" would fascinate. These amateurs with perverted taste, adorers not of art but of the *veau d'or* [golden calf], of the *beau d'or* [beauty of gold], provide Stendhal with a play on approximations which leads to *Bordeaux*. The prohibition which weighs on the word Bordeaux and which is set up by the apologue explains, in the final analysis, the "forgetting" of the word "corbeaux." The oddities of this passage therefore end up taking on meaning, and everything happens as if, at the end of a triangular journey between Bordeaux, *veau d'or*, and *corbeaux*, the first word had hidden the last.

If that were so—which I am wary of asserting, content, in the realm of the subconscious, with proposing a hypothesis—, the drawn triangle, which the pictured redundancy of the already written word only renders more strange, is perhaps a way of visualizing the system of permutation of the consonants in the three words surrounding the absent "corbeau." Stendhal's confusion, underlined by the provocative and repeated affirmation that he is a bad Frenchman, perhaps justifies both the forgetting of a word and the wandering of the mind which hooks deformed equivalents onto the *beau d'or* of the Philistine shopkeepers, amateur supporters of the Theater of Bordeaux.

The importance of sketches—neither drawings, nor graphics, nor maps—, such as this triangle, seems all the greater, (even if it is particularly dangerous to place interpretations on this shaky ground), since a number of them remain strictly enigmatic. Such sketches, it seems, defy explanation. Why did Stendhal feel the need to add them to his text when they seem neither to complete the information nor clarify points of knowledge? Their approximate character, in any case, renders them unsuitable for supporting knowledge, save perhaps memory.

One must then imagine a completely different function for them, free from the pedantic precision for which Stendhal reproached Mérimée so often. This precision is, rather, a product of the working of the imagination. I am speaking here of those sketches from which all general topographical or architectural references have been removed. Only a sign remains, a column or a frontispiece. Apparently, the imagination should not need these signs in order to sustain within itself the image of a triangle or of a "very high column," [Colonne fort élevée] (Ibid., 617); all the more so that the drawing of this last item does not picture it as high *at all*.

And yet these drawings intervene enigmatically in the middle of the text, whence one must readily concede that it is the *rupture* that they impose on the text which is important, and not what they portray. Indeed, by interrupting the flow of discourse, the sketch puts the sensibility back at the heart of understanding. As if to reassure himself that it was, indeed, the column he saw which gave him the strong impression of height, and not some Corinthian-style column pictured in all guidebooks, Stendhal interrupts discourse with image. The intelligible flow stops and the imagination forms an image which the hand transcribes immediately onto the page. I should like, in reference to Kant, to call such images *monograms*—i.e., visual forms suited to the *imagination* as a faculty. Within this drawn form, and through this monogrammatic form, that particular sensation, felt on one 27 March 1838, is linked with all the perceptions summed up in the concept of Corinthian column.

So to go beyond the tourist guide or to interrupt its discursive flow, is, for Stendhal, to affirm the specificity, and the primacy, of one's sensibility to a work. It is, to borrow the terms used by Roland Barthes, to prefer *punctum* to *studium*. The sketch—I speak here of the one which takes the form of a monogram—is, in a way, the trace of this; it is that image which is created at the pivotal point between understanding—that is to say concepts—and sensibility, the *image-concept* which, according to Kant, is the only one capable of linking a particular experience to conceptual generality, sensation to discourse.

To assert that these mysterious sketches of Stendhal are monograms, in that sense which Kant gives to the notion in his chapter on transcendental schematicism, is to set oneself the task of putting sensation back into the heart of the cognitive mechanism, as required by Stendhal: "I lack the words, I am so occupied by sensation." Occupied, here, means *possessed, invaded.* Now if Kant has placed the monogram at the juncture between the visual image and the discursive, it is precisely because he could not avoid taking into account the insufficiency of language to be always an afterthought of sensation, as Rousseau had postulated. Thus the place he reserves for imagination, at the very heart of the *Analytique transcendentale,* bears witness to his concern with synthesis and, at the same time, with the position that the image-concept, the monogram, must play in this synthesis.

These few remarks inspired by Stendhal's sketches thus aim, modestly, to point to the existence of this same quest for synthesis between imagination and understanding, monogram and concept, in the description of objects which set one's sensibility in motion.

The construction of Stendhal's text, insofar as this construction puts into play pictures, drawings, graphics, etc., tends, in my opinion, to preserve, on the level of reading, an awakened sensibility, and, on the cognitive level, the possibility for the imagination to carry out the synthesis between sensibility's excitement and understanding's capacity to provide itself with a universalizable form of this in discourse.

—Translated by John Thompson

ALAIN BUISINE

Crossed Drawings* (Rimbaud, Verlaine and Some Others)

Un jour peut-être il disparaîtra miraculeusement
—*Délires I, Une Saison en Enfer*[1]

He runs, he runs, the ferret, and it really isn't easy to catch him, to seize him as he passes by. But where exactly has he got to in this year 1876, Arthur Rimbaud, the eternal absconder, the indefatigable vagabond? What has become of him? What is he doing? What has happened to him? How is he and how does he live? Is he still on the road, or has he set himself up provisionally, like some merchant or other, before returning, once more, to his distant wanderings? In France, his friends, with Paul Verlaine at the fore, speculate about his wild peregrinations and make fun of his misadventures, affabulating his activities and his discourse:

> Oh la la, j'ai rien fait de ch'min d'puis mon dergnier
> Coppée ! Il est vrai qu'j'en suis chauv' comme un pagnier
> Percé, qu'j'sens queut' chos' dans l'gosier qui m'ratisse
> Qu'j'ai dans le dos comm' des avant goûts d'un rhumatisse,
> Et que j'm'emmerd' plusseuq' jamais. Mais c'est-n-égal
> J'aurai prom'né ma gueule infecte au Sénégal
> Et vu Sainte-Hélèn' ! (merde à Badingue !) un' rud' noce,
> Quoi ! Mais tout ça n'est pas sérieux. J'rêve eud' négoce
> Maint'nant, et plein d'astuss', j'baluchonn' des vieilles plaqu's
> D'assuranc', pour revend' cont du rhum aux Kanaks.*

*Because of the transfer of the Fonds Doucet to the Bibliothèque Nationale, we were regretfully unable to supply the relevant pictures for this article.

*In this rough translation I do not attempt to reproduce Verlaine's slang, his imitation of Rimbaud's accent or wordplays such as c'est-n-égal/Sénégal. Wherever possible, I have used published translations, and all such quotations are attributed. Where no reference is supplied, the translation is my own.—Translator's note.

1. Arthur Rimbaud, *Oeuvres Complètes*, edited, presented and annotated by Antoine Adam (Paris: Gallimard, Bibliothèque de la Pléiade, 1972), 106; *A Season in Hell* trans. Enid Rhodes Peschel (London: Oxford University Press, 1972), 75.

YFS 84, *Boundaries: Writing & Drawing*, ed. M. Reid, © 1994 by Yale University.

Oh dear, I haven't been on the road since my last
Coppée! It's true that I'm as bald as I'm
Broke, that I feel something scratching in my throat
That in my back, I've got the beginnings of rheumatism,
And that I'm more fed up than ever. But no matter
I'll have shown my ugly face in Senegal
And seen St Helena! (Shit to Badingue!)[†] A hell of a time,
What? But none of that was serious. I've got business on my mind
Now, and, very shrewdly, I pack up old insurance plates
And trade them for rum with the canaks.

It was doubtless the very end of 1876 or the very beginning of 1877 when he learned that Rimbaud, having got as far as Java in a round trip that took him via Brussels, Rotterdam, Le Helder, Southampton, Gibraltar, Naples, Suez, Aden, Sumatra, the Cape, Saint Helen, Ascension, the Azores, Queenstown, Cork, Liverpool and Le Havre—"un petit voyage, presque rien" [a little trip, really nothing to speak of],[2] quipped his friend Delahaye—was finally back in Charleville, that Verlaine wrote this ten-line poem, in the center of which he drew an astonishing *Rimbaud en canaque.* Rimbaud as a Negro, his face tattooed, a thick lock of hair sticking up from his skull, with earrings and a huge bracelet on his wrist: he is smoking a pipe (of opium?) and holding a large glass, most likely of rum. But even more remarkable than the pittoresque nature of this figuration is its position: properly, concretely intratextual, the drawing is surrounded by Verlaine's coppée, literally coiled-up among its verses. As though the disenchanted words which the poet lends him have the power to evoke his face, to restore his form.[*] A near-magical evocation like that of the ancient homeric *nekuia* which brings the dead back from Hell—and the Bridegroom was, in his time, infernal![†]

It should therefore come as no surprise to note that in his poems, however lewd and slangy the *coppée,* Verlaine also meticulously respects Rimbaud's Ardennes accent. Had he not written in the margin of an earlier drawing of 1876, *"Dargnières nouvelles"* [*Latest News*][‡]

[†]Badingue was the nickname of Napoleon III.—Translator's note.

[*]"d'evoquer son visage, de lui rendre figure" literally: to evoke his face, to render/restore his form/face.—Translator's note.

[†]This is a reference to the Bridegroom of *A Season in Hell,* usually rendered in English as the *Satanic* Bridegroom.—Translator's note.

[‡]Also imitating Rimbaud's accent.—Translator's note.

2. Letter to Ernest Millot, 28 January 1877, quoted by Frédéric Eigeldinger and André Gendre in *Delahaye témoin de Rimbaud* (Neuchatel: A la Baconnière, 1974), 254.

which represented Rimbe stark naked (having been stripped by a cab driver in Vienna): "L'accent parisiano-ardennais desideratur?" [The Parisiano-Ardennais accent desideratur?] Verlaine, who textualises his drawings by having them emerge from the poems themselves, hopes in these *coppées* to recover Rimbaldian orality, as though the restitution of the particularities of his voice could also conjure up his image, and if many of his drawings (including "*Ultissima verba*" and "*La sale bête!*" are accompanied by a *Coppée*, it is in order that the words lent to the other also render him figurally present.* In this, Verlaine is simply conforming to a device of Rimbaud's, if for the author of the *Illuminations*, the joining of vision is indeed fundamentally subordinate to sonority and its aural reception, to musicality and orality, and the hallucinatory capacity of the poet first requires an audio-oral stimulus.[3]

By a significant reversal, in Verlaine, Arthur Rimbaud's portrait is the phylactery of reconstituted orality. However parodic, satiric and derisory these dizains—doubtless scribbled down in haste between two straight absinthes—may be, they nevertheless constitute a magic act, securing an iconic presentation of the poet. To provide himself with an image (far more than an idea) of Rimbaud: this, for Verlaine, is the primary object in reproducing the voice of him who was the master of the "Vierge folle" ("the Foolish Virgin").

This passion of Verlaine for Rimbaud's face, his "visage parfaitement ovale d'ange en exil, avec ses cheveux châtain-clair mal en ordre et des yeux d'un bleu pâle inquiétant" [perfectly oval face, that of a fallen angel, with its dishevelled light-brown hair and troubling pale-blue eyes][4] would never fail. If, in the preface to the *Poètes Maudits*, which he added to the 1884 Vanier edition, he insists on the authenticity of all the portraits which he supplies in the volume, it is apparently Arthur's face which most preoccupies him:

> Étienne Carjat photographiait M. Arthur Rimbaud en octobre 1871. C'est cette photographie excellente que le lecteur a sous les yeux, reproduite . . . par le procédé de la photogravure.
>
> N'est-ce pas bien "L'Enfant sublime", sans le terrible démenti de Chateaubriand, mais non sans la protestation de lèvres dès

---

*"Sa présence figurale:" his figural or facial presence or form.—Translator's note.
   3. On this subject, cf., the rich analyses of Anne-Emanuelle Berger in *Le Banquet de Rimbaud. Recherches sur l'oralité* (Éditions Champ Vallon, 1992).
   4. Paul Verlaine, "Arthur Rimbaud," *les Poètes maudits, Oeuvres en Prose complètes*, edited and with notes and an introduction by Jacques Borel, (Paris: Gallimard, Bibliothèque de la Pléiade, 1972), 644.

longtemps sensuelles et d'une paire d'yeux perdus dans un souvenir très ancien plutôt que dans un rêve même précoce? Un Casanova gosse, mais bien plus expert ès aventures, ne rit-il pas dans ces narines hardies, et ce beau menton accidenté ne s'en vient-il pas dire: "va te faire lanlaire" à toute illusion qui ne doive l'existence à la plus irrévocable volonté? Enfin, à notre sens, la superbe tignasse ne put être ainsi mise à mal que par de savants oreillers d'ailleurs foulés du coude d'un pur caprice sultanesque. Et ce dédain tout viril d'une toilette inutile à cette littérale beauté du diable!

Etienne Carjat photographed Mr. Arthur Rimbaud in October 1871. It is this excellent photograph which the reader has before him, reproduced . . . through the process of photoengraving.

Is this not the "Sublime Child," without the terrible démenti of Chateaubriand, but not without the protest of lips that have long been sensual and of a pair of eyes lost in a very ancient memory rather than in a yet precocious dream? A boy-Casanova, though far more expert in love-affairs, does he not laugh in his bold nostrils, and doesn't his handsome, rugged chin seem to say "go to hell" to any illusion which does not owe its existence to the most irrevocable will? Finally, to my mind, only knowing pillows, crumpled by an elbow in a pure sultanesque caprice, could meddle with this superb mop of hair. And the entirely virile disdain for a *toilette* superfluous to this literally diabolic beauty!"[5]

It is known that anyone who came into contact with Rimbaud felt the fascination of his face. Ernest Delahaye, evoking the Rimbaud of 1871, insists on the extreme beauty of his "yeux d'un bleu pâle irradié de bleu foncé—les plus beaux yeux que j'ai vus—avec une expression de bravoure prête à tout sacrifier quand il était sérieux, d'une douceur enfantine, exquise, quand il riait, et presque toujours d'une profondeur et d'une tendresse étonnantes" [eyes of a pale blue irradiated with dark blue—the most beautiful eyes I have ever seen—with an expression of gallantry, as if ready for all sacrifices, when he was serious, of exquisite, childlike gentleness when he smiled, and almost always of an astonishing depth and tenderness].[6] When he saw him again in 1879, he was once again struck, in this face in which the "fraîche carnation d'enfant anglais" [rosy complexion of an English child] had given way to the

5. "Avertissement à propos des portraits ci-joints," ("Foreword concerning the attached portraits"), *Les Poètes Maudits,* op. cit., 635.

6. *Manuscrit Casals,* Bibliothèque littéraire Jacques Doucet, page 15, quoted in *Delahaye témoin de Rimbaud,* op. cit., 159.

"teint sombre d'un Kabyle", [dark coloring of a Kabyle], by "ses yeux, si extraordinairement beaux!—à l'iris bleu-clair entouré d'un anneau plus foncé couleur de pervenche" [his eyes, so extraordinarily beautiful!—with a pale-blue iris, ringed by a darker periwinkle-blue).[7] It was Verlaine, who, more than any other, created this veritable fixation with his former lover's face. He "commentait et critiquait de près les portraits qu'il connaissait de lui—tous insuffisament resemblants—, enquêtait sur ceux qu'il n'avait jamais vus, essayait d'en faire exécuter d'autres. Iconographe de Rimbaud, il projetait d'établir "une édition aussi complète que possible" de ses oeuvres "de grand luxe", dont "la *great attraction* subsidiaire" devait être cinq portraits du poète par lui-même, Forain, Régamey, Manet et Fantin-Latour [commented on and minutely criticized the portraits of him which he knew—all insufficiently lifelike—made inquiries about those which he had never seen, and tried to have others executed. Rimbaud's iconographer, he planned to put together "as complete an edition as possible" of his works, an édition de luxe whose "great subsidiary attraction" was to be five portraits of the poet by himself, Forain, Régamey, Manet et Fantin-Latour).[8] Verlaine, iconographer of Rimbaud—this is an understatement: he was manifestly an iconophile. Everything was done as though it were essential, primordial to make Rimbaud visible, to recover his nearest likeness, as he emphasizes in his "Arthur Rimbaud" "1884," which includes a (posthumous!) portrait of "Arthur Rimbaud, Twelve Years-Old" by Paterne Berrichon, dated *Roche, 29 April, 1897.*

Ne pas trop se fier aux portraits qu'on a de Rimbaud, y compris la charge ci-contre, pour amusante et artistique qu'elle soit. Rimbaud, à l'âge de seize à dix-sept ans qui est celui où il a fait les vers et faisait la prose qu'on sait, était plutôt beau—et très beau—que laid comme en témoigne le portrait par Fantin dans son *Coin de table* qui est à Manchester. Une sorte de douceur luisait et souriait dans ses cruels yeux bleus clair et sur cette forte bouche rouge au pli amer: mysticisme et sensualité et quels! On procurera un jour des ressemblances enfin approchantes. [*Oeuvres en prose complètes,* 803.]

One should not put too much faith in the portraits we have of Rimbaud, including the caricature opposite, however amusing and

7. Ernest Delahaye, "Rimbaud," *Revue littéraire de France et de Champagne* (Reims-Paris: 1905), 185.

8. Hélène Dufour, *Arthur Rimbaud. Portraits, dessins, manuscrits,* 53.

artistic it may be. At sixteen or seventeen, the age at which he composed the poetry and wrote the prose which we know, he was handsome—even very handsome, rather than ugly, as Fantin-Latour's portrait of him in *The Corner of the Table*, now at Manchester, suggests. A kind of gentleness shone and smiled in his cruel pale blue eyes and on that strong red mouth with its bitter crease: what mysticism and what sensuality! One day we will finally obtain resemblances which come close.

In Verlaine's Eyes—the expression is appropriate—writing about Rimbaud was necessarily to reactivate the memory of his face, as life-like as possible. For his edition of the *Complete Works* of Arthur Rimbaud, published by Vanier in 1895, he drew from memory two famous portraits. In the first, "Arthur Rimbaud: June 1872," the poet, who has his hands in his pockets and is smoking a pipe, resembles, with his long hair, his hat and his smart cardigan, a young peasant lad dressed up in his Sunday best and on his way to town. His body, somewhat awkward, slender and even rather meager and skinny, is exactly that of a young adolescent just past childhood. In the second drawing (of which there are actually several versions), we see Rimbaud wearing the same hat, leaning on his elbows at a table, and dreamily smoking. Why this imperious necessity to figure the poet when publishing his works? Was it mere nostalgia on the part of an inconsolable lover who would never again find so seductive a companion? In reality, Verlaine, in his desire to graphically freeze and fix "l'homme aux semelles de vent"* is sim-ply playing out to its final consequences this will to *identify* Rimbaud which no one can avoid feeling in reading his work-life. For his many sketches, be they cruelly sarcastic around 1876 or melancholically touching around 1895, are identity-drawings, just as we speak of identity-photos. And if Verlaine seeks an ever greater resemblance to the original, is it not because he in fact feels that Rimbaud never resem-bles himself, that he continually escapes the narrow and constraining identificatory configuration of self-resemblance? Always *other* to the way in which he was imagined . . . elusive, unfigurable . . .

During the same year of 1876 in which Verlaine put his vengeful *cop-pées* in the nomad's mouth, Ernest Delahaye made three drawings of Rimbaud as a savage. In the first, *"A Missionary Who Comes from*

---

*As Verlaine baptized Rimbaud: "The man with the wind at his heels," or literally, "the man with soles of wind."—Translator's note.

Charleville," one sees Rimbaud, face and chest tatooed, wearing a sort of loin-cloth and a hat pierced by an arrow, brandishing an enormous bottle of "fire water" and equipped with a "Hottentot dictionary" attached to his belt by a strap, busy training a ring of boisterous savages, the men stark naked and the women bare-chested. In the background some palm trees and a cactus seem to confirm that Rimbaud is now in some distant and exotic elsewhere. In the second drawing (penciled on the back of the first), *Rimbaud Among the Kafirs,* wearing a cowboy hat, a bracelet on each wrist, his nose pierced by an arrow, and with a tie floating on his bare chest, tatooed with a glass and a bottle (one of his arms is also tattooed with two crossed pipes), the poet exclaims to a native: "These Kafirs, wonderful hips!" Lastly, in a third drawing, still from 1876, *Rimbaud King of the Savages,* the poet, complete with pipe and crown and protected by two body guards, is curled up absurdly on the seat of his royal throne while two imploring subjects, respectfully prostrate at his feet, await his sovereign decisions.

Still in 1876, Germain Nouveau, in a letter sent to Verlaine on 4 August, drew a young man running after his top hat which has blown off. When we recall that this letter contains a poem entitled "Negro Landscape," it is not impossible to imagine that this drawing (there is no need for supplementary evidence given the very high degree of complicity between the two poets), refers to Rimbaud, off on his African adventures. All these images prefigure the "Rimbaud, Now King of a Tribe of Savages," of which Maxime Gaucher would later speak, very pejoratively, in his *Causeries littéraires, 1872–1888,* a work published in 1890, in which he criticizes the "decadents," without, of course, understanding that this African destiny is already inscribed in the work of the poet who "aboutit au nègre comme figure privilégiée de l'altérité voulue, ou même la seule altérité possible mais en même temps interdite" [ends up as Negro—the privileged figure of willed alterity, or even, the only alterity possible, but at the same time, forbidden]:[9] "Je suis une bête, un nègre" [I am a beast, a Negro] exclaims the poet in *Une Saison en Enfer.*[10] In a contradictory double movement, Verlaine and Delahayes' drawings accord Rimbaud (even before he settled in Africa) the alterity of negritude which he had been claiming

9. Michel Courtois, "Le mythe du nègre chez Rimbaud," *Littérature* no. 11, (October 1973): 85.

10. *"Mauvais Sang," Oeuvres Complètes,* 97; trans. Enid Rhodes Peschel, *"Bad Blood," A Season in Hell,* 53. Op. cit., henceforth in the text as *O.C.* and *S.H.*

since *Mauvais Sang*, while in large measure annulling it, since the figuration confers a unique and determinate—and thus reassuring— identity on him who would always escape both others and himself. By depicting Rimbaud as a Negro, Verlaine and Delahaye fail to capture him, especially given that, once firmly established in Harar, Rimbaud, relentlessly working to amass a small capital and secure a life-income for an improbable old-age, was retransformed into a White, faithful to the commercial and capitalist values of the West. It is not inconceivable that in Harar, Rimbaud expended a considerable part of his energy in eluding all identification *in act*, as he had formerly done *in poetry:* Life "elsewhere" as the passage to action of the poetic.

In short, the function (if not the only, then at least one of the principal functions) of this epistolary triangle, constituted at the time by Paul Verlaine, Ernest Delahaye, and Germain Nouveau seems to be the figuration of Rimbaud, whose wanderings never ceased to remove him from their sight. The three correspondents send a network of intersecting illustrated letters to compensate for Rimbaud's absence. They play at "cross-drawings" so that they may hold on to the illusion of knowing who their former friend was. When Ernest Delahaye writes (28 January 1877) that "la débauche illustratoire . . . vaut mieux que tout commentaire" [of illustrations debauchery . . . is worth more than any commentary] (*O.C.*, 302), he means first and foremost that it alone harbors any hope of catching up with Rimbaud, of recapturing and sabotaging him, in other words, of unmasking him and determining his identity. On 1 May 1875, Verlaine, who in the first part of his letter to Delahaye, has just affirmed (by denial, of course) his superb indifference towards Rimbaud, nevertheless concludes with this symptomatic *post-scriptum:* "Ne tarde pas trop à m'accabler de paragraphes et de dessins et de nouvelles. Nouveau y compris, puisque Nouveau il y a." [Do not hesitate to bombard me with paragraphs and drawings and news. Nouveau (the new) included because *Nouveau* (new) there is.][11] In the same vein, in a letter dated 3 September of the same year, he addresses this pressing advice to him: "Renseigne, can-canne, dessine" (ibid., 109) [Inform, gossip, draw.] Even though Ernest Delahaye was the author of many drawings, it was Verlaine who acted as foreman, requesting, inciting, and activating their production. For, far more implicated and compromised by his past than either Delahaye

---

11. *Correspondance de Paul Verlaine*, published from the original manuscripts with a preface and notes by Ad. Van Bever, (Geneva-Paris: Slatkine Reprints, 1983), vol. 3, 108.

or Nouveau, he needed to convince himself that the "*Oestre*" was, up to a certain point, the same.

Still on the part of the author of the *Fêtes Galantes*, there was this same desire to bring Rimbaud back through the art of caricature which, according to Delahaye, he adored: "Il aimait la caricature—pour la gaieté et l'imagination qui en font une sorte de poème—et aussi à cause de son goût pour le grotesque et la contorsion. Gill et Alfred Le Petit étaient ses favoris, ... Puis les choses d'Edm. Morin, à cause de leur vie intense et de leur non-prétention "à la ligne" [*Delahaye té-moin de Rimbaud*, 194] [He loved caricature—for the gaiety and imagination which make of it a kind of poem—and also because of his taste for the grotesque and for contorsion. Gill and Alfred Le Petit were his favorites. . . . He also liked Edm. Morin's things for their intense life and their lack of pretension "to the line"]. In drawing, Rimbaud appreciated "l'attitude, le geste curieux, ou bien l'interprétation amusante, forcée, perverse, des traits et des mouvements: régal pour le poète des *Assis*" (ibid., 194) [posture, the curious gesture or the amusing, forced or perverse interpretation of features and movements: majestic for the poet of the *Assis*]. We still possess a few caricatures in Rimbaud's own hand, notably his Daumieresque short-winded, nervous Bourgeois, one of whom has just received a kick in the behind. Rare drawings, very rare drawings, really no more than a few drawings in letters to Ernest Delahaye and in the *Album zutique*, as though Rimbaud himself, for whom creation was first and foremost a matter of oral imagination, had wished to leave as few properly figurative traces as possible.

Of course, the drawings of Verlaine and his friends are derisory mockeries, that one should not be too quick to inflate with an overly weighty metaphysical significance. In this sense, it is not entirely wrong to consider them the simple caricatures of a few undisciplined schoolboys prolonging beyond adolescence the practices of their schooldays: little sketches in the margins of textbooks or dictionaries or on the back of the plates in a Geography Atlas; marginalia rapidly pencilled alongside the exercises in notebooks; caricatures deeply engraved for future generations in the wood of classroom tables, or circulated on little pieces of paper under the master's nose; sketches made in real life situations, on the corner of a café table, by Verlaine, who always liked to draw in pencil rapidly, nervously the faces and postures of his friends. But this is precisely the point. . . . This was a practice that was careless and clandestine, swift and humorous. These drawings do not, strictly speaking, constitute a work, they are not in any sense monumentalized, like those of a Victor Hugo, for example. Moreover, a good many of them belonged to a correspondence. Fragile and threatened, precisely because of their aleatory postal destiny, which could ensure only a precarious survival (and there is no doubt that many of them have been lost), capricious and epidermic because they repercute the daily moods of the correspondents, they are all the more symptomatic because they do not constitute a work.

It is apparent by now that the goal of my analysis is not to compare the graphic practice of a writer with his literary work, in an attempt to determine the modes of articulation, aesthetic, phantasmal, or other, of writing and drawing. My concern is rather to measure how the graphic interventions of his friends literally symptomatized reaction to the Rimbaldian posture, with all that was inconceivable and even unbearable for those who had by no means decided to go to such extremes or to take such risks. I also want to examine how these interventions, even if they were burlesque in tone, attempted to normalize his situation by integrating the ex-poet within a relatively coded destiny which, if not completely banal and predictable, at least conformed to certain existential schemas with which others had already experimented. Thus, when around 1876, Verlaine drew a Rimbaud in suit and top-hat, arriving at the station and shouting "M . . . à la Daromphe! J'foul'camp à "Wien!" " [Sh—to *Daromphe!* I'm off to "Wien], he reduces the escapade to the kind of passing crisis which all adolescents experience at some time or other, by entitling his sketch "Les voyages forment l jûnesse" [Travel broadens the mind of the young]. So this is just a case of momentary rebellion against the mother. . . . One reassures oneself as best one can!

"Au matin j'avais le regard si perdu et la contenance si morte, que ceux que j'ai rencontrés *ne m'ont peut-être pas vu,*" (In the morning, I'd have such a lost look and such a dead countenance that those whom I encountered *possibly did not see me*), writes Rimbaud in *Une Saison en Enfer* (*O.C.,* 97; *SH,* 53). If Rimbaud takes pains to underscore these few words, it is because he is referring to Saint Matthew's Gospel (*XIII, 13*): "because seeing they do not see, and hearing they do not hear, nor do they understand."[12] Rimbaud would remain invisible to those who encountered, without really seeing him. Already absent, in other

12. As Jean Luc Steinmetz suggests in his edition of *Une Saison en Enfer* (Paris: Garnier-Flammarion, 1989), 196.

words, impossible to delimit and to identify, even when he was still physically present . . .

This being the case, one can better understand why, in the only sketch which represents the three comrades, Delahaye, Verlaine, and Nouveau together, the artist represents himself with a telescope which he needs to see the poet. This drawing, *Rimbaud "vers des horizons inconnus,"* is by far the most complex of the series undertaken by Delahaye. Lazily sprawled on a mountain slope, with his back turned to the scene, Germain Nouveau puffs at his cigar: "Nouveau qui s'en fiche" ['Nouveau, not caring less'], specifies Delahaye. Under the sea, just beneath the surface, floats Rimbaud's face. "La lune qui rigole" "sert de chapeau à Rimbe" ['The laughing moon' 'is a hat for Rimbe']. A modern version of Aeolus, the ancient god of the winds, Verlaine blows into his pipe the lid of which is actually a "marvellous" steamer, carrying the poet off "vers les horizons inconnus," as, from the boat's chimney, there rises a vast plume of smoke. In other words, this subaquatic Rimbaud, as he heads for the farthest destinations, is no longer visible to his friends: Nouveau has completely given up trying to see him; Delahaye persists with the aid of a telescope. As for Verlaine, far from trying for the umpteenth time to meet with, to catch up with his friend, he now blows to hasten his flight. And if the solid steamer which bears Rimbaud away is nothing like a drunken ship [*bateau ivre*] it will carry the poet off all the more surely on his definitive exile.

He has gone. . . . But then who saw the poet before his departure? And indeed, was he really seen? Yes, he was in fact seen, as Félix Fénéon finds it necessary to emphasize, remarking, in a fine article published in *The Symbolist* in October 1886 that, "tandis que l'oeuvre, enfin publiée, enthousiasme plusieurs personnes et en effare quelques autres, l'homme devient indistinct. Déjà son existence se conteste, et Rimbaud flotte en ombre mythique sur les symbolistes. Pourtant des gens l'ont vu, vers 1870. Des portraits le perpétuent" [while the work, which has at last been published, fills some with enthusiasm and others with trepidation, the man is becoming indistinct. His existence is already being contested, and Rimbaud floats like a mythic shadow over the symbolists. However, people did see him in around 1870. Portraits recall him].[13] Rimbaud was not yet dead, and it had been only six years since his definitive departure for Africa, yet it was already

13. "Arthur Rimbaud, Les Illuminations," in *Oeuvres plus que complètes*, texts assembled and presented by Joan U. Halperin (Geneva and Paris: Droz, 1970), vol. 2, 572.

necessary to give proof of his existence, to compensate for his disappearance.

The sun, shining with all its rays wore a broad smile that day, the better to show how generously it warms the Earth. In a field, a thin, bearded peasant wearing a tall, pointed hat with a bird perched atop, rests for a few minutes, leaning on his spade. Along a path, another peasant comes towards him, he too is wearing clogs and a tall, pointed hat. The first peasant, noticing the arrival of this acquaintance whom he had doubtless not expected to see exclaims: "Well, well!" while the other immediately replies: "Oh, sh—!" Needless to say, the former is none other than Verlaine, at the time when he was doing his best to take care of his rural affairs in Juinville, to the south of Rethel, and the latter Rimbaud who, scarcely thirty kilometers away, was working for his mother at the Roche farm, prior to his imminent departure for Cyprus. This drawing by Delahaye, "*Rencontre imaginaire de Rimbaud et de Verlaine,*" which was executed some six years after those analyzed above, is like a full stop, bringing to a close the attempt at a graphic resurrection of Rimbe. It's over! The poet of *The Illuminations* has finally torn himself away, and even the sketches of earlier days will no longer serve any purpose.

Is it pure chance that the victim of one of the most memorable disputes between Arthur Rimbaud and one of his contemporaries, was the photographer Étienne Carjat, who produced portraits, notably of Rimbaud himself? It was in 1872, at the time when Verlaine and his friends held their *assises** "on the first floor of a wine merchant occupying the corner of the rue Bonaparte and Place Saint-Sulpice, opposite a second-hand bookstore." (Preface, *O.C.*, 963). One February or March evening at the *Vilains Bonshommes* [a literary dinner], Rimbaud, excited from too much alcohol, apparently punctuated with a resounding "shit" an abusive recital of an unending stream of poems. "Sur quoi, M. Étienne Carjat, le photographe-poète de qui le récitateur était l'ami littéraire et artistique, s'interposa trop vite et trop vivement . . . , traitant l'interrupteur de gamin. . . . Rimbaud, qui se trouvait gris, prit mal la chose, se saisit d'une canne-épée à moi . . . , et par dessus la table large de près de deux mètres, dirigea vers M. Carjat . . . la lame dégainée" [Upon which, M. Étienne Carjat, the photographer-poet of whom the reciter

---

*A rough equivalent would be "held court in. . . ."—Translator's note.

was a literary and artistic friend, intervened too hastily and with too much force . . . , calling the offending speaker a brat. . . . Rimbaud, who was drunk, took it badly, seized a sword-stick of mine, and across the table, which was almost two meters wide, aimed the unsheated blade at M. Carjat. . . ."] Reportedly, M. Carjat, horrified by this attack, even if he had suffered only a very minor graze to his hand, destroyed, with the exception of the two which still survive, all the other photographic plates of Rimbaud which he kept in his studio in rue Notre-Dame-de-Lorette. Even if this is mere legend, it is appealing and satisfying because it already inscribes an initial effacement of Rimbaud's face. And how can one not relate the destruction of these negatives to the disappearance of the four self-caricatures of Rimbaud, which Verlaine was so fond of and which he had left with his wife in the rue Nicolet? When these disappearances (accidental or not, this is no longer at issue), begin to form a series, they also shape a destiny.

A further consequence of this scandalous outburst against Carjat was that some of the artists originally approached by Fantin-Latour to figure in his *Coin de Table* did not wish to be present in the canvas beside the couple formed by Verlaine and Rimbaud. It was thus that the poet Albert Mérat refused, and that Fantin-Latour compensated for his own defection with a huge vase of flowers. The presence of Rimbaud was thus sufficient to create an absence, to erase a face . . .

Rimbaud, he is impossible to figure out and impossible to figure? But had not his sister Isabelle succeeded in representing him in a drawing which she had given to the editor Léon Vanier, A Rimbaud in oriental costume, playing the Abyssinian harp? One might in truth wonder how such a graphic exploit had proved possible, given that Isabelle had never been to Abyssinia! In reality, Isabelle Rimbaud (as Steve Murphy has demonstrated) had merely traced a drawing by a certain E. Ronjat, based on a photograph taken by Messieurs Chefneux and Audon to illustrate an article by Audon, published in the *Tour du Monde* in 1889 and entitled "Voyage au Choa." Though it is true that Audon (one of the creditors of his associate Labatut) suffered the same misfortunes as Rimbaud, since, following a gangrenous infection he had to have his right foot amputated and return to France, there is absolutely no reason to think that his harpist was in fact Rimbaud. And in any event, this harpist was actually a Negro whom Isabelle whitened: her sketch "garde fidèlement la position que le dessin du *Tour du Monde* donnait à la tête, se contentant quant à elle de la rendre plus émaciée, de la doter d'une moustache plus européenne qui cache le haut des lèvres et de réduire l'apparence crépue des cheveux" [faithfully retains the position of the head in the drawing which appeared in *Round the World*, merely rendering it more emaciated, endowing it with a more European moustache which conceals the upper lip, and reducing the kinky appearance of the hair].[14] But the most astonishing thing is that, having seen this sketch at Vanier's, Verlaine was so convinced by it that he wrote a poem "Des clients perdus se tanneront. A. Rimbaud: La Saison en enfer" [Lost clients will get tanned. A. Rimbaud: The Season in Hell"], dedicated "à Arthur Rimbaud, d'après un dessin de sa soeur" [to Arthur Rimbaud, after a drawing by his sister"]:

> Toi mort, mort! mort! Mais mort du moins tel que tu veux,
> En nègre blanc, en sauvage splendidement
> Civilisé, civilisant négligemment . . .
>
> You dead, dead! dead! But at least dead as you wish,
> As a white Negro, as a savage splendidly
> Civilized, civilizing negligently. . . .[15]

There can be no doubt that Verlaine wanted nothing more than to be convinced. What a pleasure for him to see his Rimbaud reincarnated in a lyrical image, even if deep down he suspected that this naive image was a mere counterfeit! Too bad! What counted was that he manifest himself, that he appear to his worshippers.

This initial sketch by Rimbaud's sister was to generate a whole line of faux-Rimbauds, since Paterne Berrichon's *Rimbaud vers trente ans* was inspired by it, and Isabelle herself returned to this first matrix in later sketches. Thus, for example, the drawings of Rimbaud shortly before his death, which she claimed to have done from memory in 1896, are in fact nothing but clumsy variations on this initial tracing. Her *Arthur Rimbaud mourant* conserves the inclination of the head and a trace of the hair from the drawing which appeared in the *Tour du Monde*. As for her *Rimbaud à Roche* of 1891, which strangely resembles a colonial soldier, one of Pierre Loti's Spahis surprisingly lost in the Ardennes wilderness, it once again has recourse to the same physiognomy.

And as if this were not enough, Isabelle would feel herself obliged to

---

14. Steve Murphy, "'J'ai tous les talents": Rimbaud harpiste et dessinateur,' 34.
15. Paul Verlaine, *Oeuvres poétiques complètes*, ed. Jacques Borel (Paris: Gallimard, Bibliothèque de la Pléiade, 1962), 601.

produce drawings—purported to be in Rimbaud's own hand!—of the distant countries in which he had sojourned, and this by the same method—tracing. In fact, as Steve Murphy has shown, these drawings ("Environs de Farré. Abyssinie", "La maison de Soleillet," "Ankober"), which have sometimes been attributed to Rimbaud were in fact traced by Isabelle from illustrations which appeared in the *Tour du Monde* which she had bought to inform herself about this mysterious region of Choa where her brother was trafficking.

In short, it was once again, as always, a question of compensating for a lack, a haunting absence. For it does not suffice to say that Isabelle sought to consolidate and turn to profit her brother's growing fame by churning out faux-Rimbauds. In a more profound sense, she too symptomatized the unbearable impossibility of having a picture of her brother on hand. "La vie étrange et légendaire de Rimbaud, son destin haché et les mystères qu'il exhale constituent une véritable provocation aux identifications" [The strange and legendary life of Rimbaud, his fragmented destiny and the mystery which emanates from it constitute a veritable incitement to identification];[16] and Isabelle would respond to this incitement by engendering, with the self-serving assistance of her husband, a whole, reassuring line of Rimbauds, which has comfortably survived to the present day, a reflection of our incapacity to figure the "true" Rimbaud. When Yves Bonnefoy insists that it is "indécent que l'on s'acharne à suivre les traces de qui a fait retour à l'existence anonyme" [it is indecent to pursue the traces of someone who has returned to an anonymous existence,][17] he is incontestably right, except that in this case—and this changes almost everything—the anonymity, far from being the simple result of circumstances and distance, is also a Rimbaldian gesture, a creation. In his case the effacement is concerted.

Indeed, all this trumped-up and inflationary iconography produced by the family would ultimately meet its match in the most derisory self-portrait imaginable: purely abstract, as we now say of a certain kind of painting. But before reaching this extreme, Rimbaud had first tried to short-circuit his legend through his photographic self-portraits. The

---

16. Alain de Mijolla, 'Rimbaud multiple', in *Rimbaud multiple*, Colloque de Cerisy (Gourdon, D. Bedou, 1986), 223.

17. Yves Bonnefoy, *Rimbaud par lui-même* (Paris: Éditions du Seuil, coll. "Écrivains de toujours," 1961), 173.

move from drawings to photographs is in itself already significant: a move from the old techniques of representation to the industrial age of technical reproducibility. It is obviously always possible to overinvest, affectively and aesthetically, in the three negatives which we possess of Arthur Rimbaud, to overemphasize their dramatic sobriety. It nevertheless remains true that they represent a *degré zéro* of exoticism when compared to the flashiness and picturesquesness of Orientalist iconography, mass-produced in France in the wake of the famous plates which Maxime du Camp brought back from his journey to Egypt in the company of Gustave Flaubert. Nothing could be starker than Rimbaud's self-portraits: if one of them represents him "les bras croisés, dans un jardin de bananes" [arms folded, in a garden of banana-trees] whose [very relative] luxuriance could, up to a certain point, evoke the fertility of an oasis, the two others, on the other hand, select ascetic decors: in the first, he is half-way up a stony hillock covered with scrawny scrubs, in the second he is on a terrace, one hand on the railing, the other pressed to the collar of his jacket. In neither is there anything which might cause his family to fantasize about the fabulous dimension of his exotic odyssey. And this complete absence of picturesque appears even more pronounced when these self-portraits are compared with any of Rimbaud's other negatives—those which were meant to be sold, commercialized—his *douboulas-maker* photographed in Harar in 1883, sitting next to two large columns, makes a good pseudoethnographic post-card, of the kind favored by the innumerable photographers who held sway in the French colonies at the beginning of the twentieth century. In the same way, when Sottiro is also photographed next to some banana trees (though this time they were in the foreground, so that their indented foliage would give the effect of an oasis), he takes on an appearance which is both picturesque and martial, very Tartarin de Tarascon, complete with hat and his gun. To all appearances, Rimbaud scrupulously reserves for others anything which creates a spectacle. As for himself, he recoils from it . . .

"Ceci est simplement pour rappeler ma figure, et vous donner une idée des paysages d'ici" [This is only to recall my face and to give you an idea of the countryside hereabouts],[18] Rimbaud warns in a letter to his family on 6 May 1883, to which he adjoins two of his self-portraits. In

18. *Oeuvres complètes*, 365. Trans. Paul Schmidt in *Arthur Rimbaud, Complete works* (New York: Harper and Row, 1967), 259.

other words, from his point of view, such portraits contain nothing of the aura that was beginning to surround him in France. Their only value was that of a "degré zéro" of figuration and of the face. A mimetic objectification of the current state of his person, purely mechanical, which corresponds to his new dreams of engineering. He also remarks that "tout cela est devenu blanc à cause des mauvaises eaux qui me servent à laver" [It has all become pale because of the bad water I have to use for rinsing them] (Rimbaud, *O.C.*, 396; Schmidt, 259), as though the threat of effacement must inevitably overtake any portrait of Arthur Rimbaud." . . . Il me blanchit un cheveu par minute. Depuis le temps que ça dure, je crains d'avoir bientôt une tête comme une houppe poudrée" [. . . it is turning me white at the rate of one hair a minute. With the time that it takes, I fear that my head will soon be like a powder-puff], (ibid., 382), Rimbaud would write to his mother in 1890. The blanching of negatives and hair. As though all things were indeed in league to prevent the image of Arthur from ever crystallizing.

Less than two years later, in the letter to his family dated 15 January 1885, Rimbaud abandons even this simple mimetic reminder of his person "Je ne vous envoie pas ma photographie; j'évite les frais inutiles. Je suis d'ailleurs toujours mal habillé; on ne peut se vêtir ici que de cotonnades très légères" [I am not sending you my photograph; I carefully avoid all useless expenses. Moreover, I'm always badly dressed; all cne can wear here is very light cotton].[19] But do the cost of the views and the relative, very relative eccentricity of his clothing really serve to justify the abandonment of these photographic dispatches? In this case, the expense is doubtless a mere pretext, justifying the way in which he himself contrived his own effacement by refusing to transmit his image. His refusal of all vestimentary baroque is in keeping with this concerted strategy, for it signifies Rimbaud's refusal of all visible signs which might bring him to another's attention. The result: a virtually anonymous Rimbaud, except to the members of his family, who knew him before and could recognize him in spite of his changes. As early as 1883, when the Secretary General of the Geographical Society of Paris, which at the time wished to "collect in its Albums the portraits of those people who had made a name for themselves in the geographical sciences and in travel (Schmidt, 382), asked

19. *Ibid.*, 396. Trans. Wallace Fowlie in *Rimbaud, Collected Works, Selected Letters* (Chicago: University of Chicago Press, 1966), 347.

him to send his photograph, Rimbaud did not respond to the request. And even if he confided to his family his fear of disappearing "au milieu de ces peuplades du Harar, sans que la nouvelle en ressorte jamais" [in the midst of these tribes, without news of me ever getting out] (Schmidt, 365, Fowlie, 343), he actually seemed to do everything in his power to program this forgetting.

Rimbaud's last drawing would radicalize this occultation of his body. Since the beginning of the year 1891, his knee had been swelling continuously, and was increasingly causing him atrocious pain. It was absolutely essential that he return to France to be treated, but the pain was by then so intense, the ankylosis so debilitative, that he could no longer either walk or ride. He therefore decided to have himself transported on a stretcher, and at the beginning of April he himself drew up a plan for its construction. This litter strangely resembles a coffin awaiting its corpse. It was actually a sort of long crate with two shafts for the bearers, simply surmounted at either end by stems woven into an upside-down *V*, bound together by another bar, doubtless supposed to support a cloth which would protect the invalid from the oppressive ardor of the sun. An almost abstract geometry of design, an engineer's working drawing, bare and arid like the travel journal which he would keep during his evacuation. *L'Itinéraire de Harar à Warambot* is indeed nothing more than a minimalist listing of time-tables, departures, arrivals and names of places traversed, of a terrible stenographic dryness, in the same way that the stretcher is itself reduced to the bare minimum.

Self-portrait of the poet in the form of an empty stretcher—it was all as though Rimbaud retained only the empty frame: frame of the litter and frame of the painting. The body had disappeared. In other words, the Rimbaldian silence, which has provoked so much discourse, is complemented, reduplicated by his visual effacement. Rimbaud was so forcefully propelled into all his undertakings, even his catastrophic return to Europe, that he left nothing tangible or visible behind him: "l'existence de Rimbaud paraît comme n'ayant pas de chemin de retour, comme n'étant pas une construction. Elle ne peut se stabiliser, ne peut prolonger le présent, présent qui n'existe même pas parce qu'il se consume avant même de s'installer, comme une trace qui s'efface au moment même où elle se marque" [Rimbaud's existence appears to have no return road, not to be a construction. It cannot be stabilized, it cannot prolong the present, a present which doesn't even exist, for it is consumed before it can even take hold, like a trace erased in the very moment that it is made].[20]

"Tout ecrivain laisse après lui, aux yeux de son lecteur, une sorte de *spectre*. Mais s'il est tellement difficile de se représenter Rimbaud (et d'abord physiquement), n'est-ce pas parce que nous éprouvons à le lire la vaine obsession qui fut la sienne: voler un jour, en même temps que le feu, sa propre image?" [In the eyes of their readers, all writers leave behind them a kind of *ghost*. But if it is so very difficult to represent Rimbaud (to begin with, physically), is it not because in reading him, we feel his own vain obsession of one day stealing, along with fire, his own image?"][21] But steal it from whom? From himself, in order to avoid seeing himself rapidly ageing in his absurd commercial evolution into a shopkeeper? Or from others, to prevent them from contemplating his portrait because, no longer a poet, he is no one? In fact, it is really a matter of stealing it simultaneously from others and from himself. Of fleeing from any recognizable image which would involve a congelation, a fixture of identity.

Is there any need to emphasize that Rimbaud produced the most abstract image of himself at a time when his body was making its horrible return in the most caricatural manner possible? He became his very own caricature—Arthur Rimbaud as a pumpkin:

> . . . je suis réduit à l'état de squelette par cette maladie de ma jambe gauche qui est devenue à présent énorme et ressemble à une énorme citrouille.

> . . . I have shrunk to the state of a skeleton through this sickness in my left leg which has now become huge and looks like a huge pumpkin.

["Letter to his mother and sister," *O.C.*, 665; Fowlie, 361.]

Arthur Rimbaud as hunchback, as a hopping marionnette:

> . . . De temps en temps, je me lève et sautile une centaine de pas sur mes béquilles, et je me rassois. Mes mains ne peuvent rien tenir. Je ne puis, en marchant, détourner la tête de mon seul pied et du

---

20. Livius Ciocarlie, "Le 'texte' de la correspondance africaine de Rimbaud," *Arthur Rimbaud*, no. 3, *La revue des lettres modernes* (Paris: Minard, 1976), 33.
21. Gérard Macé, "Rimbaud 'recently deserted,'" *ex libris* (Paris: Gallimard, 1980), 74.

bout des béquilles, la tête et les épaules s'inclinent en avant, et vous bombez comme un bossu. Vous tremblez de voir les objets et les gens se mouvoir autour de vous, crainte qu'on ne vous renverse pour vous casser la seconde patte. On ricane à vous voir sautiller. Rassis, vous avez les mains énervées et l'aisselle sciée, et la figure d'un idiot.

. . . Every once in a while I get up and hop a few steps on my crutches then I sit down again. I can't hold anything in my hands. When I walk, I can't turn my face from my single foot and the ends of my crutches. My head and shoulders sink, I look like a hunchback. You tremble when you see things and people moving all around you, for fear they'll knock you over and break the leg you have left. People laugh to see you hopping around. You sit back down, your hands are worn out, your shoulder is sawed through, you look like a lunatic. ["Letter to his sister Isabelle," 15 July 1891, *O.C.*, 690; Schmidt, 293]

Even in their most malicious sketches, for example, when they imagine Rimbaud in a cellar, lying dead drunk in front of two barrels, Delahaye and Verlaine had not dared to go so far. Once again, Rimbaud had roundly defeated them. He himself became the grotesque puppet, the living caricature, even more lopsided than the "doddering old fools" (*"gâteux"*) whom he had mercilessly sketched as a child. Already, with his stay in Harar drawing to a close, he felt himself becoming an object of curiosity:

Je regrette de ne pouvoir faire un tour à l'Exposition cette année. . . . Ce sera donc pour la prochaine; et à la prochaine je pourrai exposer peut-être les produits de ce pays, et, peut-être, m'exposer moi-même, car je crois qu'on doit avoir l'air excessivement baroque après un long séjour dans les pays comme ceux-ci.

I'm sorry I can't come to visit the Exposition this year. . . . I'll save it for the next one; and at the next one maybe I can exhibit the products of this country, and maybe exhibit myself; I think you must get to look exceedingly baroque after a long stay in a place like this.

["Letter to his mother and sister," 18 May 1889, *O.C.*, 543; Schmidt, 274.]

In other words, first a little in Harar, and then very brutally when his leg swelled monstrously before it had to be amputated in Marseille, Rimbaud took on the appearance of the caricatures which had delighted his friends, but at an inopportune moment, ten years later. Now that his works were more and more widely circulated, and his fame as a poet was being established, he became the grotesque by which he had once been portrayed. Yet again, he escaped the image which might be held of him.

By way of an apologia to these few annotated vignettes whose sole purpose is to mark the effects of impossible identificatory assignation always produced by the false presence of the poet, I offer this last return of Arthur Rimbaud, in the sacred form of an icon. It was on 8 June 1899 when, *in a church*, the *mother* saw, once again, in a kind of hallucination, her Arthur who had been dead for seven long years:

> Hier donc, je venais d'arriver à la messe, j'étais encore à genoux faisant ma prière, lorsque arrive près de moi quelqu'un, à qui je ne faisais pas attention; et je vois poser sous mes yeux contre le pilier une béquille, comme le pauvre Arthur en avait une. Je tourne ma tête, et je reste anéantie: c'était bien Arthur lui-même: même taille, même âge, même figure, peau blanche grisâtre, point de barbe, mais de petites moustaches; et puis une jambe de moins; et ce garçon me regardait avec une sympathie extraordinaire. Il ne m'a pas été possible, malgré tous mes efforts, de retenir mes larmes, larmes de douleur bien sûr, mais il y avait au fond quelque chose que je ne saurais expliquer. Je croyais bien que c'était mon fils bien-aimé qui était près de moi.

> So yesterday, I had just got to Mass, I was still on my knees saying my prayer, when someone came up beside me, I wasn't paying attention to him; then before my eyes, I saw a crutch like poor Arthur had being layed against the pillar. I turned my head to look, and was completely overcome: it was Arthur himself: same height, same age, same face, his skin a grayish white, no beard, but a little moustache; and then he had one leg missing too; and this boy was looking at me with such extraordinary tenderness. I couldn't in spite of all my efforts, hold back my tears, tears of pain, of course, but deep down there was something which I can't explain. I truly believed that it was my beloved son who was by my side.[22]

Rimbaud, finally resembling himself so that his mother could recognize and bless him. The Assumption of the hallowed son (cf., Gérard Macé; "Rimbaud 'recently deserted,'" 70–71). The hallucination thus

---

22. Letter from Mme Rimbaud to her daughter Isabelle, 9 July 1899, quoted in *Madame Rimbaud, essai de biographie suivi de la correspondance de Vitalie Rimbaud-Cuif* by Suzanne Briet (Paris: Minard, Lettres modernes, 1968), 108.

had exactly the same function as the earlier sketches by Verlaine and Delahaye: that of giving a face to the one who had always frustrated others' desire to capture him.

In the same guise, when Allen Ginsberg, mythical figure of the Beat generation, told his friends that he clearly saw the ghost of the poet when in 1982 he slept at 5 bis, quai de la Madeleine, where Rimbaud had lived with his mother, what was he saying if not that Rimbaud, now in the heaven of poetry, is a saint, and can appear to the faithful? And indeed it suffices to be a believer, as Verlaine already was. But when one considers the relentlessness with which Rimbaldians track Rimbaud, piously collecting the most minor documents and testimony, to attain a better knowledge of who he was, are they not all, are we not all, believers? For this is doubtless the only way of coming to an acceptable and bearable compromise with the Absolute, which subsists only in its perpetual withdrawal.[23]

—Translated by Madeleine Dobie

SELECT BIBLIOGRAPHY

Abeles, Luce. *Fantin-Latour: Coin de table, Verlaine, Rimbaud et les Vilains Bonshommes*. Paris: Les Dossiers du Musée d'Orsay, 18, Editions de la Réunion des musées nationaux, 1987.

Carré, Jean-Marie. *Autour de Verlaine et de Rimbaud, dessins inédits de Paul Verlaine, de Germain Nouveau et d'Ernest Delahaye*. Paris: Cahiers Jacques Doucet, 1949.

——. *Dessins d'écrivains français aux XIXème siècle*. Paris: Maison de Balzac, 1983–84.

Guyax, André, and Hélène Dufour. *Arthur Rimbaud. Portraits, dessins, manuscrits*. Paris: Les dossiers du Musée d'Orsay, Editions de la réunion des musées nationaux, 1991. [To date, this is the most complete and reliable volume devoted to Rimbaldian iconography.]

Etiemble, René. "Supplément ou complément aux iconographies d'Arthur Rimbaud," in *Le Mythe de Rimbaud: Genèse du mythe*. Paris: Gallimard, 1954.

Houin, Charles. "Iconographie d'Arthur Rimbaud." *Revue d'Ardenne et d'Argonne* 11, 1901 and *Le Sagittaire* October–November, 1901.

Matarasso, Henri, and Pierre Petitfils. *Album Rimbaud*. Paris: Gallimard, Bibliothèque de la Pléiade, 1967.

Murphy, Steve. " 'J'ai tous les talents!': Rimbaud harpiste et dessinateur," *Parade sauvage, Bulletin* 6, 1990.

Petitfils, Pierre. *Album Verlaine*. Paris: Gallimard, Bibliothèque de la Pléiade, 1981.

Regamey, Félix. *Verlaine dessinateur*. Paris: Floury, 1896, reprint, Geneva: Slatkine, 1981.

23. To reduce the number of notes in this article to a minimum, I am providing here an alphabetically arranged bibliography of the principal books and articles devoted to the drawings of Arthur Rimbaud and Paul Verlaine. See *Select Bibliography*.

Ruchon, François. *Rimbaud. Documents iconographiques.* Geneva: Editions Pierre Cailler, 1947.

————. *Verlaine. Documents iconographiques.* Geneva: Editions Pierre Cailler, 1947.

Taute, Stéphane. *Arthur Rimbaud dans les collections municipales de Charleville-Mézières.* Charleville-Mézières, 1966, 1969.

Van Bever, Ad. and Maurice Monda. *Bibliographie et iconographie de Paul Verlaine.* Paris: Messein, 1926.

CLAUDE GANDELMAN

The Artist as "Traumarbeiter": On Sketches of Dreams by Marcel Proust

Si je travaillais, ce ne serait que la nuit. Mais il me faudrait
beaucoup de nuits, peut-être cent, peut-être mille. Et je vivrais dans
l'anxiété de ne pas savoir si le maître de ma destinée, moins
indulgent que le sultan Sheriar, le matin, quand j'interromprais
mon récit, voudrait bien surseoir à mon arrêt de mort et me
permettre de reprendre la suite le prochain soir.

—Marcel Proust[1]

"DREAMWORKERS"?

This neologism just came to my mind as a possible derivation from
Freud's well-known concept *"Traumarbeit"* [Dreamwork], the work of
distortion operated by the dream process itself. For, indeed, artists are
"dreamworkers" in their own right and do record visually—as well as
verbally—their nightly dreams and visions. Long before Füssli, or Fu-
seli, had made his nightmarish visions the essential themes of his
work, and long before English Romanticism, Albrecht Dürer sketched
a watercolor drawing in which he tried to record a nightmarish dream
which had left him "trembling all over" when he woke.

This drawing (1410 in Panofsky's pictures list)[2] shows huge streams
of water pouring from the sky. Dürer's explanation follows:

> In the year 1525, after Whitsuntide in the night between Wednesday
> and Thursday, I saw this vision in my sleep, how many big waters fell
> from the firmament. And the first hit the earth about four miles

1. Marcel Proust, *A la recherche du temps perdu*, ed. Pierre Clarac and André
Pierre (Paris: Gallimard, Pléiade, 1954), vol. 3, 1043; *Remembrance of Things Past*, trans.
C. K. Scott-Moncrieff (London: Chatto and Windus, 1957). All citations from the *Recherche* will be indicated in the text and, unless otherwise indicated, will be taken from
these two editions.
2. See Erwin Panofsky's *Dürer* (Princeton, N.J.: Princeton University Press, 1943),
vol. 1, 12–13. Cf., 135, vol. 2, plate MCMXLIII. In the second volume, the dream-picture
is listed as 1410. "Landscape flooded with waters from Heaven (Dream Vision). Pen and
watercolor Vienna Kunsthistorisches Museum. Dated 1525, the drawing represents a

YFS 84, *Boundaries: Writing & Drawing*, ed. M. Reid, © 1994 by Yale University.

from myself with great violence and with enormous noise, and drowned the whole land. So frightened was I thereby that I woke before the other waters fell. And these were huge. Some of them fell far away, some closer, and they came from such a height that they seemed to fall with equal speed . . .

Panofsky comments: "Even in the grip of a nightmare, Dürer could not help obscuring the exact number of miles which seemed to separate him from the imaginary event, and to draw logical conclusions from the apparent speed of the falling waters to the distance whence they came." Thus, according to Panofsky, even in his visual transcription of a dream, Dürer remained a paradigm of the science-oriented Renaissance man. And indeed, this is what the neo-Kantian and Cassirerian Panofsky meant to prove from the outset, namely that Dürer was a Renaissance paradigm of the scientific positivism of the period. Needless to say, quite another approach to the drawing is possible.

For instance, a Freudian approach would certainly have some grounds for claiming that we have here a visual transcription of a vision of the famous "*Urszene*," the "primal scene" (no matter whether this Freudian concept refers to a reality or to a fiction). It is this scene that, according to Freud, is at the root of neurotic phantasies (especially phantasies of a hysterical character): the vision of the threatening ejaculation of the almighty father. If so, what Dürer recorded here might be said to be a sort of "cosmic ejaculation," that of a threatening cosmic (or "heavenly") "father."

A third possibility of interpretation, however, is that Dürer's dream *refers to the creative process in the artist's mind*. After all, "splashing" color against the flat surface of the canvas or the wood of the palette is a rather *banal* occurrence in a painter's day—but not one that is without theoretical implications. Dürer's unconscious mind may have been preoccupied with Cicero's famous problem concerning the possibility of splashing color as a method of pictorial creativity, as when the great orator asks: "Pigments flung blindly at a panel might conceivably form themselves into the lineaments of a human face, but do you think the loveliness of the Venus of Cos could emerge from paints hurled at random?"[3]—or, closer to him, he was certainly familiar with Leonardo's

---

deluge dreamt by Dürer under the impact of the widespread belief that the world would be destroyed by a flood in 1524."

3. Cicero, *De divinatione*, 1, 13. Cf. the bilingual edition of Arthur Stanley Pease (University of Illinois Studies in Language and Literature, 6, 1922–23), 123 ff.

recommendation to "look at walls splashed with stains,"[4] and with his reporting in his notes on painting that "Our Botticelli said that [all] study was vain, because by merely throwing a sponge full of diverse colors at a wall, it left a stain on that wall, where a fine landscape was seen" (Leonardo, *Treatise*, vol. 1, 59). Whether or not Dürer was acquainted with the ideas of Leonardo (the *Tratato* was published after his death), he certainly knew his Latin classics and was familiar with this problematic of the "masterpiece made by chance" that was always "in the air" during the High Renaissance in Italy. Thus, dreams and sketches of dreams may be indicative of aesthetic preoccupations— and not just indices of anxiety or obsession.

However one may interpret this specific dream vision of Dürer, it is clearly designated as "dream." Similarly, Füssli clearly identified some of his paintings as the rendering of dreams, as "dream pictures." A title, "The Nightmare," referring to what is probably his most famous picture, is explicit enough. Yet, generally speaking, artists leave it to the art historian to decide whether the painting he is contemplating is a mere phantasy or a recorded dream.

An example of such carelessness in matters of identification that comes to mind in the work of a major artist is to be found among the drawings of Philip Otto Runge preserved in the Ashmolean Museum, at Oxford. One does not really know whether a sketch representing two grimacing giants holding hands around a conglomerate of hideously grinning masks refers to the private mythology of Runge, or whether it might not be the very picture which the artist's brother, Daniel, described as "The Sheet with the Dream Faces."[5]

Closer to our time, and again, belonging to the German—or rather Austrian—tradition, is the Expressionist Alfred Kubin. He was primarily a graphic artist and a draftsman but also wrote a rather nightmarish "dreambook," *Die Andere Seite* [The Other Side], which contains both the description of some dreams and his visual transcriptions of them.

So far, I have talked primarily of draftsmen and painters. But what about artists who worked primarily "in the verbal medium"? They, too, it appears, are often dream-painters, or dream-sketchers, draftsmen of their own nightly visions. Thus, a drawing by Franz Kafka shows a man walking on a roof (Fig. 1).

4. Leonardo da Vinci. *Treatise on Painting*, ed. A. Philip MacMahon (Princeton, N.J.: Princeton University Press, 1956), 50ff.

5. "Das Blatt mit Traumgesichtern," reproduced in *Runge in seiner Zeit*, Hamburger Kunsthalle 21. Oct. 1977–Jan. 1978 (Prestel Publishing House), 82.

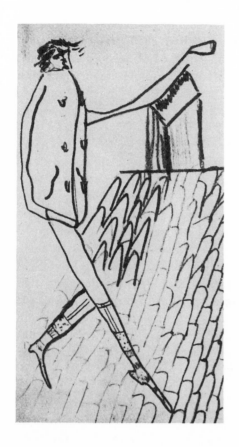

1. Franz Kafka, "Man on a Roof, or Somnambulist."

This man seems to be advancing gingerly in his socks held to his calves by suspenders. He is without trousers. His eyes are closed. He may be asleep. This may refer to a dream of Kafka not recorded in his *Diaries*. Or have we here a self-portrait of Kafka as a somnambulist? Or is it an allusion to Arthur Hollistscher's *Der Schlafwandler* [The Somnambulist], published in 1917?[6]

I have selected *offhand* examples which came "naturally" to my mind's eye. It is perhaps not entirely due to chance that they came from within the German tradition (in his relation to dreams, Füssli, indeed,

6. Arthur Hollitscher, *Der Schlafwandler* (Berlin: Fischer Verlag, 1919). Curiously, the "Holitscher connection" with Franz Kafka has never been explored. Yet Kafka mentioned this writer to Gustav Janouch as someone who influenced him. He certainly knew his *Golem* (1908) and his *Reise durch das jüdische Palästina*, which appeared in 1922 (two years before Kafka's death).

must be considered "German" rather than English). And it is certainly no chance phenomenon if "the Dream" (both the literary descriptions of it, or the novel delineated as an enlarged "oneiric description") became one of the main themes of literary German Romanticism.[7] But mention must also be made of another tradition of "dreamwork," and one that will bring me closer to the heart of my subject. I am speaking of the French tradition.

It was André Breton who, in the twenties, coined the phrase *Rêves d'encre* to make it the title of his first published tachist book made up of random splashes of ink.[8] But this very phrase, *dreams of ink*, was certainly inspired by Victor Hugo's poetic description of his own abstract inkblots as *soleils d'encre.* Concerning Hugo's work, there is no doubt that many of the half-abstract blots and stains, as well as the other random drawings he produced with the help of "spiritist" techniques, are related to dreams and to his endeavor to reach the depths of the oneiric world. It is this species of inkblot-based drawings that people have described as "veritable delirium of the hand and of the mind . . . monstrous creatures which seem a hodgepodge of the animal, vegetable, and mineral kingdoms."[9] I have dealt elsewhere with the idea of a possible connection between Hugo's tachism and the German tradition of *Kleksographien*, and also with the British tradition as represented by the theories of Alexander Cozens.[10]

Victor Hugo never indicated that his drawings were attempts to depict actual dream visions he might have had. Yet, Hugo's *carnets de brouillon* are full of bizarre figures in zigzag which might, actually, be attempts at recovering dream images through "automatic" techniques. But, in Hugo's work, there is at least one drawing which can surely be identified as the rendering of a nightmare: it shows a hand that reaches out of the surface of a lake or a sea like a mute shout for help (cf. Cornailles and Herrsher) (the head and body of its owner have been already swallowed up by the water and are no longer to be seen). This sketch is undoubtedly related to the frequent dream visions Hugo tells us he had of his elder daughter drowned in the Seine.

7. On this subject suffice it to mention the classic Albert Béguin, *L'Âme romantique et le rêve* (Paris: Corti, 1953).

8. André Breton, *Rêves d'encre* (Paris: Corti, 1954).

9. See R. Cornailles and G. Herscher, *Victor Hugo dessinateur* (Paris: Editions du Minotaure, 1953), 55.

10. Cf. Claude Gandelman, "Victor Hugo et le 'Mouvement Tachiste International,'" *Neohelicon* (Budapest), 17/2, 239–49.

Closer to us, other *Cahiers de Brouillon,* those of another major French writer also show sketches of private dreams.

MARCEL PROUST AS DREAMWORKER

In an often quoted passage, Proust expressed his nostalgia for the art of the painter:

> Le littérateur envie le peintre, il animerait prendre des croquis, des notes, il est perdu s'il le fait. Mais quand il écrit, il n'est pas un geste de ses personnages, un tic, un accent, qui n'ait été apporté à son inspiration par sa mémoire, il n'est pas un nom de personnage inventé sous lequel il ne puisse mettre soixante noms de personnages vus dont l'un a posé pour la grimace, l'autre pour le monocle, tel pour la colère, tel pour le mouvement avantageux du bras. Et alors l'écrivain se rend compte que si son rêve d'être peintre n'était pas réalisable d'une manière consciente et volontaire, il se trouve pourtant avoir été réalisé et que l'écrivain, lui aussi, a fait son carnet de croquis sans le savoir.
>
> [*Le Temps retrouvé,* 899–900]

> The man of letters envies the painter, he would like to take notes and make sketches, but it is disastrous for him to do so. Yet when he writes, there is not a single gesture of his characters, not a trick of behaviour, not a tone of voice which has not been supplied to his inspiration by his memory; beneath the name of every character of his invention he can put sixty names of characters that he has seen, one of whom has posed for the grimaces, another for the monocle, another for the fits of temper, another for the swaggering movement of the arm, etc. And in the end the writer realises that if his dream of being a sort of painter was not in a conscious and intentional manner capable of fulfilment, it has nevertheless been fulfilled and that he too, for his work as a writer, has unconsciously made use of a sketch-book.
>
> [*Time Regained,* 936–37]

Proust himself left no indication that such a substantial sketch-book was to be found also in the margins of his draft copybooks. He was painfully aware that drawing or sketching was a sort of "semiotic enclave" that could destroy literature as a finished product (*Il est perdu s'il le fait. . .*) if it became visible. Yet, in his manuscripts, some hundred doodles ranging from simple graphic annotations to more elaborate caricatures are scattered throughout the margins, on the flyleaves, on pages left blank in the body of the manuscripts, on the back of written pages—and sometimes superimposed on the text itself and often on the slips attached to the pages by a hinge, Proust's famous *béquets* which were the despair of the Gallimard printers. Many of these sketches are, indeed, representations of characters in the written work of the author. In several previous studies, I have called attention to these strange graphic productions of Proust.[11] In this paper, however, I intend to deal exclusively with one drawing which, undoubtedly, represents a dream of Proust, and what is more, a dream that is also "verbally" described at the very beginning of the *Recherche du temps perdu*.

The sketch of this dream is in a draft copybook number 16645 of the "Fond Proust" at the Bibliothèque Nationale in Paris (exactly on p. 110 of the copy book) (Fig. 2). It corresponds to the following text:

> Quelquefois, comme Eve naquit d'une côte d'Adam, une femme naissait pendant mon sommeil d'une fausse position de ma cuisse. Formée du plaisir que j'étais sur le point de goûter, je m'imaginais que c'était elle qui me l'offrait. Mon corps qui sentait dans le sien ma propre chaleur voulait s'y rejoindre, je m'éveillais.
>
> [*Du côté de chez Swann*, vol. 1, 4]

> Sometimes, too, just as Eve was created from a rib of Adam, so a woman would come into existence while I was sleeping. Conceived from some strain in the position of my limbs, formed by the appetite that I was on the point of gratifying, it was she, I imagined, who offered me that gratification. My body, conscious that its own warmth was permeating hers, would strive to become one with her, and I would awake.
>
> [*Swann's Way*, 3]

The drawing shows the dreamer as he is suddenly sitting up in his bed, as though suddenly awakened by a nightmare, while trying to clutch the bed sheets and hold them against his chest. The body of a woman is superimposed against that of the startled dreamer. Her head is seen in

---

11. Cf. Gandelman, "The Drawings of Marcel Proust," *Adam*, ed. Miron Grindea, Nos. 394–96, Fortieth Year, 1976, 21–57, and a chapter in my book, *Le Regard dans le texte: Peinture et écriture du Quattrocento au XXe siècle* (Paris: Méridiens-Klincksieck, 1986), dealing with the drawings of Marcel Proust: chap. 6, "Proust Caricaturiste," 119–53.

2. Marcel Proust, "Parturition dream."

profile, standing out against the chin of the dreamer—as though she were one of these cubistic representations, "profile against face," that are to be seen in the early work of Picasso. She is fully dressed, and her feet can be discerned in her high-heeled shoes, as though jutting under the bed.

The woman, Proust writes, "was born of the pleasure I was on the verge of attaining: she had been formed by the dream just in time to make me believe that it was she who was the cause of the pleasure." The psychological significance of this dream of ejaculation *cum* parturition is manifold.

In the first place, the dream glorifies or glamorizes autoeroticism. It testifies to the self-sufficiency of the male dreamer who proclaims that he does not need women to experience pleasure. Better yet, it implicitly claims that parturition is possible for men! In dreams—so it asserts—hermaphroditism is a natural thing. From the depths of the Proust psyche, no doubt, the "hermaphroditic" dream-birth expressed the wish to be able to give birth in the biological sense. If the dreamer gives birth "like a woman," it is because he "is" himself a woman, a "mother." It is probable that the dream, here, represents Proust's desire of identification with "she who gives birth," that is, the mother, his own mother.

Secondly, the dream announces the presence of a recurring motif, that of the hermaphroditic birth that we find, again and again, in *A la recherche du temps perdu*. It prefigures such passages where Proust expounds his theory of oneiric sexual metamorphosis, writing that dreams are capable of "putting a woman inside your skin" (*"vous mettre une femme dans la peau"*). Perhaps we should even see in the title *Jeunes filles en fleur* first and foremost an allusion to those self-fertilizing flowers[12] in *Sodome et Gomorrhe*, which are capable of reproducing themselves unaided:

> Comme une antitoxine nous protège de la maladie, comme la glande thyroïde règle notre embompoint, comme la défaite vient punir l'orgueil, la fatigue le plaisir, et comme le sommeil, à son tour, dépend de la fatigue, ainsi un acte exceptionnel d'autofécondation vient à point mettre le frein et . . . ramène à la normale la fleur qui a transgressé.
>
> [*Sodome et Gomorrhe*, vol. 2, 603]

12. For more detail on Proust's botanical metaphor, see Rina Viers, "Evolution et sexualité des plantes dans *Sodome et Gomorrhe*," *Europe* 53 (1971): 100–13.

As an antitoxin protects us against disease, as the thyroid gland regulates our adiposity, as defeat comes to punish our pride, fatigue, indulgence, and as sleep in turn depends upon fatigue, so an exceptional act of autofecundation comes at a given point to apply its turn of the screw, its pull on the curb, brings back within normal limits the flower that has exaggerated its transgression of them."

[*Cities of the Plain*, part 1, 4]

Note the significant proximity of the words *sleep* and *autofecunda-tion*. Actually, sleep, like the dream, is a "hermaphrodite" phenome-non: "La race qui l'habite, ce sommeil, est, comme nos premiers an-cêtres humains, androgyne. En lui un homme apparaît, un instant plus tard, sous la forme d'une femme," [*Sodome et Gomorrhe*, 981] [The race that inhabits its sleep is, like that of our first human ancestors, androgynous. A man in it appears a moment later in the form of a woman [*Cities of the Plain*, part 2, 174–75].]

Thirdly, the dream, and especially Proust's sketch of it, is a sort of "trademark" of Proustian "oneiricism." It signals the eruption of phantasms into the narrative as the origin and foundation of the novel itself—what Marthe Robert, in the footsteps of Freud calls "le roman du névrosé."[13] Indeed, like Dürer's, Proust's dream-sketch represents a sort of "primeval scene": it refers to a pleasurable ejaculation of the dreamer and to a coitus experienced during the night *at the very beginning* of the narrator's great search, the *"recherche du temps perdu."* Located as it is on the second page of the book, one might say that this "primal scene" *cum* parturition dream functions like an *inci-pit* to the *Recherche*. It is the sign that a literary *genesis* of a specific kind is about to take place. Over and beyond its strictly psychological implications, therefore, the dream-description acts as an *Urszene* in relation to the whole *œuvre*.

And the sketch is also a sign of what is to follow, a sort of pictorial *table des matières*. Whether verbally described or sketched, the dream of parturition is a sign of the one and only "matter" that (in the ulti-mate analysis) *matters* in the book: creation, artistic and literary cre-ation, and subsidiarily, self-creation as self-parturition through the act of writing.

Thus—this is the fourth aspect of Proust's "dreamwork"—the presence of the dream is meaningful also for aestheticotheoretical rea-

---

13. Cf. Marthe Robert, *Roman des Origines et Origine du Roman* (Paris: Gallimard, 1977).

sons, as was Dürer's dream cited at the outset of this study. From the very beginning this "dreamwork" signifies to the reader that Art is to be regarded as the product of a sort of aesthetic hermaphroditism. A writer, it implies, creates his characters through a hermaphroditic parturition. In this respect, the character of Swann is absolutely paradigmatic:

> Swann endormi tirait de fausses conclusions tout en jouissant en même temps de tels pouvoirs créateurs qu'il était capable de se reproduire lui-même par simple acte de division, comme certains organismes inférieurs; de la chaleur qu'il sentait dans sa propre main il modelait le creux d'une main étrangère qu'il croyait tenir et par des sentiments et des impressions dont il n'était pas conscient, il parvenait à produire, par des péripéties imaginaires, ce qu'aucune chaîne logique n'aurait pu faire: la personne dont il avait besoin pour recevoir son amour ou pour le secouer et l'éveiller.
>
> [*Du côté de chez Swann*, 1, 380]

> Swann in his sleep drew false deductions, enjoying, at the same time, such creative powers that he was able to reproduce himself by a simple act of division like certain lower organisms: with the warmth that he felt in his own palm he modeled the hollow of a strange hand which he thought he was clasping, and out of feelings and impressions of which he was not yet conscious, he brought about vicissitudes which, by a chain of logical sequences, would produce, at definite points in his dream, the person required to receive his love or to startle him awake.
>
> [*Swann's Way*, part 2, 225]

The recurrence of the hermaphroditic motif is important because it is a symbol of Proust's vision of his own creative process. In the same way as the woman in the dream is literally projected out of the thigh of the narrator, he, the narrator, projects his self outward, onto the blank page. But in the same way as the woman was penetrated by the male dreamer (unaware as he was, that she was the product of his own act of parturition) the writer is also "penetrated" by images.

The *Recherche du temps perdu*, is, ultimately, an extended description of the apperceptive process of any narrator-writer. In a manner inverse to that through which the writer projects his ideas upon the world, the image of men and women "penetrates" him, and his creative process absorbs (digests) images. Fictitious models for this "absorption" and "digestion" appear in the *Recherche*. There are creatures in the *Recherche du temps perdu* which "absorb" the world around them—this world which penetrates them. A character stemming from the youthful readings of the narrator, is Golo, the very paradigm of this type of creative technique:

> The body of Golo itself, being of the same supernatural substance as his steed's, overcame all the material obstacles—everything that seemed to bar his way—by taking each as might be a skeleton and embodying it in himself: the doorhandle, for instance, over which, adapting itself at once, would float invincibly his red cloak or his pale face, never losing its nobility or its melancholy, never showing any sign of trouble at such a transubstantiation.
> [*Côté de chez Swann,* 1, 9–10; *Swann's Way,* 1,10.]

Proustian perception—like Golo's body—incorporates the world into itself. This enforced "swallowing" of the world can be observed throughout the *Recherche,* for instance in the metaphor of the boa constrictor that is an "allegory" of the writer himself: "Like a boa constrictor that has just swallowed an ox, I felt myself painfully distended by the sight of a long trunk which my eyes had still to digest;" or in the metaphor of penetration by "images of women":

> And . . . whenever the image of different women penetrates our senses, unless we are able to forget it or the competition of other ideas eliminates it, we know no rest until we have converted those aliens into something that is compatible with ourselves, our heart being in this respect endowed with the same kind of reaction and activity as our physical organism, which cannot abide the infusion of any foreign body into its veins without at once striving to digest and assimilate it.[14]

Note that the penetration of the narrator by a woman's image is the exact inversion of the process of its projection outward (outside the "thigh" of the narrator) in the act of dreaming that is the subject of this essay. But this obsession with the process of absorption has repercussions on the act of literary creation. As writer, Proust is prey to anxiety concerning the difficult digestion of the elements that he has to assim-

---

14. *JF,* 801–02; *Within a Budding Grove,* Part Two, 140–41. I have permitted myself to correct slightly the Scott-Moncrieff translation in accordance with the French text, which has "chaque fois que l'image de femmes différentes pénètre en nous" and not "whenever the idea of women who are so different from us penetrates our senses."

ilate. This anxiety is discernible in his comparative analysis of the style of Flaubert and of Balzac, in *Pastisches et mélanges.* The following passage in *Contre Sainte-Beuve* is very explicit on the subject of the duality projection/absorption (outward/inward) in the creative process: "Dans le style de Flaubert . . . aucune impureté n'est laissée . . . Tout ce qui était hétérogène a été converti et absorbé . . . Au contraire, dans les œuvres de Balzac, des éléments mal digérés coexistent . . ."[15]

Thus, the hermaphroditic dream represents the antithetical couple projection/absorption. The male act of projection, that is, of overlaying the external world with projected images or ideas, matches the anguished absorption of the world by the sort of feminine matrix which—in a writer—constitutes the "absorbing" apperception of surrounding world. Image-projecting consciousness (Riegel's *Kunstwollen*) is constantly ("see-sawingly," one might say) relayed by the parturating sensation and apperception. It is, indeed, this second type of consciousness, the "penetrated" and absorbing, the feminine, that is the creator or recreator of the portions of "involuntary memory" or "epiphanic time" presented by Proust as his supreme goal. In effect, these parcels of "recovered time" enter into us through the orifices of our senses, through the "mouth" of our apperceptive matrix: whether it is the *madeleine* which, swallowed, makes for "epiphanic" time;[16] or a tepid odor in a public convenience in the Champs Elysées which enters through the nostrils; or the gurgle of water in the bedroom pipes, the sound of a spoon (suggesting digestion) against a saucer (the ear—it is well-known—is a secondary sexual orifice). Whether it is the steeples of Martinville, the hawthorne edge near Balbec; the contact of the napkin against the mouth (this other sexual orifice). All this partici-

15. *Contre Sainte-Beuve,* (Paris: Gallimard, Edition de la Pléiade). "The mind of the poet is full of manifestations of all kind. . . . They aspire to issue forth from him, because all that is made to endure aspires to issue forth from all that is fragile and ephemeral. . . . Similarly, the idea of the mysterious laws of poetry . . . aspire to escape from ephemeral man. . . . It aspires to escape from him in the shape of masterpieces." My translation.

16. On the sexual nature of the *madeleine,* see Serge Doubrovsky, *La Place de la madeleine: écriture et fantasme chez Proust* (Paris: Mercure de France, 1974); see also Philippe Lejeune, "Ecriture et Sexualité," *Europe* 53 (1971). Elsewhere, Proust describes the invasion of the involuntary memory under the impulsion of the madeleine dipped in the cup of tea and the unequal paving stones. He speaks of this absorption into an unreal place in terms of an alienating voyage in time, like that of H. G. Wells's hero (a voyage that really involves a loss of self for him, for he adds, "If my actual location in time had prevailed immediately, I believe that I would have swooned."

pates in the process of penetration of reality *into the writer*—and it is this penetration that produces the "Epiphany."[17]

From all this comes to the fore with great clarity the vision of a process of literary creation that is split into a double movement of androgynous or hermaphroditic character: on the one hand it consists in the "male" act of projection—the projection of one's self or one's ideas over the world; on the other hand, this projection is followed by a parturition, by an act of feminine apperception through the ingestion and absorption of all the images of the world and of the men in this world—images that penetrated you. Here Proust makes manifest (obviously) psychic trends located deep in his own psyche, but he also inscribes himself within the thought of the great Neoplatonic philosophers of the Renaissance, such as Ficino, Pico de la Mirandola, Nicolas de Cusa, and others, for whom the most perfect form was that of the divine androgyne or "divine hermaphrodite"—a form that was perfect because it was complete (man and woman), and autonomous or self-sufficient, capable of procreating and parturating at one and the same time, creator of its own self.

"CUBIST" DREAM?

"All of this is very interesting, but what," our reader may ask, "does the *sketch* that Proust made of the dreamer and the woman issuing forth from him *add* to the verbal description?"

What is "added" concerns specifically the style of the *Recherche du temps perdu* insofar as it relates to the modern movements in art. The style of the "oneiric drawing" reproduced here, it seems to me, evinces a distinctive affinity with Futurism and Cubism. For instance, the upper part of the sketch distinctly shows a "profile" (the profile of the woman to whom the dreamer has just given birth) delineated within the contours of a face (the face of the dreamer). As one knows, this "simultaneity"—as Apollinaire called it—is one of the chief characteristics of Cubist portraiture.

There is no doubt whatsoever that this profile of the "dreamt

---

17. Only one sensory experience of this type does not seem to be linked to the idea of orifice and penetration. This is the stumble caused by the irregular paving in the courtyard of the Guermantes hotel. Nevertheless, this "false step" also has a connection with sexuality: it may be the physical equivalent to "falling" (for a woman, a man?) and a miniature "Fall" like that of Man "fallen into sexuality" at the beginning of *Genesis.*

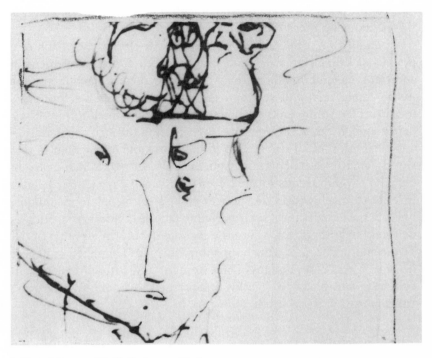

3. Marcel Proust, "Cubistic face profile."

woman" *inscribed* within the face of the dreamer belongs in the same category as the following drawing, this picture of a profile within a face (with its three eyes on the right-hand side: an eye *de face* and one *in profile*) (Fig. 3).

Literary research has dealt at length with the supposed affinity between *A la recherche du temps perdu* and Impressionism and with the similarities between Proust's painter-character Elstir and the American painter Whistler.[18] Thoroughly documented catalogues have also been drawn up of the works of art cited in the *Recherche*.[19] However, practically nothing has been written about the influence of Futurism and Cubism on the author. And yet, I have found three passages in *A la recherche du temps perdu* where the words "cubism" and "cubist painter" occur. It is remarkable that the first of these three

18. Cf. J. Monning-Hornung, *Proust et la peinture* (Geneva: 1951); J. M. Cocking, "Proust and Painting" in *French Nineteenth Century Painting and Literature* (London: Harper and Row, 1972), 305–25.

19. Cf. M. E. Chernowitz, *Proust and Painting* (New York: 1944); and especially E. Graham, *The Imagery of Proust* (Oxford: Blackwell, 1966).

passages associates Impressionism, Cubism, and Futurism in the same praise of modern art. "No doubt," Proust writes,

> one can easily imagine, by an illusion similar to that which makes everything on the horizon appear equidistant, that all the revolutions that have hitherto occurred in painting or in music did at least show respect for certain rules, whereas that which immediately confronts us, be it impressionism, a striving after discord, an exclusive use of the Chinese scale, cubism, futurism, or what you will, differs outrageously from all that have occurred before. Simply because those that have occurred before we are apt to regard as a whole, forgetting that a long process of assimilation has melted them into a continuous substance . . . Let us try to imagine the shocking incoherence we should find, if we did not take into account the future, and the changes that it must bring about if a horoscope of our own riper years were presented to us in our youth.
>
> [*Within a Budding Grove*, 1, 532]

In other words, the Impressionist artist, and also the Cubist or Futurist renounces from the outset the "long process of assimilation" effectuated in the consciousness by time, by the procession of centuries and the habits of seeing which they transmit. The avant-garde artist effectuates a veritable "time reduction" and seizes in the present instant a part of the future that is situated normally at the end of an enormous mass of time.

The second passage is located in *La Prisonnière*, when the narrator compares Baron de Charlus's indignation at a remark made to him concerning homosexual behavior to that which "a disciple of Claude Monet speaking of the Cubists" (*The Captive*, 2, 137) would feel toward their style of painting. Proust, one realizes, had no illusions about the sort of relations that might exist between the supporters of (at the time of his writing already "old fashioned") Impressionism and those of Cubism.

A third reference is to be found in *Le Temps retrouvé* in the passage where the "narrator" is describing the ravages of age perpetrated on the faces of once youthful persons. Some of the ladies' metamorphoses, says the narrator in a footnote, "are like those illustrious ladies in the eighteenth century who became religious, they lived in flats full of cubist paintings, both a cubist painter working only for them, and they living only for him" (*Time Regained*, 3, 946). But what is remarkable is that these devotees of Cubism or their coevals are described in almost cubistic terms. Proust speaks of the "revolution [effectuated by time] in the geology of the human countenance," of the "erosions that had taken place beside the nose," the "immense deposits on the cheeks which enveloped the face with their opaque and refractory mass." While the terms are geological, we are nevertheless reminded of those faces composed of partially unformed but tortured masses belonging to heads sculptured by Picasso in 1908 and 1909. Actually Proust was acquainted with the work of Picasso and had already written about him in a preface to Jacques Emile Blanche's *Propos de peintres.* There, he speaks of "the great, the admirable Picasso, who has concentrated all the features of Cocteau in an image of such noble rigidity that beside it, the most charming Carpaccios of Venice are somewhat devalued in my memory of them."[20]

Whether Proust was acquainted or not with the theory of "simultaneity" which is rather Futuristic than Cubistic, the fact is that he uses it in his doodles of the human face—as shown above. The dream, such as Proust depicts it in his sketch of the hermaphroditic parturition "uses," one might say, "a cubistic technique" in his representation of the human face. The "dreamwork" behaves like a cubist painter.

At the same time, the dream is a prefiguration of important characters in the *Recherche,* such as the Princess of Guermantes, or Albertine, who quite frequently appears as a *discontinuum* of juxtaposed profiles. "I ought to give a different name to each of the Albertines who appeared before me," he writes. "Never the same, like . . . those seas that succeed each other on the beach . . ." (*Within a Budding Grove,* 2, 346) This theme of the multiplicity and juxtaposition of the profiles of Albertine recurs constantly: "For I possessed in my memory only series of Albertines, separate from one another, incomplete, snapshots; and so my jealousy was restricted to an intermittent expression, at once fugitive and fixed . . ." (*Captive,* 1, 196)

As for the Duchess of Guermantes, Proust presents a veritable catalogue of her "whole series of different faces . . . faces that occupied a relative and varying extent (in space) . . ." (*Guermantes Way,* 1, 28–29) This apprehension of Albertine as a sea of juxtaposed profiles allows us

---

20. Cf. *CSB,* 580: "Le grand, l'admirable Picasso, lequel a précisément concentré tous les traits de Cocteau en une image d'une rigidité si noble qu'à côté d'elle se dégradent un peu dans mon souvenir les plus charmants Carpaccios de Venise." The portrait to which Proust refers might be the 1917 sketch of Cocteau reproduced in C. Zervos, *Picasso,* vol. 3, 1917–19, fig. 17.

to give a somewhat different sense from the accepted one to the title of one of the books of *A la recherche, La Fugitive*. In effect, if Albertine is "the fugitive," this is not only because of her flight away from her lover, Marcel; more probably, it is because Albertine's being escapes entirely and only exists in the state of ephemeral "profiles"—never as a totality. If I dwell to such an extent on the word "profile"—as opposed to "face," that is never to be captured—it is not only because of Cubism—it is also because this word makes me think of a philosophical vision of the world which is not without reference to Cubism—Phenomenology.[21] As a matter of fact, it is this word, *"profile,"* that is used in French to translate the term *"Abschattung"* (*"shading"* in English), introduced by Husserl to describe each instantaneous content of apperception. As to the "nucleus," the thing itself, Husserl writes, "it will never be perceived but will always, always remain a virtual reconstruction from 'profiles.'" Cubism, in its time, was an attempt at such a reconstruction, and it was a juxtaposition of profiles—and often of profiles set against a "face"—that analytic Cubism employed pictorially in order to reconstruct a face or a body as a totality. Let us think for a moment of the "faces/profiles" juxtaposition which was to become systematic in Picasso's later portraits. No matter what the aesthetics of Cubism might be, no matter their emphasis on a new kind of beauty linked to the geometrization of the human figure, it is this paradoxical juxtaposition that was the essential feature. Did it not have the signification of showing us, by visual means, the impossibility of attaining through apperception alone the "irreducible core" of a being? And is not the same philosophical statement that is made by *A la recherche du temps perdu*, both concerning the *being* of man and the *being* of Time?

21. The question of the relationship between the two movements was much debated in the fifties and sixties. The main studies on the subject are those of L. Van Haecht, "Les Racines communes de la phénoménologie, de la psychanalyse et de l'art moderne," *Revue Philosophique de Louvain* 51 (1953): 568–90; Robert Klein, "Peinture Moderne et Phénoménologie," in *La forme et l'intelligible* (Paris: NRF, 1970), chapter 21, 411–29 (actually this chapter reproduces an article which appeared long before in a Parisian art journal). And even before these two authors, already in 1925, Ortega y Gasset had broken new ground in this direction in his *La Deshumanisación del Arte*.

SERGE BOURJEA

Rhombos
Eye, Dance, Trace: The Writing Process in Valéry's Rough Drafts

> Nadelman dessine au compas et sculpte en assemblant des rhombes.
> Il a découvert que chaque courbe du corps s'accompagne d'une courbe
> réciproque qui lui fait face et lui répond.
> —André Gide. *Journal.* 25 April 1909.

The transcription of Paul Valéry's *Cahiers* indicates the exceptional nature of this document in the history of modern literature; it constitutes a genuinely unique event (the *effect*) of its handwriting process. Even if it were only a question of applying conventional publishing rules, the necessary organization of an essentially vague and uncertain set of words, already quite remarkable in its final result,[1] would not really resemble the original document. It is only distantly related, literally incommensurable with this essential *rough sketch* (sketchy, scrambled, scratched—such is the idea suggested by this expression, in which the inventiveness of/in Valéry's writing lies). Instead of the strange and essentially irregular gestures which appear during the writing process, we find "something else," another reality, one which is probably easier to read but which can only be read according to the framework and the finite code of a *corpus* of writing.

While following in the poet's footsteps, trying to investigate these non-categories of the vague and uncertain, the sketchy and irregular, we would like to emphasize what is at stake on the surface and in the depths of Valéry's rough sketches. We will try to distinguish a process from the final product or, better still, what is characteristic of the writing process and separates it dramatically from the immutable being of the texts (in the way that these texts are bound together and read

---

1. Paul Valéry, *Cahiers 1894–1914.* Integral edition. Four volumes published to date (Paris: Gallimard, 1987, 1988, 1990, 1992). It should be noted that between 1957 and 1961, the C.N.R.S. published 29 facsimile volumes of the complete set of the *Cahiers.* It is revealing to compare the two editions in order to understand the exact nature of this document, which is made up of roughly 30,000 handwritten pages.

YFS 84, *Boundaries: Writing & Drawing,* ed. M. Reid, © 1994 by Yale University.

according to the Book and its chosen model). When Valéry tries to define for himself, not the reasons but rather the nature of the tireless activity he pursued for fifty years (jotting down early in the morning "whatever inventions come" ["ce qui s'invente soi-même"]), he reaches the point of representing and *figuring* the relationship between a small number of operations which appear, unreliably and yet insistently, again and again.

—For the poet the writing process is first and foremost *a matter of sketching.* A graphic gesture, which seems to be perfectly independent at first sight, sets down on paper the multiform variety of arabesques that a pen, as an extension of the hand or the whole body, is capable of inventing. No doubt this is what explains the abundance of sketches by a hand holding a pen strewn throughout the *Cahiers* and serving as their emblematic figure.

—Next, there is *a certain gaze* which one could instantly call "divided" (as if it were distracted or withheld), a gaze which seems to characterize the act of inscription. Not only does the eye seem to be preoccupied by the obsessive image of the hand which, in turn, frequently sketches it (eye and hand necessarily and reciprocally obsessed by the activity of the other); but what is written by this incredible "hand of the eye" (in Valéry's phrase) is accomplished according to the ambiguous mode of a paradoxical vision. At this point, the whole project seems to be *to see without seeing,* or to disclose furtively something which is nevertheless willfully hidden from sight, that which cannot really be seen or constitute a scene. "What a headless man can see" writes the poet rashly, although the phrase appears in a rough draft which was never rewritten or published.[2]

—Finally, before considering any intellectual aim or intentionality, the poet invariably leads us to the main idea of *pleasure,* which in no way precludes the anguish nor the working through of a mysterious mourning. The writing process had no other end for him than this raw liberation, lacking any true destiny, of a desire to write, a desire which Valéry often formulates as a "dance," as an energy lavishly spent by a body vibrantly drunk with its uncontrolled movement.

Eye, dance, trace—but also the links between these terms, the complex relationship that incessantly leads the reader from one notion to

2. One of Valéry's unpublished rough drafts, *Ovide chez les Scythes:* fourteen manuscript pages of an unfinished project which immediately introduces the image of a beech tree in the wind, the strange site of an "empty cup" ("its crazy cup of leaves"), and the object of an impossible gaze by a severed head ("the impossible vision").

the other—this is what we propose to investigate here, in a kind of redoubling of the poet's own reflections about writing, as revealed for example in the fragments of *Degas, danse dessin*.[3]

I

First, among the numerous extracts possible here, let us call attention to this subtly elaborated fragment of the *Cahiers:*

—Mon ami je viens de faire une grande, une profonde découverte!
—Parlez—
—Mais—je ne puis l'exprimer.
—Diable.
—Songez que—en quelque sorte—les mots, les langues usitées sont comme incommensurables avec elles—pas plus qu'ils ne peuvent donner l'idée de telle courbe . . . Mon secret réside dans une image que je pourrais beaucoup plus dessiner que décrire—mais je ne puis guère la dessiner non plus—car elle n'est ni seulement des traits et de la couleur—ni un object connu. Cela ne ressemble à rien—voilà pourquoi cela est puissant.—Un coup d'oeil intérieur à cette vision—m'éclaire. Je lui rapporte tout ce que la vie me propose, ou la reflexion. Je puis doser—et j'ose . . .

[*Le feu plein d'idées*]

—My friend, I have just made a great and profound discovery.
—Go on.—
—But . . . I can't express it.
—You don't say!
—You must be aware that words and commonly used languages are, so to speak, incommensurable among themselves, and can't communicate the idea of a given curve. . . . My secret lies in an image that would be easier to draw than to describe—but I can hardly draw it either, because it is not just lines and color nor a well-known object. It doesn't resemble anything—that is why it is so powerful. An inside glance at this vision—enlightens me. I bring it

---

3. Paul Valéry, *Oeuvres complètes* (Paris: Gallimard, 1970), vol. 2, 1163 ff.: *Degas, danse, dessin*. A set of notes and fragments for the biography of the artist. Placed under the metaphor "ne pas lire d'un trait," these pages include numerous reflections on "seeing and tracing," as well as a theory of Drawing as a major Art. "All the gifts of the mind are used [in a drawing which enables] a form to be read and pronounced before writing it . . ." Valéry insists on the interest of spontaneous sketching compared to structure, as well as on the fundamentally incomplete nature of a drawing: "I believe that [Degas] thought that a work could never be called finished . . ."

everything that life or reflection offers me. I can measure it out—and
I dare to do it.

The fire full of ideas
[Paul Valéry, *Cahiers*, vol. 2, 229–30]

As can be seen, this is a dialogue which splits up reflection, cuts it
into alternative sequences and distributes it according to the gap between two voices. It does not matter that it is a false dialogue "between
me and myself " (as Valéry frequently said) or an ingenious device of
language, an easy artifice of verbal representation. One speaker states
that a revelation has occurred and the other urges him to express it.
The advantage of the process is clear. Even if on the one hand it attests
to the impossibility of putting "the discovery" into words, of grasping
it like a real object (through language), on the other hand it proves that
this discovery *did* take place and that there was unquestionably an
invention, since one calls the other to witness and announces it with
absolute certainty. The dialogue is used to affirm and present the revelation, while maintaining its essential secret (its radically separate
character). Furthermore, maintaining it in the unspeakable "I cannot,"
far from meaning an impossibility or incapacity, paradoxically saves
the powerful specificity of the discovery, keeping both its "greatness"
and its "profundity," beyond words and the laws of language. At this
point, the event *is* a certainty and a discovery *did* take place just as the
one claims, but only to the extent that "it does not resemble anything"
and cannot be compared to any known thing.

There is more in this short text. For Valéry, in the systematic "mistrust of languages" that governs the writing of the *Cahiers*, here as
elsewhere, it is verbal language that is deemed least capable of expressing the discovery. To put this another way, it is the very expression in
the linguistic code that seems already condemned to be incomplete or
insufficient. Words are never more than a representation of the impossible, obscure, or unknown object. They are incapable of grasping
the whole all at once, in the uniqueness of its appearance and the intensity of its effects. Pronouncing the word confines it within the strict
order of language and reduces it to a mere dead letter, a faded re-
representation, forever different and inadequate in relation to what has
in fact been produced.

Yet, because it is partially outside the code, the drawing immediately seems better adapted to the *figuration* of the "great" and "pro-

found" secret, as it presented itself to the mind, even if the "secret," well-named because of its fundamentally isolated character, again eludes any designation and seems to withhold all meaning. By drawing it, a real approach might be possible, given that the final product, having emerged in a flash, is *not only* made up of lines and colors (but is so to some degree). The unknown, shown only for a fleeting moment in its incommensurability, is more an image (in the pictorial rather than the metaphoric sense), that can more easily be seen than heard or abstractly understood. "My secret lies in an image." That is precisely where the secret is located, even if this place is not really a place, only somewhere between two places (forever divided by the differences between the two), in the *inter* which at the same time links them together and yet distinguishes the two protagonists of the dialogue. In this strange yet positive non-place for the discovery (in all places at once, yet in none them), it is precisely "an image" that sight alone can fantasmatically discover and truly reveal.

The lesson of this brief dialogue can be easily seen. For the writer who is concerned with the writing process, that is to say with the production at the very heart of the dialogue, the discovery or invention will encounter the insufficiency of a language that, whatever its possibilities, can only offer a poor image instead of power. Yet this image will have a special status. Even if it is virtual, it consists of a number of qualities attributed to real "forms" ("curves," "lines," "color" . . .) and it offers a certain perspective, other than the graphic drawing, that makes a statement possible. A glance at it will keep this exquisite ambiguity from remaining indifferent to inside and outside, to the interior (reflection in the intellectual sense of the word) and exterior (what "life offers me"), in what is justly called an enlightening "vision" which is just as imaginary or fantasmal as it is real and definite.

Even the very figure of the text with its irregularities and its surface effects, makes possible a view or more precisely an *inter-view* of this vision. The plural pronoun "them" (in French, the feminine "elles") is not attached to a definite antecedent (since the syntax does not allow it to designate the discovery), and the graphically interesting association of "je puis doser" and "j'ose" just barely explains a mad audacity in the visual proximity of these two verbs, due to the double reduction.[4]

4. Double reduction: "je" > "j' "; "doser" > "ose."

II

Let us take one more step towards the drawing, in its fundamental relationship with the writing process, armed now with a presentiment of this relationship. With an explicit arrow, a fragment of *Cahier* XXV (about 1935) links a short text placed under the authoritative title "Form," with a drawing which is more complex than it appears to be at first sight (Fig. 1).

1. Paul Valéry, drawing, "Forme," from the manuscript of *Cahier* XXV.

Forme—

La main et l'oeil *suivent* la courbe commencée et lui cherchent la *grâce successive* et lui raccordent d'autre a[i]res qui *plaisent aux deux*—

Form—

The hand and eye *follow* the curve begun and try to find the *successive grace* for it and connect it to other are[a]s that *are pleasing to both*—

[Paul Valéry's *Cahiers;* vol. XXV—édition photocopiée du C.N.R.S.—554]

The interpretation of this fragment does not present any major difficulties. Once again it asserts the agreement between the hand and the eye in their relationship to the line and, as is frequent in Valéry's works, insists on the dual reciprocity that unites them. In a first gesture the predominance of the line is indicated (since the hand and eye literally "follow" the displayed curve). A second gesture moves in the opposite direction (for it is now a "gracious" act that seems to antici-

pate the line). Moreover, the "form" sketched out in this way is fundamentally linked to the effect of pleasure which is precisely what links
the hand to the eye, the body to the mind, in an act of scriptural
invention.

However a word crossed-out, a disturbance [*trouble*] created by the
written form in an otherwise clear fragment introduces a certain wavering and a brief hesitation. The French grapheme "ares," indicating a
specific surface or a spatial expanse, seems to suggest "areas" [*aires*][5]
which, although it may appear to mean the same thing, does involve
the additional idea of orientation or directionality. This reading is all
the more plausible because Valéry was well aware of the idea and used
it several times, notably under the marine category "Rhumb."

On the right side of the page, the drawing (evidently done quickly
and carelessly) illustrates, completes, and profoundly modifies what
the written word states. Above all, it is an attempt to create a simple
representation in another language of the relationship between the
hand, the eye, and the trace. On a closer look, however, several elements not suggested in the written version become visible:

—The line set down in front of the hand that points at, and indeed
seems to follow it, has a series of obvious connotations. A small snake,
an "irrefutable worm" (*Le Cimetière marin*), sperm or gene—in any
case an undulating form set down there, not to show a reality directly
but to let it be felt, to offer a pre-view of its possible genesis.

—The arrow linking the writing and the drawing designates directly a strange look. The wide-open eyes, noticeably disproportionate
and covered with lines (eyelashes, eyebrows, shadows, and various
marks) in comparison with the face as a whole, not only fail to look at
what they are supposed to be following along with the hand holding the
pen, but also they seem to be directed at something beyond the page, at
something seen in the margin that seems withdrawn from any true
apprehension. A strange thing is divined, a thing seen/unseen, invisible and perhaps unrepresentable, a secret "object," maintained in its
radical absence (because objectively it is not there and has left no trace).
Yet somehow it is present because the look, at least as it is represented,
seems to stare and reflect some memory of it on the paper's surface.

—But the most interesting motif is definitely the one that no writing can echo. On one side of the face, instead of an ear there is what

5. Note that the letter *r* is oddly drawn and does not correspond to the way it is
written on the rest of the page. Here it would appear to be an *i*. "Aire" [Area of wind]
directly refers to the rhomb (or rum or rhombos) as an angular quantity.

appears at first sight to be an ambiguous form (not directly identifiable) which takes up a considerable amount of space. It presents itself to the reader as if *the eye were listening*[6] to the ineffable through the drawing and was becoming aware of, or at least was in touch with, another truly unnamable universe. There is definitely something there that really doesn't belong to the order of a text, that cannot be read nor heard directly, that can only be seen. A truth or a perceptible reality exists which however is lost in the writing without fading away completely and which cannot be ignored in the dialogue, in the gap between the text and the drawing.

—This strange form appeals to the imagination. A regular reading of Valéry's poetic manuscripts makes it possible to identify this form with other fairly similar drawings which the poet designates mysteriously as "sea cages" (in the manuscript of the poem *Eté* for example). The hull of a ship imagined by an architect looms dimly, a wreck of which only a faint hint remains, the memory of its past movements, a cradle perhaps or the bosom of the sea as some maternal force. But in this particular representation, what can be discerned seems to be a type of top presented more in its spinning and its humming, its effects, than in its spheroid structure or its physical shape.

Consequently this fragment can be read in the following manner: the "form," in the drawing as well as in the writing, exists both before and after taking shape. Undoubtedly it originates once again from the subtle concordance of the hand and the eye, but more precisely from the incommensurable effect of the "inside glance" and "the vision" (as defined by the preceding text) that may be glimpsed. In other words—and here we are approaching the essence of Valéry's theory of the line—there is an irreducible gap between what is created on the surface of the paper, under the eyes which anticipate it and the hand which invents it, and what is pro-posed as an invention, a discovery or a revelation, which justifies the writing or drawing.

The complex design of what we are calling Valéry's writing process (in French *l'écrire*) can be captured by the mathematical notion of the Rhombo, in the most widely accepted sense. Indeed, etymologically the Greek *rhombos* is mainly a "top," an unstable toy seeking its equilibrium, an unstable spinning toy. Even in its uncertainty the top

6. On this point, Valéry is fairly close to Claudel's "second logic" of the Art (see: Paul Claudel, *Art poétique* [Paris: Mercure de France, 1941]), even if he denies himself any attempt to decipher what the world scene at times offers him. Yet his landscape is that of the sea "toujours recommencée" and not that of a firmly rooted "forest."

is ludic; it enables one to gamble on its irregular movement, as if it could represent perfect equilibrium. Yet this term is also the mathematical representation of this movement, in the form of a perfectly regular diamond. Valéry's manuscripts do not say anything else. The top (with the elusiveness of a vortex, noise, hum, and irregularity) appears in the writing as only a diamond, i.e., as a regular shape and structure, entirely cognizable, whereas the movement that this diamond refers to suggests the inexhaustibility or impossibility of its apprehension. Thus the manuscripts constantly manifest the need for both a transgression and a transaction in the writing process. What is "desired" in this process belongs to the disorganized character of the unnamable, of what has not yet been structured, of what would paradoxically be held in abeyance forever, or at least as long as possible, from any language.[7] On the contrary, what is accomplished by and in the writing is different, only indirectly connected with what takes its life from the scriptural activity, as if there were an irreducible gap, an absolute incongruity between the two universes.

Undoubtedly Valéry, with some self-satisfaction, took pleasure in this indirection, in the felicity of a division within the writing process. Consider what he said in the remarkable preface of *Rhumbs:*

> The sea term "Rhumbs" has fascinated quite a few people. . . . Just as the needle of a compass remains fairly constant while the course changes, so can we watch the whims or the successive applications of our thought, the diversity of our desires, of our emotions and of our impulses, like the differences defined in contrast to I know not what consistency in the profound and essential intention of the mind, a sort of presence to myself that opposes it at every moment. The fragments composing this book consist of such differences . . . : hence Rhumbs.
>
> [Valéry, *Oeuvres,* vol. 2, n. 597.]

---

7. This idea will surprise followers of Valéry's tradition. It is however quite powerful in the poet's work. One could refer, for example, to the beautiful "lettre-préface" written by Valéry in 1943 for the inauguration of the Musée Historique du Papier at the Moulin Richard-de-Bas in Ambert d'Auvergne. In it the writing process first appears to be pure suspension, in the intensity of desire, of the wish to draw something: "In reality, any blank page declares to us that there is nothing more beautiful than that which does not exist. On the magic mirror of its white expanse, the soul sees in front of it a miraculous space which could be brought to life with signs and lines. This presence of absence both overexcites and paralyzes the pen's act of no return. In all beauty there is an *interdiction* to touch. Something sacred that suspends the gesture emanates from it . . ." It must be observed that the Mallarmean "angoisse" makes room here for this very pleasure when faced with the blank page.

This preface, not without humor, opposes (just as it links through contrast) consistency to variability and whims to intentions, in what could be perfectly grasped as a generalized metaphor of writing. It vouches for the insurmountable gap, the difference between one position and another, yet without pronouncing any divorce. And it is indeed a "Je ne sais quoi," an insistence on a strange order (neither the complete disorder of the unnamable nor the unchanging order of the language structure) which at the last moment legitimizes the rhumbs of the writing, these "fragments composing this book."

III

At this point, it would appear that an explanation has been found for Valéry's strong preference for handwriting ("There is nothing more beautiful than a beautiful rough draft" *Cahiers XV,* 421), as well as the surprising disproportion that marks a work made up more of diverse rough drafts and scraps, contained in the secret *Cahiers,* than of completed and published texts. The new "genetic criticism," which emphasizes these drafts and claims to extract another conception of literature, seems fully justified by these considerations.[8] Valéry seems adverse to the evolution (which is repeatedly confessed to be entropic), the drift towards the articulation of an utterance, entirely thrust outside of the perceiving subject and thus rendered visible and readable. His whole writing project (but at this point it would probably be preferable to speak of a simple *jet,* of a scriptural "jaculation" and consequently of a *sub-je(c)t* of the writing process) consists of maintaining for as long as possible what reveals itself in front of the hand that is writing it and the eye which is *not* looking at it, in the whirl and irregularity, in the hesitation of a radical indeterminacy which is essentially graphic. It is the vibration of a gesture, a thrust and drive, the rhythmic yet much more impulsive and unmotivated movement of a "dance" of the writing process that seems to be the only thing that matters, at least the only thing worth something beforehand, in the founding instant of a beginning—and not the intellectual intention, the intelligible operation, far beyond constant vigilance. . . .

8. See Serge Bourjea, Jeannine Jallat, Jean Levaillant: *Cahiers de critique génétique* no. 1 (Paris: L'Harmattan, 1991). This reflection on writing, based on the manuscript of Valéry's *La Jeune Parque,* establishes a clear distinction between the "text" (as a signifying structure) and the "rough draft," as the place to present forms which cannot be reduced or computed.

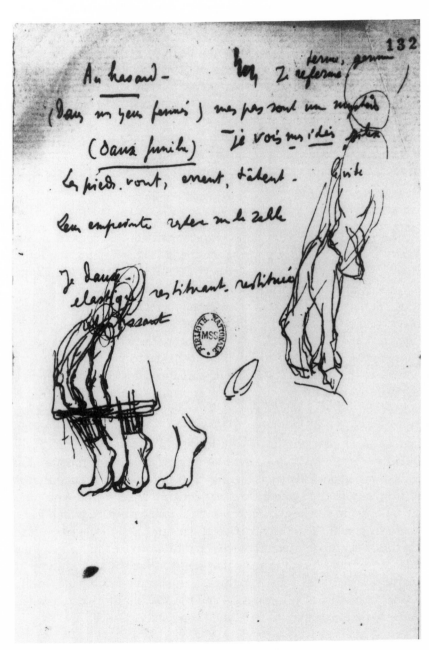

2. Paul Valéry, drawing of a dance from the manuscript of *La Jeune Parque.*

This demonstration would probably require much time and would dramatically modify the tenacious image of Valéry as a poet of pure intellect. In the following lines we will therefore limit ourselves to the quotation of one last fragment, this time taken from the rough draft of a poem, in which the trope already reveals the intention (Fig. 2).

                              terme, germe
Au hasard —   J(S)e referme,

(Dans mes yeux fermés) mes pas sont un mystère

                    —
   (Danse funèbre)   je vois mes idées   Silex

Les pieds . vont, errent, tâtent-   le vide

Leur empreinte reste sur le sable

Je danse -
   élastique restituant - restituée
   retentissant

---

                              term, germ
   At Random—   I return,

(In my closed eyes)   my steps are a mystery

                    —
      (Funeral dance)   I see my ideas, Flint

The feet are going, wandering, groping-   the emptiness

Their trace remains in the sand

I dance-
   elastic releasing - released
      resounding

This page of the "dance" is taken from the manuscript of *La Jeune Parque*.[9] It is certainly possible to think that such a work has a thematic aim and that it strives to include a specific trope or motif in the poem. The search for a rhyme ending in *erme* in French, and the sketch of a figure in motion (of a dancing subject: "I dance"), would readily confirm this hypothesis. But it is worth noting that on the one hand, this project had no future and does not seem urgent since it was not included in the final text and does not fit into the published work. On the other hand, it is the purely gestural exteriority that must be underscored, this energy of the line freely displayed on the page, that immediately attracts one's attention and turns this page into an authentic *scene of writing*. It is not so much the potential for meaning unfolding here as the very power of the scribbling which catches the eye and seems to constitute the interest of the page (beyond words: cross-outs, scratches, waverings, and swirls). This self-justifying "scene" gives a glimpse of a number of *tensors* in the writing that make it possible:

—The pouring out "*At random.*" A dissemination, a scattering of "term(s)" and "germ(s)" on the writing surface, the manuscript sheet is as it were placed under the authority of this sign of "randomness"; the expression is underlined and, through its careful writing as well as the space that it occupies in the organization of the pages, takes the place of the programmatic title. On the other hand, the mention of emptiness, of an appreciably different kind of writing—less labored, more uncertain, more wavering—curiously is found at the heart of a vague and moving silhouette, which spontaneously suggests more of an agitation, a fading or a flux in the writing itself than a dance. The writing is destined to emerge from the gap between these two terms and in the evacuation of the space into which the dice are cast once more. . . .

—The "trace" of a step. This hesitant or troubled movement, literally "wandering" and "groping," shows that under the emergent thematic, the traces are still perceived as a mystery. Once again these traces are secret and hidden, incapable of total revelation in a realization "with eyes closed," as if the very movement, the absolute fact of proceeding at random without an acknowledged goal, could allow them to be characterized. Beyond that, the idea of a "trace," a tangible mark left on an uncertain surface likely to be blurred such as "sand," is formed as a result of this step. The wandering and the groping at least

9. Bibliothèque Nationale. Manuscript of *La Jeune Parque*, dossier no. III, sheet 132. Reproduced here with the generous permission of Mme. Agathe Rouart-Valéry.

will have left a sign that they have occurred, an obvious mark albeit fragile of an otherwise complex movement which it could sum up or reduce.

—Finally the dance "step." The French word *"pas,"* meaning both an absence or denial *and* the affirmation of a movement, offers to us a dual sign ("double game" and "double bind"), simultaneously a completely gratuitous and exasperated exertion and also its negation in the "death sentence" of the language and its obliteration beneath the words, as if what the dance is saying could be annulled and sentenced to immobility at each moment. Characteristically this "dance" manifests itself once again as divided by a gap (in the graphic re-presentation of a parenthesis) and so to speak "funereal." It constitutes a sacred (secret) activity enacted around the "corpse" (as a symbol of the missing object), perhaps destined to allow this missing object to be transformed into a true work of mourning. But even if the dance was initially linked to death, it is still entirely turned towards the celebration of life, especially in Valéry's works. It is the very movement of life, the affirmation of an existence in "the beyond" of the lack and the absence.

Who or what is dancing before our eyes? Once again it is first and foremost the writing process itself, drawing and tracing the remembrance of the moving forms that haunt the mind and the senses at the moment of their "discovery." They present the energetic "graceful" exertion of the body as it fits into the writing process without having the resulting forms take on any meaning other than they originally had. This is what the two drawings (one could hardly call them doodles or scribbles) seem to be saying in a dialogue, in a strange ballet. Feet are conspicuously and almost compulsively visible; there are no fewer than five, sometimes perfectly rendered with a distinct and repeated gesture, sometimes evoking a whirling agitation. Some deeper, more inward movements are hinted at by the interlacing of the blurred lines that constitute the life of the formless forms captured in the flux of their oscillations, their intimate quivering or trembling. . . .[10]

10. This recalls a few pages by Michel Serres, *Genèse* (Paris: Grasset, 1982), cf., 26, on the foot (or the step) of "La Belle noiseuse": "the work is made up of forms, the masterpiece is a formless fountain of forms. . . . Only that which we call the phenomenon, the avatars of a Proteus in its secrets, are known or cognizable: they emerge from the resounding [*noiseuse*] sea. "La Belle noiseuse" is not a painting, it is the "noise" of beauty, the bare Multiple, the numerous sea whence is born, whence is not born, according to the case, the beautiful Aphrodite. We always see Venus without the sea or the sea without Venus, we never see physics appearing suddenly, *anadyomen,* out of metaphysics . . ." (*Genèse,* 39,40). Beyond these remarks, it must be stated that we fully

Here again, this is what the wavering of the lines seem to affirm in the effort and the thrust of their inscription, just as they become legible and decipherable before their filtering by the mind. In order to see the effort well, it would be necessary to blink and half-close one's eyes. From this point of view, in the first line, centered at the top of the page, in place of an initial inaugural division, there is a striking heavy inscription (graze, incision, scarification, or an intelligible message—who knows?). Its form is most mysterious; it is a true "trace," which either betrays the hand's nervous impatience (and would thus be merely a simple and meaningless crossing-out) or else the violence of a rejection. A "non" appears which is clearly the "non" of the Parque confronted with the momentary denial of her life.

It is definitely a question of vision and perhaps of double vision. If what lay before one's eyes were internalized too soon, to be quickly forgotten, one might reach the hasty conclusion that these manuscript documents are incomplete and imperfect, a not-yet-pure or worthless composition that never could be compared to the perfection of a finished text carried through to its completion. Yet maintaining the rough draft in its confusing "visibility" (what is perceived at first glance) offers an opportunity to apprehend what is lost in its elaboration, in the progression towards a "definitive" version. Everything vague and uncertain, every physiological and corporeal shock and disturbance (every "émoi" as the poet himself said) not only regularly accompany scriptural invention but also undoubtedly constitute its pressing necessity. The first document that we have shown, the most elaborate and complete one, was accompanied by a sort of unattached appendix. Nothing proves that this appendix is definitely linked to the brief dialogue that we have analyzed. In the lower right-hand corner there is a seemingly unrelated comment: "The fire full of ideas." Yet the manuscript sheet itself indicates "I see my ideas—Flint." This is what the wide-open eyes of the one who is writing sees without seeing. Within himself and at the same time in front of him, unnoticed and yet below him, he sees "in my closed eyes" the flame of a fire, the sudden spark or flash of a scraped piece of flint. He sees a blinding burst of "ideas," the content of

---

subscribe to the project (radically opposed to the structuralists' "scenographies") of elaborating an (impossible) "ichnography" of works of art. For Serres, *ichnography* is precisely "a set of possible profiles.," "Proteus himself." (In Greek, *Ichnos* means "the trace of a step.")

which is less important than the intensity of the glance that can be cast at them.

Strangely enough, this rough draft "dance" reappears again several years later as the germ of a text in prose on the dance ["l'état dansant"], aptly entitled *Philosophie de la danse*[11]—not at all comparable to *La Jeune Parque*. Now this text, unjustly ignored by Valéry's critics, enables us to retrace the connection which, we believe, profoundly binds the three documents and constitutes their essential link, despite their apparent disparity.

It is easy to find here the strange gaze as we have described it, i.e., blind or closed but at the same time hyper-lucid. The wonder-struck observer watching the "dancer" (who can also be understood as "the verbal dance" [1400] or the formal movement of all works of art in the making) possesses "the extraordinary eyes which transform everything they see into the prey of the abstract mind" (1396). Yet "the dancer," who seems to be enclosed within another separate and secret world, cannot really be seen for what she is and cannot return the glance that is cast towards her. Her dancing body also elicits the comment "that it does not see anything and that its eyes are absolutely useless, are mere gems or gleams."[12]

Indeed the dance does enclose her in another space and time which can be defined only in an infinite series of self-transformations and self-modifications, in the enchantment of *"transports"* which however lead nowhere, nor do they limit or arrest the dance in any way. The most obvious characteristics of this "dance" cannot be defined. Rather they are constantly inviting the reader to *un-read* them; they are ceaselessly undoing any possibility of being read or deciphered. "It [the dance] is instability, it exudes instability, traverses the impossible and takes advantage of the improbable" (1398).

However this act, which is comparable only to that of a "flame," is

11. Valéry, *Philosophie de la danse, Oeuvres complètes*, vol. 2, 1390 ff. The pagination of our quotations refers to the publication of Valéry's lecture on the Spanish dancer "l'Argentina." It must be pointed out that dance (much more than music, considered too abstract and intellectual) is the privileged metaphor in Valéry's work through which the activity of writing can be entirely understood.

12. In *Degas, danse, dessin*, this "blind look" is described as follows: "the eye, through its movements on what it sees, must find the path of the pencil on the paper, just as a blind man, by feeling his way, accumulates the elements of contact of a form." Op. cit., 1194.

paradoxically a product of the *drawing*. Valéry noticed that the dancer "weaves with her steps and constructs with her gestures" (1398) an elusive universe destined for an infinite incompleteness. In the same way, when speaking of Athikte's friends, in the dialogue *L'Ame et la danse*, Socrates affirms that "their hands speak and their feet seem to write." Every scriptural "dance," because of its successive outbursts, subverts and rewrites an unlimited text, just as dance and choreography transcend walking, "this prose of human movement." Indeed the paradox is that the trace is destined to be ephemeral and can only be grasped as a print in the sand as we have seen (for Valéry, rewriting Plato, writing is like writing *on the sand*). Essentially fragile is the trace which lies halfway between the "letter" (the writing itself, transitive and destined to have meaning) and the drawing (of the curve or the line, not intended to mean anything). It is constantly on the brink of revision here or there, of falling into what it can never really be in itself. Yet it is this very fragility of Valéry's writing process that the rough drafts seem deliberately to maintain, in accordance with their dual impossibility, as if a particular pleasure were attached to the pure dancing activity of an inscription in the drawing. For Valéry, nothing proves that the eye of the reader, any more than the hand of the writer, tries to transcribe or translate instantaneously what it sees and feels: to write "in letters." The line and the drawing were undoubtedly there first and immediately say something, perhaps the essential thing, about what is being readied and directed towards language. Is the eye not initially seduced by the scratches on the page, the vacillations and wormlike tremblings of what is not yet a true sign, in order to communicate and captivate the gaze? And is not the hand quivering, nervous, muscular, reflecting the inexpressible pleasures of the body, before becoming the docile instrument of thought? The blind Eye and Hand, far more than *L'Oeil et l'esprit*—this is, contrary to Merleau-Ponty's phenomenology,[13] what should be said of the pictorial activity on the written page.

After Valéry, Blanchot would say it: the entire writing process lies on the unthinkable crest that separates the clarity of a beautiful language which is spoken" from "the opaque meaning of something that is consumed and consumes, turns to ashes and is resuscitated in a vain effort to turn itself into nothing."[14]

Not only is the body of the dancer poised entirely on this crest, but

13. Maurice Merleau-Ponty, *L'Oeil et l'esprit* (Paris: Gallimard, 1983), 22.
14. Maurice Blanchot, *La Part du feu* (Paris: Gallimard, 1949), 27.

also that of the writer and the reader. "One would say that [the body] is having a battle of wits" ["joue au plus fin"], said Valéry of its blissful fragility: "it is as if it were gifted with an extreme resiliency that could capture the impetus of each movement and could immediately release it" (1397). (The manuscript had already proclaimed: "As I dance I am fluid /releasing /released /resounding" ["Je danse / élastique restitu-ant restitue /retentissant"]. And once again we find the only image that takes this resiliency into account: the top which is writing its strangely unstable balance in the rhomb:

It is trying to go deeply into the mystery of a body which
suddenly, as if under the effects of an internal shock, enters into a
life both strangely unsteady and strangely steady, at the same time
strangely instinctive, yet strangely knowing and firmly
elaborated. . . . *It recalls the top which stands on its point and
reacts so sharply to the slightest contact.*
[*Philosophie de la danse*, 1397. My emphasis.]

—Translated by Liliane Greene and the author.

JACQUES DERRIDA

Maddening the Subjectile*

I would call this a scene, the *scene of the subjectile*, if there were not already a force at work there already to make little of what always sets up the scene: the visibility, the element of representation, the presence of a subject, even an object.

Subjectile, the word or the thing can take the place of the subject or of the object—being neither one or the other.

Three times at least, to my knowledge, Antonin Artaud names *"what is called the subjectile."* He says exactly that: "what is called . . ." Indirect nomination, invisible quotation marks, allusion to the discourse of the other. He uses the word of the others but perhaps he will have it say something else, perhaps he will tell it to do something else.

All three times, it is to speak of his own drawings, in 1932, 1946, and 1947.

Nevertheless, is it likely that he really *spoke about* his drawings? And above all that we can or are allowed to? We won't tell the story of the subjectile, rather some remembered details of its *coming-to-be*.

The first time (later, we will be attentive to what only happened *once* for Artaud), on 23 September 1932, he concludes a letter to André Rolland de Renéville like this: "Herewith a bad drawing in which what is called the subjectile betrayed me."

Wait a minute: a subjectile can betray you?

And let's watch out, when Artaud evaluates his painting or his

*This is an excerpt from Jacques Derrida and Paule Thévenin, *Artaud: Portraits, Dessins* (Paris: Gallimard, 1988). With the kind permission of Jacques Derrida and the translator, Mary Ann Caws.

YFS 84, *Boundaries: Writing & Drawing*, ed. M. Reid, © 1994 by Yale University.

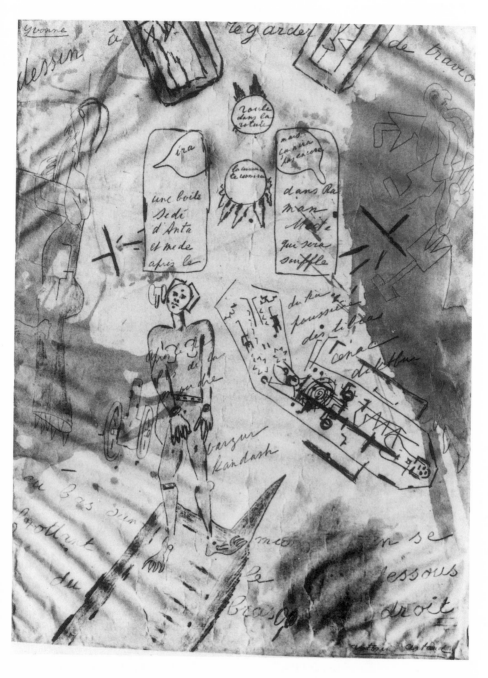

1. Antonin Artaud, *La Machine de l'être*.

drawings, when he speaks badly of them ("a bad drawing"), a whole interpretation of the bad reinforces it. Already in 1932, it is not simple to figure out what he is indicting here: it is not only a question of technique, of art, or of skill. The indictment is already leveled at God. He is denouncing some treason. What must a subjectile do to commit treason?

In 1932, the word could seem to have been created recently. The current dictionaries had not yet admitted it in the spoken tongue. So the legitimacy of a "subjectile" remains in doubt. Paule Thévenin (who has said everything that has to be known about Artaud's drawings and whose work I am presuming everyone knows)[1] judges it necessary to be more precise in a note: "It's perhaps in the part torn from this letter that the drawing was to be found. Antonin Artaud, having definitely found it too revealing, is said to have taken it away, tearing off the bottom of the page. He certainly wrote *"subjectile,"* (Artaud, vol. 5, 274).

This note tells us at least two things. First a drawing can *be a part of* a letter, it's completely different from accompanying it. It *joins* with it *physically* because he is only separate as the expression "part ripped off." And then *to betray* can be understood in a very particular sense, to fail in one's promise, to belittle the project, take one out of its control but by doing this, to control while at the same time *revealing* the project as it is thus betrayed. Translating it and dragging it out into broad daylight. Betraying the subjectile would have made the drawing "too revelatory," and of a truth sufficiently unbearable so that Artaud judged it necessary to destroy its support. This latter was stronger than him, and because he had not mastered the rebellious one, Artaud is said to have snatched it away.

"He really wrote *subjectile.*" Paul Thévenin warns those who, because they do not know this rare word, might be tempted to confuse it with another.

With what other word could we have confused the drawing itself, in sum, the graphic form summing up the 'subjectile'? With "subjec-

1. I am thinking in particular of Paule Thévenin, *Recherche d'un monde perdu* and above all of *Entendre/voir/lire* (Hearing/Seeing/Reading) in *Tel Quel* 39 (Fall 1969) 40 (Winter 1970). See also *Notes de travail sur les mots forgés par Antonin Artaud dans ce texte* (un commentaire sur *la maladresse sexuelle de dieu*) in *Peinture/Cahiers théoriques*, no. 1, 2nd trimester 1971: *Lettre à Henry-Claude Cousseau sur les dessins d'Antonin Artaud*, Cahiers de l'Abbaye Sainte-Croix 37, (1980); *Dessin à regarder de traviole* in *Café* 3, (Fall 1983); catalogue of the exhibit *Écritures dans la peinture*, April–June 1984. Centre national des arts plastiques, Villa Arson, Nice.

tive," perhaps, the treason close up. But so many other words, a great family of bits and snatches of words, and Artaud's words are haunting this word, drawing it towards the dynamic potential of all its meanings. Just to begin by subjective, subtle, sublime, also pulling the *il* into the *ile,* and finishing with projectile. This is Artaud's *thought.* The body of his thought working itself out in the graphic treatment of the subjectile is a dramaturgy through and through, often a surgery of the *projectile.* Between the beginning and the end of the word (*sub/tile*), all these persecuting evils who emerge from the depths to haunt the supports, the substrata, and the substances: Artaud never stopped naming, denouncing, exorcizing, conjuring, often through the operation of drawing, the fiends [*suppôts*] and succubi, that is the women or sorcerers who change their sex to get in *bed* with man, or then the vampires who come to suck your very substance, to subjugate you to steal what is most truly yours.

Through the two extremities of his body, such a word, itself subjectile, can, like the drawing of a chimera, stand to mingle with everything that it is not. Although it seems too close to them, it draws them towards the lure of an entire resemblance: the *sub*jective and the pro*ject*ile.

What is a subjectile? Let's go slowly, not rushing things, learning the patience of what is developing, and make it precise: what is "called the subjectile"? For Antonin Artaud doesn't speak of the subjectile, only of what "is called" by this name. To take account of the calling, and what is called. A subjectile is first of all something to be called. That the subjectile *is something,* that is not yet a given. Perhaps it comes across as being *someone* instead, and preferably something *else:* it can betray. But the other can be called something without being, without being a being, and above all not a subject nor the subjectivity of a subject. Perhaps we don't know yet what "is called" like this "the subjectile," the subjectility of the subjectile, both because it does not constitute an object of any knowing and because it can betray, not come when it is called, or call before even being called, before even receiving its name. At the very moment when it is born, when it is not yet, and the drawing of Artaud situates this *coup de force,* a subjectile calls and something betrays. That's what I can say about it to begin with.

At least in this language. In French, we think we have known for a short time what the word "subjectile" means, in its current sense. We believe it to be contemporaneous with Artaud. Contemporary dictionaries date it from the middle of the twentieth century. But they are wrong, they are really reactivating an old word, French or Italian.[2] The notion belongs to the code of painting and designates what is in some way lying below (*sub=jectum*) as a substance, a subject or a succubus. Between the beneath and the above, that is at once a support and a surface, sometimes also the matter of a painting or a sculpture, everything distinct from form, as well as from the sense and representation, which is not representable. Its presumed depth or thickness can only be seen as a surface, that of the wall or of wood, but already also that of paper, of textiles and of the panel. A sort of skin with holes for pores. We can distinguish two classes of subjectile, and according to a criterion which will decide everything in the surgery of Artaud: in this apparently manual operation that is a drawing, how does the subjectile permit itself to be traversed? For we oppose just those subjectiles that let themselves be *traversed* (we call them *porous*, like plasters, mortar, wood, cardboard, textiles, paper) and the others (metals or their alloys) which permit no passage.

About the subjectile we would have to—yes—write what is untranslatable. To write according to the new phrasing, but discreetly, for resistance to translation when it is organized, noisy, spectacular, we

2. I am adding *three* details, which all depend on texts I have just become acquainted with, now that this manuscript has already gone to the printer's. a. As for the "Italian" source, I refer to the Letters of Pontormo to Varchi, edited by Jean-Claude Lebensztejn in *Avant-guerre* (1981, 2, 52–55). Here we read: ". . . Sculpture is such a dignified and eternal thing, but this eternity has more to do with the marble quarries of Carrara than with the value of the Artist, because it is a better subject for that, and this subject, which is to say, relief . . ." Lebensztejn notes here that "subject, soggetto, designates the material substance of art, its substratum, *subjectum, hypokeimenon.*" "Pontormo's argument about the subject, he adds, was already present in Leonardo (without a subject). We find it again in Bronzino's letter to Varchi (with a subject). This time it is 'in più saldo subbietto.'" b. The very beautiful book that Georges Didi-Huberman just published with the title *Painting Incarnate* (Paris: Minuit, 1985) calls the subjectile "the old notion of the *subjectile*" and refers to Jean Clay to whom "we owe its theoretical reestablishment." (38). c. Paule Thévenin has just given me a text she recently discovered, about which everything lets us suppose that Artaud had read it. The word *subjectile* appears in it *three times.* It is an article that Tristan Klingsor devoted to *Pierre Bonnard* in 1921 (in *l'Amour de l'art*, second year, no. 8, August 1921): "The use of a subjectile, so infrequent until now, that is cardboard, facilitates his research. The way the cardboard absorbs so readily lets him get rid of the oil colors. . . . In addition, Pierre Bonnard, with a seeming negligence, lets this subjectile show through here and there. Since it is rather warm in nuance, generally golden, it contrasts with the cold tones laid down by the painter and gives them the most exquisite finesse. Even better, it guarantees a general harmony to the work. . . . Once the nuances that cardboard gives have been discovered, the artist will transport them to his canvas, he keeps his orchestration in changing the subjectile."

already know it has been repatriated. In truth its secret should only be shared with the translator.

A subjectile can appear untranslatable, that is axiomatic and organizes the bodily struggle with Artaud. By which two things can be meant. First, the word "subjectile" is not to be translated. With all its semantic or formal kinship, from the subjective to the tactile, of support, succubus or fiends with a projectile, etc., it will never cross the border of the French language. On the other hand, a subjectile, that is to say the support, the surface or the material, the unique body of the work in its first event, *at its moment of birth,* which cannot be repeated, which is as distinct from the form as from the meaning and the representation, here again defies translation. It will never be transported in another language. Unless it is taken over bodily and intact, like a foreign substance. So we shall be able to conclude: 1) What exceeds translation really belongs to language. 2) What so drastically exceeds linguistic transfer remains on the contrary foreign to language as an element of the discourse. 3) The word "subjectile" is itself a subjectile.

How to measure the consequences of this paradox? I will dare to make the claim that we have to embroil ourselves in the paradox in order to approach the painted or drawn work of Artaud. This spatial work would be first of all a corporeal struggle with the question of language—and at the limit, of music.

No way of passing over this fact: what I am writing here in French, in a language what was up to a certain point and most often that of Artaud, should first be appearing in a language said to be foreign. You are reading in German here[3] what was first destined to offer a subtle resistance to translation. But since you are reading me in German, it means that this text has nevertheless been translated, whereas at no moment would one have thought of translating the drawings or the paintings, nor indeed the words or phrases contained in them—by Artaud's own hand. Incorporated, that is to say, inscribed in the graphic corpus *in the very substance* of the subjectile.

To defy the foreigner, not in order to write in good old French, but on the contrary to undertake the *experiment, to translate* the crossing of my language, to the point of forcing the French, my natural language, the only mother tongue able to serve as an ultimate support to what I

3. At the moment when these pages were written they were supposed to appear first, in fact only, in translation.

am calling upon first. The French language is the one in which I was *born*, if I may say, and in which *I find myself* even as I debate with it or against it. I am writing *in the substance* of the French language. (How will they translate that?)

Now at the moment of speaking the language said to be maternal, I remember the last arrival of the subjectile, the ultimate occurrence of the word *in the hand* of Artaud. Father and mother are not far off: "The figures on the inert page said nothing under my hand. They offered themselves to me like millstones which would not inspire my drawing, and that I could probe, shape, scrape, plane down, dew, unsew, shred, tear up, and sew together without the subjectile ever complaining through my father and mother." (1947)

How can a subjectile, untranslatable, betray, we were wondering just a moment ago. What must it have become now, in the return of the word fifteen years later, in order never to complain "through father or mother," at the moment when I am attacking its unresisting body with so many *coups de force* and in so many ways, delivering myself up to him in order to deliver him so many operations with my hands, when the surgeon that I am demands to probe, shape, scrape, plane down, dew, unsew, shred, tear up, and sew together without the subjectile ever complaining through my father and mother." (1947)

What had happened in the interval (1932–1947) Something? An event, once, on such and such a date?

> And since a certain day in October 1939 I have never
> again written without drawing.
> Now what I draw
> is no longer themes of Art transposed from . . .[4]

No longer to have to transpose, to translate. Must we write against our mother tongue to do that? Precisely in order to *render* what is untranslatable?

But no one can say calmly that French was Artaud's only mother tongue, nor that language is just a support, as you might say of a paper or a textile, of a wall or a panel. Unless you treat it in its turn as a subjectile, this sort of subject without a subject, with this manner or this maneuver betraying all whole story in an instant, in fact the story of a betrayal. Being and god would be implicated in this trial of the subjectile: perversion and malfeasance, subterfuge or swindle.

---

4. *Dix ans que le langage est parti . . .* 1947, in *Luna-Park* no. 5, October 1979, 8.

So it would be necessary to write while drawing by hand, against this language, and have it out with the so-called mother tongue as with any other, making oneself scarcely translatable, starting from it but also within it (I am speaking of *Auseinandersetzung*, of *Ubersetzung* and, why not, of *Untersetzung*), in it where I am supposed to have been *born:* but where I was still, Artaud would say, in the twist it imposes on the syntax of this word *innate.* This supposed natural tongue, this tongue you are born with, it will be necessary to force it, to render it completely mad, and in it again the subjectile, this word which is scarcely even French, in order to describe the support of the pictogram which is still resonating with the trace left in it by a projectile. This came to perforate its surface feeling but sometimes resistant, the surface of a subjectivity appeased and reassured: the precarious outcome of the work.

The Germans don't have any word *subjectile,* although they were the first to project this great corpus of Antonin Artaud's pictograms, and to publish it separately, even though it is inseparable. As certain dictionaries tell us, we didn't have this word in French either a short while ago, but at least it suits our Latinity. The Germans—think of Fichte or Heidegger—have always tried to take back their language against Rome. Artaud too, and this isn't the only thing they have in common, however horrifying this seems to some. In other conditions, with time enough and taking the necessary precautions, I would be tempted to insist on the possible encounters which didn't take place between Heidegger and Artaud. Among many other themes, the one of the *innate* and the *Ungeborene* in Heidegger's reading of Trakl, and the question of being, quite simply, and of *throwing* [*jeter*] and of *giving* [*donner*].

Artaud, then, against a certain Latinity. What he says on this subject about the *mise-en-scène* is also valid, as is always true, for the pictogram and for what doesn't necessarily happen or does so only through words:

In opposition to this point of view, which strikes me as altogether Western or rather Latin, that is, obstinate. I maintain that insofar as this language begins with the stage, draws its power from its spontaneous creation on stage, and struggles directly with the stage without resorting to words . . . it is *mise en scène* that is theater, much more than the written and spoken play. No doubt I shall be asked to state what is Latin about this point of view opposed to my own. What is Latin is the need to use words in order to express ideas that are clear.

Because for me clear ideas, in the theater as in everything else, are ideas that are dead and finished.[5]

The Germans have no subjectile, but how would we know that without Artaud who never only uses it but attacks it, quarrels with it openly, seduces it, undertakes to pierce it through, puts it through the wringer, and first of all, names it? Not so much in order to dominate it but to deliver from a domination, to deliver someone or something else that isn't yet born. He attacks it like a Latin word. Without having any fear of the word: like a Latin thing, like this historical sedimentation of a thing and a word consolidated together not far from the subject and the substance, from Descartes' "clear ideas."[6]

I don't know if I am writing in an intelligible French. To madden the subjectile, is that still French?

Forcené, this word that I wanted to decompose surreptitiously, subjectilely, in *for, fort, force, for*, and *né*, letting all the words in *or, hors, sort* incubate in it, I thought it was limited to its *adjectival* usage as a past participle. The infinitive seemed to me excluded, foreclosed in fact, and I thought I was inventing it for the needs of a cause requiring some forcing of language. But that isn't it at all, for *forcener* exists, even

---

5. IV, 39. AA, 234. *AA* refers to the *Writings of Antonin Artaud*, ed. Susan Sontag (New York: Farrar Straus Giroux, 1976). The numbers refer to pages in this volume.

6. Artaud does to the French language what he does to the subjectile. He blames it, scolds it, *operates* on it, mistreats it in order to seduce it, etc. From now on, the reader can translate in "French," by "the French language" said to be the mother tongue everything concerning the "subjectile." But to write *against*, absolutely against one's mother tongue what you can do best is to *leave* it, rest in it, bet on it, *leave it* also for the necessary departure and separation: "We have to vanquish French without leaving it, / For fifty years it has held me in its tongue. / Now I have another tongue under (sic) tree." "To manage that, / starting with the fact that I am French / and in the way that best expresses my present force of will, actual, immediate, human, authoritarian, / and correct / for no matter what is me, my way of doing it is not that of a being. / It will always be me speaking a foreign language with an always recognizable accent." As we will see later, you have to repair the sick body, put it back to new, really, to the very beginning as an egg, have it born again. And that will be true for the subjectile as much as for French: "As for French, it makes you sick, / it is the sickest, / with a sickness, tiredness, / which makes you believe that you are French, / that is to say, *finished*, / a person finished." And at the moment of translating, precisely, what he means ("it translates quite exactly what I mean") speaking of what, we will see, inhabits or haunts the subjectile, that is, the fiend. Artaud writes: "It's the basis of the Ramayana not to know what the soul is made of, but to find that it is and always was made of something which was before, and I don't know if in French the word "rémanence" exists, but it translates quite exactly what I mean, that the soul is a fiend [suppôt], not a deposit [dépôt] but a *suppôt*, which always picks itself up and rises from what formerly wanted to subsist, I would like to say remains [*rémaner*] to dwell in order to remain, to emanate in keeping everything else, to be the else which is going to come back up." Texts quoted by Paule Thévenin in *Entendre/voir/lire, Tel Quel*, 40, 72, and 39, 55, 57, 58.

if its use is rare and outmoded. But only in an *intransitive* form. You can't *forcener un subjectile* in French without forcing the grammar of the word at the same time. *La forcènerie* or *le forcènement,* the act or the state of the *forcené* consist simply, and intransitively, in *forcener* or in *se forcener,* that is to say, losing your reason, more exactly, your *sense,* in finding yourself *hors sens, without sense (fors* and *sen.)* Littré's etymology seems reliable in this case: "Provençal: *forçenat;* Italian, *forsennato;* from the Latin *foris,* hors, and the German *Sinn* or *sens, sense:* outside of your senses. The spelling *forcené* with a *c* is contrary to the etymology and incorrect; it isn't even borne out by traditional use, and only comes from an unfortunate confusion with the word *force,* and it would be far better to write *forsené."* The word would then correspond with this German *Wahnsinnige* about which Heidegger reminds us that it doesn't initially indicate the state of a madman *(Geisteskrank),* of someone mentally sick, but that originally, what is without *(ohne)* any sense, without what is sense for others: *"Wahn* belongs to Old High German and means *ohne:* without. The demented person *[der Wahnsinnige,* which we could translate in French as *forsené]* dreams *[sinnt]* and he dreams as no one else could. . . . He is gifted with another sense [with another meaning, *ander Sinnes].* Sinnan originally means: to travel, to stretch towards . . . , to take a direction. The Indo-European root *sent* and *set* mean path."[7]

I am sure that what I am writing will not be translatable into German. Nor into Artaud's language. Should I be writing like Artaud? I am incapable of it and besides, anyone who would try to write *like* him, under the pretext of writing *towards* him, would be even surer of missing him, would lose the slightest chance ever of meeting him in the ridiculous attempt of this mimetic distortion. But we shouldn't give in either to the kind of judgment *about* Artaud which will not be, any more than his name, the subject or the object, still less the subjectile of some learned diagnosis. All the more in that it is a question of what are called his drawings and his paintings, not only of his speech. Himself furthermore, and we can verify this, never writes *about* his drawings and paintings, rather *in them.* The relation is different, one of imprecation and argument, and first of all one that relates to a subjectile, that is available for a support.

We cannot and should not write *like* Artaud *about* Artaud who

---

7. Martin Heidegger, *Unterwegs zur Sprache,* 53, French translation: *Acheminement vers la parole* (Paris: Gallimard, 1976), 56. The *trajectory* (as well as the spurt or the -ject of a projectile). In other words the path *(sent, set-)* of the *forcènement* is what we will try to follow here between a number of languages.

himself never wrote *about* his drawings and paintings. So who could then claim to write *like* Artaud *about* his drawings or paintings?

We have to invent a way of speaking, and sign it differently.

Yes or no, we must finish with the subjectile, a mime might say. And he wouldn't be wrong, for we are spectators of the scene: in this matter of the subjectile, it is certainly a judgment of God. And it is certainly a matter of *having done with it*, interminably.

Let's give up on it for the moment.

Even though a subjectile signs in advance, *for Antonin Artaud*, in this place of precipitation, even of perforation, in the very moment when such a projectile touches the surface, we have to learn not to rush to seize, to understand, we should take the time needed to absorb the ink of so many words that should deposit themselves slowly in the thickness of the body: exactly the one of the subjectile whose nature we still do not understand. Does it even have an essence?

So let's not rush to the question: what is a subjectile? What is being when it is determined as a subjectile?

The word should be translatable in German, since it has to go outside of French to come back, crossing the border several times. Unless it institutes itself the border that it itself is, between *beneath* and *above* (support and surface), *before* and *behind*, *here* and *over there*, *on this side* and *on that*, *back* and *forth*, the border of a textile, paper, veil or canvas, but *between* what and what? For can we enter, by perforation or deflowering, into what has no other consistency apart from that of the between, at least unless we lend it another one?

No doubt the Germans will insert the Latin word like a foreign body in their own language: intact, untouchable, impassive. Perhaps that is just as well. The meaning of this bodily struggle with the subjectile will probably have been: how do you address a foreign body? What about skill [*adresse*] and awkwardness [*maladresse*] in relation to the foreign body? what about prosthesis? what about "artificial fecundation" against which Artaud protests "*to have done with the judgment of God*"?

A subjectile is not a subject, still less the subjective, nor is it the object either, but then exactly what, and does the question of "what" have any meaning for what is *between* this or that, *whatever it is?* Perhaps the *interposition* of a subjectile, in this matter of drawing by hand, in this maneuver or meddling [*manigances*] is what matters.

Let's give up first of all trying to be ever *in front*, face to face with the pictograms which will never be *ob-jects* or subjects present for us. We won't be describing any paintings. The paradigm of the subjectile: the table itself! We won't ever speak of it if *to speak of* means to speak about objects or subjects.

But if, even sometimes occupying their place and being in the place of it, a subjectile is never identified with the subject or the object, is it to be confused with what Artaud so often likes to call a *motif?* No, it would *decide* on the motif, but it is true that in the very counterforce of this decision we see the hint of a place of extreme tension. What exactly is a motif? "For the motif itself, what is it?" Artaud asks in *Van Gogh, the Man Suicided by Society,* implying by the question that a motif is nothing, but so singularly nothing that it never lets itself be constituted in the stasis of a being. This word *motif* (how will they translate that?) certainly has the advantage of substituting the dynamics and the energy of a motion (movement, mobility, emotion) for the stability of a *-ject* [jet] which would come install itself in the inertia of a subject or object. What he gives up describing in one of Van Gogh's canvasses, Artaud inscribes in the center the *motif,* in the center of the "forces" and the *writing* forces ("apostrophes," "strokes," "commas," "bars," etc.) with these acts of "blocking," "repression," "the canvas," and so on as protagonists. Here we have to quote: "How easy it seems to write like this," the whole page of response "for what exactly is the motif itself?"

So I shall not describe a painting of van Gogh after van Gogh, but I shall say that van Gogh is a painter because he recollected nature, because he reperspired it and made it sweat, because he squeezed onto his canvases in clusters, in monumental sheaves of color, the grinding of elements that occurs once in a hundred years, the awful elementary pressure of apostrophes, scratches, commas, and dashes which, after him, one can no longer believe that natural appearances are not made of.

And what an onslaught of repressed jostlings, occular collisions taken from life, blinkings taken from nature, have the luminous currents of the forces which work on reality had to reverse before being finally driven together and, as it were, *hoisted* onto the canvas, and accepted?

There are no ghosts in the paintings of van Gogh, no visions, no hallucinations.

. . . . .

But the suffering of the prenatal is there (Artaud, XIII, 42–43; AA, 499).

The fact that later on Van Gogh is credited with having had "the audacity to attack a subject . . .", that doesn't mean that there was any subject for him, no matter how simple, even if it happened to be "of such disarming simplicity." In the flow of this way of speaking, it can be understood that the subject precisely attacked were not going to be or should not be any longer one. And this is the following paragraph: "No, there are no ghosts in van Gogh's painting, no drama, no subject, and I would even say no object, for what is the motif? / If no something like the iron shadow of the motet of an ancient indescribable music, the leitmotiv of a theme that has despaired of its own subject. / It is nature, naked and pure, seen . . ." (Artaud, 42–43; AA, 497).

This motif, we don't know what it is—neither this nor that—it doubtless no longer even belongs to being, nor to being as a subject. If it is "of nature" we shall have to think of nature completely differently, and the history of nature, the genealogy of its concept, in other words of its *birth* and conception: up to the *innée*, this neologism of Artaud where nature collides with its contrary, what is not born in what seems to be *inné*, the "suffering of the pre-natal" which appears as a monstrosity.

Under the surface of the word, and under the sense, *hors sens*, the passage from *motif* to *motet* doesn't obey only the formal attraction of the words, the *mots, motifs,* and *motets,* although when you let the attraction play under the meaning, you draw or sing rather than speaking, you write the unwritable. No, this passage also convokes the multiplicity of the voices in a motel in painting. It promises something essential in what Artaud still understands by painting: an affair of sonority, of tone, of intonation, of thunder and detonation, of rhythm, of vibration, the extreme tension of a polyphony.

This should be read like a book about music, according to Artaud. The "untellable antique music" tears apart the veil of a birth, revealing "naked nature," the origin whose access has been forbidden by this "nature," concealing even the source of this interdiction. The leitmotiv, this really musical motif of painting, its guiding force and its major esthetic passion, we must not mix it up with a *theme,* the meaning of an object or a subject, such as it could be *posed* there. A theme is always posed or supposed. The leitmtotif for his part doesn't always answer in itself like a stable support: no more subjectile, this last is carried away by the motif. The property of a theme is what an expropriation has deprived us, and it is as if we had been deprived of our own memory, distanced from our own birth. Across the "prenatal suffering", we cannot meet back up with innate nature (in-né) except by forcing the subjectile, rendering it *mad from birth*. You have to make it frenetically desire this birth, and to madden it from the outset in making it come out of itself to announce this next proximity: "It is nature, naked and pure, seen as she reveals herself when one knows how to approach her closely enough" (AA, 500). Music, nature, seeing: the same: seen (*vue*). Such a proximity confines you to madness, but the one that snatches you from the other madness, the madness of stagnation, of stabilization in the inert when sense becomes a subjectivized theme, introjected or objectivized, and the subjectile, a tomb. But you can force the tomb. You can madden the subjectile until—mad from birth—it gives way to the innate (*inné*), which was assassinated there one day. A violent obstetrics gives passage to the words through which however it passes. With all the music, painting, drawing, it is operating with a forceps.

Of course, Artaud was speaking of Van Gogh here. But without giving in to the cliché ("speaking in front of Van Gogh he is speaking of himself, etc.)" we have to recognize that Antonin Artaud couldn't have entered into that *relationship*, into the realm of the relation with Van Gogh except in *giving himself* over to the experiment that he was renouncing exactly that, describing the stability of a painting.

And this experiment is the traversal of this *jetée*, this trajectory. I am calling by the name of spurting or *jetée* the movement that, without ever being *itself* at the origin, is *modalized* and disperses itself in the trajectories of the *objective*, the *subjective*, the *projectile, introjection, objection, dejection,* and *abjection,* and so on. The subjectile remains *between* these different *jetées*, whether it constitutes its underlying element, the place and the context of birth, or interposes itself, like a canvas, a veil, a paper "support," the hymen between the inside and the outside, the upper and the lower, the over here or the over there, or then finally becoming in its turn the *jetée*, not this time like the movement itself of something which is thrown but like the hardened fall of a mass of inert stone in the port, the limit of an "*arrested* storm," the dam. Giving itself over entirely, hurling itself into the experience of this throwing [*jetée*], Artaud could enter the realm of relationship with Van Gogh. And all the questions we will listen to from now on resound: what is a *port*, a *portée*, a *rapport* if the subjectile is announced as the support of the drawing and painting? What does *porter* mean in this case? And throwing, hurling, sending? Is spurting [*la jetée*] a mode of sending or of giving? Might it be rather the inverse?

Must we choose? What is it? Is it the same thing? *Is it?* Is it still possible to submit that to the question *what is it?* The way Artaud treats the question of being [*être*] and of beinginess [*êtreté*] (his word)[8] will occasionally be open to doubt. Being shows up starting with the *jetée*, not the inverse. We don't even have to speak of pulsion or compulsive interest in the direction of the spurt [*jet*]. The thought of the throwing is the thought of pulsion itself, of the pulsional *force*, of compulsion and expulsion. Force before form. And I shall try to show that it is Antonin Artaud's *thought* itself. Before any thematics of the spurt, it is *at work* in the corpus of his writings, his painting, his drawings. And from the beginning, indissociable from *cruel* thought, in other words, a thought of *blood*. The first *cruelty,* is a spurt of blood. In 1922, *Works and Men:* "We have to wash literature off ourselves. We want to be humans before anything else. There are no forms or any form. There is only the gushing forth of life. Life like a spurt of blood, as Claudel puts it so well, speaking of Rimbaud. The mode now is anti-Claudel, and Claudel among us is perhaps the only one who in his good moments doesn't make literature" (Artaud, 204).

The subjectile: itself between two places. It has two situations. As the support of a representation, it's the subject which has become a *gisant*, spread out, stretched out, inert, neutral (*ci-gît*). But if it doesn't fall out like this, if it is not abandoned to this downfall or this dejection, it can still be of interest for itself and not for its representation, for *what* it represents or for the representation it bears. It is then treated otherwise: as that which participates in the forceful throwing or casting, but also, and for just that, as what has to be traversed, pierced, penetrated in order to have done with the screen, that is, the inert support of representation. The subjectile, for example the paper or the canvas, then becomes a membrane; and the *trajectory* of what is thrown upon it should dynamize this skin in perforating it, traversing it, passing through to the other side: "after having exploded the wall of the problem," as he says in *Fiends and Tortures* [*Suppôts et suppliciations*]. I hasten to quote these words and this work so as to insist that we will never hear anything about the subjectile without having the fiend and the torture resound in it. And without reading the pages that bear this title.

8. "They have dipped me three times in the waters of the Cocytus / and protecting all alone, alone in my obst*inate* beingness, / and protecting my mother Amalycytus all alone, / and why now Amalycytus this mother of an obst*inate* Anteros?" (Quoted by Paule Thévenin, *Tel Quel* 39:32. My emphasis.)

The subjectile resists. It has to resist. Sometimes it resists too much, sometimes not enough. It must resist in order to be treated finally as itself and not as the support or the fiend of something else, the surface or the *subservient* substratum of a representation. This latter has to be traversed in the direction of the subjectile. But inversely, the subjectile, a screen or support for representation, must be traversed by the projectile. We have to pass beneath the one which is already beneath. Its inert body must not resist too much. If it does, it has to be *mistreated*, violently attacked. We will come to blows with it. The *neither/nor* of the subjectile (*neither* subservient, *nor* dominating) situates the place of a *double constraint:* this way it becomes unrepresentable.

Neither object or subject, neither screen nor projectile, the subjectile can *become* all that, stabilizing itself in a certain form or moving about in another. But the drama of its own becoming always oscillates *between* the intransitivity of *jacere* and the transitivity of *jacere*, in what I will call the *conjecture* of both. In the first case, *jaceo*, I am stretched out, lying down, *gisant*, in my bed, brought down, brought low, without life, I am where I have been *thrown*. This is the situation of the subject or the subjectile: they are *thrown beneath*. In the second case, *jacio*, I throw *something*, a projectile, thus, stones, a firebrand, seed (ejaculated), or dice—or I cast a line. At the same time, and because I have thrown something, I can have raised it or founded it. *Jacio* can also have this sense: I cast down foundations, I institute by throwing out something. The subjectile does not throw anything, but it has been cast down, even founded. A foundation in its turn, it can thus found, sustain a construction, serve as a support.

Between the two verbs, the intransitivity of *being-thrown* and the transitivity of *throwing*, the difference seems from then on to be as *decisive* as temporary, that is to say, *transitory*. The being-thrown or the being-founded founds in its turn. And I cannot throw [*jeter*] or project [*projeter*] if I have not been thrown myself, at birth.

Everything will play itself out from now on in the critical but precarious difference, instable and reversible between these two. Such at least would be our working hypothesis. But what we will surely verify, is that, hypothetically, the subjectile always has the function of a *hypothesis*, it exasperates and keeps you in suspense, it makes you give out of breath by always being *posed beneath*. The hypothesis has the form here of a conjecture, with *two* contradictory motifs in one. Thrown throwing, the subjectile is nothing however, nothing but a solidified interval *between* above and below, visible and invisible, before and behind, this side and that.

Between lying down and throwing, the subjectile is a figure of the other towards which we should give up projecting anything at all.

The other or a figure of the other?

What does Artaud's drawing or painting *have to do* with such a *figuration* of the other?

Will this figuration accept limits? painting and drawing only, in opposition to the discursive text, even in the theater? Yes and no, yes in fact and up to a certain point, whose arbitrary nature covers over precisely a whole story of a dissociation that Artaud wants to *traverse*, like a limit or a wall. Not by rights and rigorously, and this is why I shall propose to give another sense to the word *pictogram* in order to designate this work in which painting—the color, even when it is black—drawing, and writing don't tolerate the wall of any division, neither that of different arts nor that of genres, nor that of supports or substances. The choice of this word pictogram may seem odd. It does not lead to any supposed primitivity of some immediately representative writing. Certainly, through the magical force something points to a proto-writing upon which we project all the myths of origin, through the efficacity of spells cast or exorcized, the incantatory or conjuring virtues, alchemy, magnetism, such a pictography would have some affinity with Artaud's drawings, paintings, *and* writings. But I shall take it to mean especially the trajectory of what is *literally* understood to traverse the border between painting and drawing, drawing and verbal writing, and, still more generally, the arts of space and the others, between space and time. And through the subjectile, the motion of the motif assures the synergy of the visible and the invisible, in other words theatrical painting, literature, poetry and music. Without any totalization and taking due account of the subjectilian wall, of this dissociation in the body of which there will always be marked the singularity of the event made work.

We can only speak of this whole pictographic work by insertion and precipitation, by the acceleration of a rhythmical projection and the inscription of a projectile, beyond what we calmly call words and images. We can then say this: these are written drawings, with phrases that are inserted in the forms in order to precipitate them. I think I have gotten to something special this way, as in my books or in the theater . . ." This was at Rodez in 1945, and we will have to take account of a trajectory, in fact that of the subjectile. But as if we were at the end of this trajectory, and in the past (I think . . . I have arrived,") a sort of destination seems to prevail after the fact. There is "this side," on this side, that is drawing, that will be distinguished *on one hand* from literature, from the theater (that is, sentences.) But *on the other hand* these drawings are written drawings that cannot just be put on one side any longer and which—here is "something special"—contain phrases and even better, sentences that are not only taken in, *stuck, inserted,* but where the insertion itself precipitates the forms. From then on, the analogy carries off the limits. What I have arrived at is certainly special, unique, irreplaceable, inimitable, but singular *like* what I "arrived at" "in my books or theater." Just as in the interior of the "written drawing," the limit has been crossed, the breaking down of the barrier in the other "arts" abolishes the border between *all* these "arts." Everything is singular each time and each time analogical: a figuration of the other.

If in the pictogram the relationship between the verbal writing, the phonogram mute line and color is analogous to what it will have been in literature or in the theater *according* to Artaud, no body, no corpus is entirely separable. The phrase inserted remains at once inscribed and quivering. It works the charter, the frame-lock of a stubborn spatiality. The phrase is not *softened,* it no more lets itself be domesticated than it masters the map. It does not lay down the law, it does not enunciate the charter of a constitution. But its protestation accelerates a rhythm, imprints intonations, pulls the form along in a musical or choreographic motion. Without this mobility, the figures would become once more, like the "clear ideas" of the Latin world, "dead and terminated." Even if we recognize some of the workings of words, the inserted phrases rise up like enticing themes, trajectories of sound and writing and not only like propositions. Once they are put forth, they destabilize the proposition, that is a certain historical relation between the subject, the object and the subjectile. A relationship of representation. From now on, "pictogram" will indicate this destabilization become work.

—Translated by Mary Ann Caws

III.

BERNARD VOUILLOUX

Drawing between the Eye and the Hand: (On Rousseau)

1. THE ORIGIN OF DRAWING

In the *Essai sur l'origine des langues,* Rousseau connects the invention of drawing to love.[1] The connection is doubly fundamental: first, it is made at the beginning of the first chapter, where it follows the distinction established between the two means of human communication, namely, movement (touch or gesture) and voice; and second, its immediate setting lends it the topical value of an argument. What is remarkable about this argument is that it maintains an apparently contradictory relationship with its context. To uphold the integrity of the argument would be to admit that if the "premiers motifs qui firent parler l'homme furent des passions" [man's first motives for speaking were of the passions] (68;12), they were also the first which prompted him to draw. But this parallel, along with the conclusion which follows from it, is put into question by the whole remainder of the essay: human needs are to be systematically associated with the origin of gesture, and passions with the origin of language. Thus we read at the opening of the second chapter, in a sentence that recapitulates the material of the first, that ". . . les besoins dictérent les prémiers gestes et . . . les passions arrachérent les prémiéres voix" [need dictated the

---

1. Jean Jacques Rousseau, *Essai sur l'origine des langues,* ed. Jean Starobinski, (Paris: Gallimard, "Folio/Essais", 1990), 60; trans. J. H. Moran and A. Gode, *On the Origin of Language* (New York: Frederick Ungar, 1966), 6. The quotations from Rousseau are given in the spelling of the time. Further references to the original text and the translation will appear, in that order, in parentheses even when the French has been eliminated; other translations are our own except where noted.—Translator's note.

YFS 84, *Boundaries: Writing & Drawing,* ed. M. Reid, © 1994 by Yale University.

first gestures and . . . passion stimulated the first words] (66;11).[2] This
would contradict not only the genealogical argument of invention, but
also the example proposed by this same first chapter of an amorous
message communicated without recourse to words: the *salam*, a gift of
small objects (pieces of fruit, ribbons . . .) whose meaning is known
only to those passionate lovers for whom they have a shared conventional value (63–64;9). Nonetheless, rather than suppose a contradiction between the argument and the example on the one hand, and the
theoretical developments regarding discourse on the other, a contradiction that would condemn a reading of the text to aporia, we can
hypothesize that the text plays on the level of semiotic elaboration
which governs the introduction of passion, and on the place and function assigned to it in each of the two communicational schemes. Either
the nonlinguistic message transmits information concerning the plans
or the situation of the lovers (this is the case with *salams:* the status of
drawing remains uncertain), or it is passion itself that is communicated, formulated, and propagated, by and in the linguistic mediation
of discourse. In the first case, only the content of the signifying
structure—as it happens its motivation [*motif*]—is passional, and the
gestural medium, in so far as it is "dictated" by need, remains subject
to a strict economy throughout, and is rigorously managed by staged
intervals of transmission: compared to articulated language, the language of gesture allows one to say "more in less time" (60;6). In the
second case, the verbal message, "torn" from the speaker by passion
and formally obedient to the rhetorical rules of expression, has the
ability "to stir the heart and inflame the passions" of the listener
(62;8): passion is no longer only, nor necessarily—thus raising the
question of sincerity—contained within the communicational triangle (*destinateur, destinataire* and *référent*); it is in the message itself,
and which impregnates the form and substance of its expression. This
is why the author of the *Essai*, just before concluding that "while
visible signs can render a more exact imitation, sounds can more effectively arouse interest" (63;9), can observe without contradiction that
"the passions have their gestures, but they also have their accents

2. Certain passages of the *Essai* presuppose that the language of voice, though
every bit as "natural," succeeded that of gesture, just as passion succeeded need. In the
Discours sur les origines et les fondements de l'inégalité, Rousseau, following Con-
dillac, explicitly held gestures to be auxiliaries to "inflections of the voice" (*Discours*,
Part one, *O. C.*, vol. 3, 148 and n. 2; except where noted, all references to Rousseau are to
the Bernard Gagnebin and Marcel Raymond edition of the *Oeuvres complètes* (Paris:
Gallimard, Pléidae, vol. 1, 1961, vol. 2, 1961, vol. 3, 1964, vol. 4, 1969).

(63;9), given that accents alone can be described as impassioned, and thus entrancing [passionants]—in other words, passions do not *have* their gestures and their accents in the same way.

The chapter on writing will teach us, moreover, that the passions also have their own writing; it will be specified that the first of the three "ways of writing" which is "to represent . . . objects directly" (73;17), either directly or by allegorical figures, "corresponds to passionate language, and already supposes some society and some needs to which the passions have given birth" (74;17). These second-generation needs complicate the filiations established by Rousseau in a peculiar way. In order to account for their status, one would have to reconsider everything in the *Essai* that relates to the epoch of the gesture. Here it will suffice to start with the note (at the beginning of chapter 9) on the American savages who, silent and isolated in their huts, communicate with their neighbors only by means of signs—a practice which should be linked to that notion of the home as tactile and visual proximity which is developed in the following pages:

> nul ne connoissait et ne desiroit que ce qui étoit sous sa main. . . .
> Hors de la portée où son oeil peut voir et où son bras peut atteindre,
> il n'y a plus pour lui ni droit ni proprieté.

> No one knew or wanted to control anyone beyond those who were at hand. . . . Beyond the range of his own vision or the reach of his arm, there are for him neither rights nor property.   [93–94;33–34]

It is clear that the state of dispersion in which the first savages live is in fact determined by needs, the very same needs that dictate their gestures. What seems less clear but just as certain is that other needs, created by the necessity of working together against a harsh natural world—those needs which will fashion the first peoples and, by an indirect consequence that must be emphasized, will be the origin of the passions—will in turn give birth to language(s).[3] Wherever gesture was dictated by need, language is wrested from those passions which other needs have helped to arouse. It is thus that language itself engenders "new needs," those implied by pictographic writing:

> Les prémiéres langues, filles du plaisir et non du besoin, portérent
> longtems l'enseigne de leur pére; leur accent séducteur ne s'effaça

---

3. Love conditions the existence of "popular tongues," the only true languages for Rousseau, who is careful to distinguish them from "domestic tongues" which are contemporary with incestuous marriage, not exogamous love—instinct, not passion, ibid., 106–08.

qu'avec les sentimens qui les avoient fait naitre lorsque de nouveaux
besoins introduits parmi les hommes forcérent chacun de ne songer
qu'à lui-même et de retirer son coeur au dedans de lui.

The first tongues, children of pleasure rather than need, long bore
the mark of their father. They lost their seductive tone with the
advent of feelings to which they had given birth, when new needs
arose among men, forcing each to be mindful only of his own
welfare, and to withdraw his heart into himself.   [108;46].

It is almost as though, in looking retrospectively at the genesis of
southern languages, Rousseau had "forgotten" the needs which, by
putting an end to the original state of dispersion, allowed for the formation of passional ties. One might even wonder whether by affirming at
the beginning of the following chapter that in southern climates need
is born of passion (in contrast to what happens in cold climates),[4]
Rousseau sacrifices to the seduction of antithesis and chiasmus the
complexity of a genealogy in which need would figure not only as
derivative of, but prior to passion, not merely in the moment of passage
into writing but also, *already*, in the moment of the formation of
peoples and thus of languages. It is in light of this originary complication, of this coimplication of need and passion, that one could interpret
the link between the pictogram and "passionate language" as the reversal of the link between drawing and love. There would then be a correspondence between drawing as invented by love, a needy invention
caused by passion, and, in the order of language, the most passional and
the most imitative of all kinds of writing, the pictogram, a passionate
invention (*moyen*) deployed by the "needs born of the passions." The
needy state of the passions would thus echo the passionate state of
need, beyond the step or the leap implied by writing, and this insofar as
writing responds precisely to these derivative needs: "L'art d'ecrire ne
tient point à celui de parler. Il tient à des besoins d'une autre nature qui
naissent plustôt ou plustard . . ." [The art of writing does not at all
depend upon that of speaking. It derives from needs of a different kind
which develop earlier or later . . .] (76;19].

Nevertheless, it remains unclear whether drawing, at least as it

---

4. Ibid., 109. More than the relationship between need and passion, what holds
Rousseau's attention is their respective relationship to language: the southern and
northern languages differ in that the former express passion (*"aimez-moi"*), the latter
need (*"aidez-moi"*), 110.

appears at the moment of its invention in the *Essai*, can be related to that substitutive function which *salams* typically perform, or if it can be assimilated to the other gestural messages cited in the first chapter or, more generally, to what is normally meant by drawing, including and especially in Rousseau's time. Something in the internal structure of the argument resists such a reduction. Yet it is typical of Rousseau's theoretical writing that the genealogy in which drawing is inscribed in the *Essai* should be patterned on fable [*la fable*], rather like the way the second *Discours* gave a reading of the origin and the foundations of inequality according to that mode of presentation, the "utopian fiction,"[5] which the *Essai's* third chapter will apply to the figurative origin of language. But, in spite of a common recourse to narrative scenarios and notwithstanding appreciable differences of extension, the "authority" of these sources is hardly comparable. Whereas in fictions of the "savage man" the founding narrative adopts, with a tone of logical certitude, the atemporal present or the hypothetico-deductive temporality (the future in the past) that is appropriate to the revelation of a structural matrix of history—the fable, by contrast, is indistinguishable from the buzz of its own articulation. The origin is lost in the murmur of tradition, as if, once it is a question of gesture and no longer of words, its history could be related only on the faith of mediations whose source is itself lost in what we have come to call the "mists of time." "Love, they say, was the inventor of drawing" (60;6). What, more precisely, do "*they*" say? Rousseau, relying on the mnemonic virtues of allusion, recalls here, without recalling it, that drawing was invented in the gesture of the young woman who first traced on the wall a ring around the shadow of her lover as he was about to leave: "Que celle qui traçoit avec tant de plaisir l'ombre de son amant lui disoit de choses! Quels sons eut-elle employés pour rendre ce mouvement de baguéte?" [How could she say things to her beloved, who traced his shadow with such pleasure! What sounds might she have used to work such magic?] (60;6). At the very moment of tracing the outline of the shadow, the sketcher, by the gesture of tracing, addresses her lover. Tradition adds, and it is a lesson Rousseau forgets, that the young woman was the daughter of the potter Boutadès. Via Pliny, tradition specifies further that it was through the daughter's invention that the father discovered the first art of modeling portraits in clay (*fingere ex argilla similitudines*).[6] From this genealogical chiasmus we will retain here only the refractory filiation of the portrait in the round [*portrait en ronde-bosse*],[7] descendant and heir, through the daughter, to an "art" entirely made up of movement in which the mediation of gesture has not yet been separated from immediate touch and where the range of vision does not go beyond an arm's length.[8]

As soon as it is no longer confused with the redundant "gesticulations" that match the speech of Europeans, the *"langue du geste"* (or *"langue des signes"* as Rousseau calls it in *Emile*) can be advantageously substituted for that of voice or words. Rousseau invokes classical eloquence, which allowed for the passage from one to the other, the suspension of the flow of *flumen orationis* in a stupefying stasis to enable the demonstration of the thing itself:

> Ce que les anciens disoient le plus vivement, ils ne l'exprimoient pas par des mots mais par des signes, ils ne le disoient pas, ils le montroient . . . L'objet offert avant de parler ébranle l'imagination, excite la curiosité, tient l'esprit en suspens et dans l'attente de ce qu'on va dire.

> What the ancients said in the liveliest way, they did not express in words but by means of signs; they did not say it, they showed it. . . . An object held up before speaking will arouse the imagination, excites curiosity, hold the mind in suspense, in expectation of what will be said.   [61;6–7][9]

---

6. Pliny, *Histoire naturalle* XXXV, xliii. The anecdote was related in Antiquity by several other authors. It retained considerable authority throughout the entire classical period, up to the end of the eighteenth century. Jaucourt's article "Peinture" in the *Encyclopédie* alludes to it (Geneva edition, vol. 25, 1777), 119, as does Diderot in his *Salon of 1763*, à propos of the portrait (*Essais sur la peinture*, ed. Gita May, suivis de *Salons de 1759, 1761, 1763*, ed. J. Chouillet, (Paris: Hermann, 1984), 194. On its appearance in the painting of the last third of the eighteenth century, cf. Roger Rosenblum, "The Origin of Painting: A Problem in the Iconography of Romantic Clacissism", *Art Bulletin* 39, (1957): 279–90.

7. *Ectypa* in Pliny's text: this interpretation is maintained by J. -M. Croisille in his edition of the text (Paris: Les Belles Lettres, 1985), n. 4 of §151, 261, and n. 7 of §152, 262–63.

8. "L'action du mouvement est immédiate par le toucher ou médiate par le geste; la prémiére, ayant pour terme la longueur du bras, ne peut se transmettre à distance, mais l'autre atteint aussi loin que le rayon visuel," *Essai* op. cit., 60.

9. The two sentences reappear almost word for word in *Emile* (Book 4, *O.C.*, vol. 4, 647).

For as long as it is not a question of "stirring the heart and inflaming the passions"—in which case only sounds and their accents can, we have seen, "arouse" the interest—for as long as the gesture is confined to imitation, then it is superior to the word [*parole*]: "one speaks to the eyes much better than to the ears." Rousseau is so convinced of this truth that he takes up the formula again in *Emile*, all the while emphasizing that "A word always makes a weak impression" (*Emile*, 645). The superiority of the gesture is due, of course, to the ease with which it is learned, to its relative independence from convention, to its expressive force, and to its economy of means (*Essai*, 60). But, more fundamentally—that is closer to its fabled origin—this superiority comes from its proximity to the thing, from the fact that it operates close to the thing itself. Very precisely, it derives its imitative or mimetic power not from the fidelity of a drawing to a given model, but from its deictic relation to the thing it shows, within gestural reach, and as though in its image. For the young woman's tracing wand *shows* the outline, by touching it, in the same way that the outline indicates (signifies graphically [*indiciellement*]) the shadow it circumscribes—this thing, this nearly nothing that is the luminous projection of a body onto a surface. Again in the same way, the shadow itself indicates the body of the young woman's lover. . . . At the very end of this chain of metonymies made up of deictic signs, signifying by a demonstrative gesture this series of contacts, the gesture of the young woman prompts us to think the unthinkable: an "immediate sign,"[10] a demonstrative "imitation", a drawing that "speaks" through its tracing [*tracer*] and not by its trace, through its pro-duction and not as a product and which, as such, presupposes the active presence of its *destinateur* and of the *destinataire* who gives form to the referent. Here the drawing, at the moment of its invention, differs not only from *salams* and from writing (even pictographic writing), but from what conventionally passes for drawing itself. All of the ambiguity of this genealogy would ultimately be linked to the oscillation of its images between immediacy and mediation, touch and gesture, the tactile and the visual. Almost all of the examples of language through movement cited in the first chapter of the *Essai* rely on a gestural mimicry performed at

10. Jacques Derrida, *De la grammatologie*, (Paris: Minuit, 1967), 333; *Of Grammatology*, trans. Gayatri C. Spivak (Baltimore: Johns Hopkins University Press, 1974) 234. On this passage from the *Essai*, I refer the reader to his admirable analysis.

a distance (comparable to the language of deaf-mutes), on either the designation or the transmission (i.e., even the exchange) of things endowed or not with conventional meaning.[11] In all of these cases, it is gesture and sight, not touch, which are primarily involved in communication. It is only in the fable which opens the paradigm that touch is truly invoked, and even here it is in a context where the stress falls on the gesture and the "wave of the wand."

In any case, however exceptional its occurrence, the "touching" gesture of the young woman is nonetheless pregnant with a future which inscribes it at the origin of representational drawing. For we must not forget that this gesture hangs upon an instant, the *adieu*, which will come to see distance, absence, and graphic mediations succeed and supplement [*suppléer*] the immediate presence of the thing. What happens when the sign is separated from the thing? We know of the theoretical motives that lead Rousseau to a radical (but not unambiguous) suspicion of the sign, language, writing, drawing, painting, representation, imitation, art. . . . in general. Thus, once the lover has left, what is left is only the outline, a trace that, if it says anything at all, no longer addresses itself to the lover: the trace no longer "speaks" for anyone but the viewer, and first of all for the young woman who—now separated from her own gesture—drew it. And the only thing it will say to her is the "thing" that was there and that is no longer there, that to which alone so many "things" needed to be said. The trace no longer speaks except to signal, deceive, supplement the presence of the one who has become only its referent. The traced line has become art, the technical mediation of the thing. And what henceforth it gives access to is no longer the thing but itself, that is, ultimately, the painter:

> "Hommes savans dans l'art de feindre
> Qui me prêtez des traits si doux,
> Vous aurez beau vouloir me peindre,
> vous ne peindrez jamais que vous."

> Men skilled in the art of deception
> Who grant me such gentle features,

11. An exception: the touch of hands by which, according to Chardin, Rousseau's source, the "*facteurs* of India communicate with one another, op. cit., (64/9–10). A little earlier Rousseau evokes the language of deaf-mutes perfected by Pereire. In any event, it is improper to maintain as does Paul de Man that "all examples destined to illustrate the "natural" language of man are acts of violence" (*Allegories of Reading*, (New Haven: Yale University Press, 1979), 140.

In vain do you wish to paint me,
For you will never paint anyone but yourselves.[12]

Leonardo said the same thing: *Ogni dipintore dipinge sé*. The portrait does resemble, but it resembles its painter, not its model. The only true portrait is the self-portrait; the only good representation works according to a reflexive modality that bends its mediations back toward the subject. Here we cannot avoid the opening sentence of the *Confessions:* "Voici le seul portrait d'homme, peint exactement d'après nature et dans toute sa vérité, qui existe et qui probablement existera jamais" [Here is the only portrait of a man, painted exactly according to nature and wholly true, that exists and that probably ever will exist].[13] The remainder—painting—is at worst a fraud, at best a "niaiserie" [foolishness].[14] No exceptions to this rule—apart from the fable. Thus, when the tutor of *Emile* recommends the practice of drawing to the children, it is "not exactly for the art itself, but in order to make one's eye accurate and one's hand flexible" (*Emile*, vol. 2, 397). And if it is so important to exercise the sense organs, and those of sight and touch above all the others, it is less in order to imitate objects than to know them, that is, to compare them in imagination or reflection—in other words, to have them nearby as it were: "In any kind of study, without the idea of represented things, representing signs are worthless."[15] It is

12. "Quatrain pour un de ses portraits", *O.C.*, vol. 2, 1157, [our translation]. On Rousseau's difficulties with his figurative portraits, cf., *Confessions*, Book 12, *O.C.*, vol. 1, 613 (the story of the portrait that was to have been made by the sculptor Lemoine); *Rousseau juge de Jean-Jacques*, Second Dialogue, ibid., 777 (his violent criticism of those portraits of him which circulated in Paris).

13. Op. cit., 3. On the question "*Comment peut-on se peindre?*", cf., Starobinski, *La Transparence et l'obstacle*, suivi de *Sept essais sur Rousseau* (Paris: Gallimard, coll. "Tel," 1976), 223–25. Paul de Man addressed the problematic of the portrait in its relation with the self using one of Rousseau's first texts, *Narcisse*, op. cit., 185 ff.

14. Consider the extreme contempt with which he treats artists in a passage from his first version of *Emile:* "ces hommes importans qu'on n'appelle pas artisans mais artistes ne travaillant que pour l'amusement des gens oisifs et des riches mettent un prix arbitraire à leurs niaiseries . . ." (*Emile*, [manuscrit Favre], *O.C.*, vol. 4, 191–92). And a little further on: "Un patissier est surtout à ses yeux [i.e., d'Emile] un homme très respectable et il donneroit toute l'Academie Royale de peinture pour le moindre confiseur de la rue des Lombards," ibid., 193. See also the passage from the *Discours sur les sciences et les arts* in which he censures painters and sculptors who prostitute their talent (Part two, *O.C.*, vol. 3, 21–22. The tone and argumentation are similar to those of Diderot blaming amateurs for the "decadence" of painting (I refer the reader to my study "Diderot, Jacques, le Maître, le Spectateur et l'Amateur," *Argumentation* 6:4, (Fall 1992).

15. Ibid., 347. We know that in both the *Essai* and *Emile* imagination is a condition of imitation, as that *transport* which carries one out of oneself, making pity possible.

in order to possess himself through self-knowledge that Rousseau will paint his own portrait [*"se peindra"*]. "As a general rule, never substitute the symbol of the thing signified, unless it is impossible to show the thing itself."[16] My purpose here is not to test the conditions of application of this prescription to the work of Rousseau, nor to expose or discuss the thought revealed by the literary texts, and the autobiographical and theoretical writings, in the complexity of their development, their articulations, and their "contradictions," but to reflect [*réfléchir*] on the role which origin plays in Rousseau's fiction, the origin which the *Essai* assigns to drawing and to imitation, to imitative drawing, between on the one hand love, need and passion, and on the other hand, between vision and gesture, gesture and touch, imitation and indication: to bring these patterns to agree with the "portrait" of Julie that we read in *La Nouvelle Héloïse;* thus to *read* this written portrait, that is to produce its system of writing, to tease out both its "literary" and theoretical implications. Saint-Preux, thinking that he is seeing Julie in person, is said to exclaim, while writing about it to her: "I see you." I will examine here what he meant by *seeing* and what he allows us thereby to *see* and to *hear.*

2. A TOUCHING PORTRAIT

At the origin of the portrait Julie has commissioned from a passing painter, there is a "friponnerie" [prank],[17] a subterfuge, a game of doubles in the form of a quid pro quo. Since Claire and Julie's mother want to have her portrait, Julie asks the painter to make, "secrètement," a second copy which she will send to Saint-Preux. So a second copy is made. Is it made directly "on" the model? If so, it is difficult to see how this copy (along with the first copy) is less original than the original. Or is it rather made indirectly, from the original itself (which alone would have been painted *on* the model, as the saying goes)? But Julie does not say whether this copy is intended for Claire or for Madame d'Etange. Clearly, for her it is not important: "Ensuite sans m'embarrasser de copie ni d'original, je choisis subtilement le plus ressemblant des trois

---

16. *Emile,* Book 3, op. cit., 434; trans. B. Foxley (London: Dent and Sons, Everyman's Library, 1955 ed.), 133.

17. *Julie, ou la Nouvelle Héloïse,* Part two, letter XXIV, *O.C.,* vol. 2, 290 (including the following quotations; only references to another letter or page will be mentioned; trans. Judith H. McDowell, (London: The Pennsylvania State University Press, 1968), 216.)

pour te l'envoyer" [Then without troubling myself about the copy or the original, I slyly chose the best likeness of the three to send to you]. The original and the two copies, the avowed copy and the secret copy, placed on the same level, co-appearing [comparaissant] together, are compared to the model: this is a condition of judgment. Judgment of what? There is no a priori rapport between the original and resemblance to the model: the greatest likeness [ressemblance] can be found just as easily in either of the two copies as in the original.[18] Julie's trickery goes far: it betrays not only the trust of those around her, but also a certain sense of propriety insofar as it governs the judgment of taste. In fact, if discrimination between the original and the copy haunts classical thought, it is only because it is constitutive of what is proper to art: both the originality and the originarité of the work are based on a proper name effect that can be guaranteed only through the authenticity of the signed and finished work. Not only the signature, but also the workmanship, bear the mark of the painter. We know that traditional art history and the expertise which guarantees it continue to this day to exploit the theoretical and economic resources of this diffuse effect in which the genius of a workmanship [un faire] is deposited. The casualness with which Julie does away with this effect serves to restore the integrity of the portrait as and only as an image of the model, thereby restoring to judgment it legitimate jurisdiction: the evaluation of the link of resemblance between the portrait (original or copy) and the model. The search for the original will never be anything but a strategy intended to assure the painter's control of the painting at the expense of the latter's relation to the "thing." For Julie as for Rousseau—in contrast to a certain amateur ironically invented by Diderot—a "bad copy" is worth more than a "sublime original,"[19] if the first resembles the thing more closely than the second.

18. In Fragment 9 of Mon portrait one finds a slightly different problematic of the literary (physical or moral portrait as copy and the original as model: "Toutes les copies d'un meme original se ressemblent, mais faites tirer le meme visage par divers peintres, à peine tous ces portraits auront ils entre eux le moindre rapport; sont-ils tous bons, ou quel est le vrai? Jugés des portraits de l'ame"; O.C., vol. 1, 1121–22; see also fragments 6 and 8.

19. Denis Diderot, Jacques le Fataliste et son Maître, ed. S. Lecointre and J. Le Gaillot (Geneva-Paris: Droz, 1976), 255. (See the article cited above n. 14). Diderot, in his Salon of 1763, immediately after recalling that the gesture of the young woman is at the origin of painting and sculpture (text cited above n. 6) made resemblance the first quality of the portrait: "Entre deux portraits, l'un de Henri quatre mal peint, mais ressemblant; et l'autre d'un faquin de concussionaire ou d'un sot auteur, peint à miracle, quel est celui que vous choisirez? . . . D'où je conclus avec vous qu'il faut qu'un portrait soit

Why does this resemblance matter? It matters only insofar as it matters *to* someone: not to Claire nor to Madame d'Etange who have the model in person before their very eyes and within reach every day, and for whom possession of the portrait will rather be a gauge of affection, but to Saint-Preux who, being far away, can make up for [*suppléer*] the absence of the beloved with her painted representation. In this case then, it is crucial that the portrait be as exactly faithful as possible:

> les homages que tu rendrois à une autre figure que la mienne
> seroient une espece d'infidélité d'autant plus dangereuse que mon
> portrait seroit mieux que moi, et je ne veux point, comme que ce soit
> que tu prennes du goût pour des charmes que je n'ai pas.

> the homage you would pay to a face other than mine would be a sort
> of infidelity, all the more dangerous in that my portrait would be
> better than I, and I do not want you in any manner whatsoever to
> acquire a liking for charms I do not possess.

Aware of the substitutive function of the portrait, Julie therefore lucidly measures the transfer economy into which it will enter. The conversion of Saint-Preux's—the spectator's—feeling as he moves from the portrait to the model, progressing from the painted hypostasis to the real person, can be realized only if the portrait resembles the model as faithfully as possible. Failing this, these feelings would refer to another, embellished or idealized, face, and even the face of another. Now, what can better determine this resemblance than passion? But whose passion? If passion did not guide the brush of this "painter of miniatures" from Italy, whom we can suppose imbued with the Academy's dogmatic principles, there is at least reason to believe that passion animates the eyes of the spectator. His eyes? Indeed.

The first mention Julie makes of the portrait is figurative: like the savage who calls other men he encounters for the first time "giants", she playfully calls a mere portrait a "talisman."[20] She announces enigmatically to Saint-Preux the imminent arrival of a package containing a "petit meuble," that is an object that one can transport and carry around with one, and perhaps even wear, as the allusion to a "kind of

---

ressemblant pour moi, et bien peint pour la postérité"; one should notice nonetheless that the example is not straightforward: it seems that for Diderot there can be no *ressemblance* except from a good model, that is from a model who is himself an "image" of virtue.

20. Letter 20, 264; trans. 212. The figurative nomination performed by the 'savage man' is narrated in chapter 3 of the *Essai*, op. cit., (68–9/13).

amulet" suggests. Resemblance therefore does not entering into the picture. The figured enigma here encodes the strange properties of a magical object—we can recognize three of these distinctly. The first is empathy, which operates by means of sight and which becomes effective, within the framework of a strictly regulated ritual, by the mode of *penetration:* "Contemplate it every morning for a quarter hour until you feel penetrated by a certain tenderness." The second property: sympathy, which proceeds from the application of the amulet to the eyes, the mouth, and the heart, and whose operation is that of a "prophylactic" [*préservatif*], since it protects the officiant (also called the "faithful one") from the "fetid air of the land of gallantry." The third property, linked to some "electric quality" operates only between "faithful lovers" by telepathic impression: "The idea is to communicate to the one the impression of the other's kisses from more than two hundred leagues away." After the direct action exercised on the officiant by the amulet (visual penetration, tactile application), there follows, at a higher degree of initiation, action at a distance, beyond what the *Essai* thematized as "an arm's length" and range of sight, beyond earshot. Through the channel of the magical object, giver and receiver come into communication.

In fact, Saint-Preux will test these powers immediately. After going to pick up the package and overcoming his impatience with great difficulty, he waits until he is home to open it, in accordance with Julie's wishes. On the way, in his carriage, he succumbs to the temptation to "feel through the wrappings" the enigmatic object.[21] Unable to see, he touches. Not, however, without having "some suspicion of the truth" —of the truth which, as a figure of the feminine, is concealed as though behind a veil beneath the wrappings which, once home, he takes off one by one, down to the last wrapping. Unveiling and revelation: "Julie! . . . Oh my Julie! The veil is torn. . . . I see you." . . . The epiphany of Julie, appearing in her tangible truth, unfolds with all the force of the "silent eloquence." Of that orator who won the acquittal of the famous courtesan Phryné by undressing her in front of her judges, referred to among other examples cited by the *Essai* (and it is remarkable here,

---

21. Letter 22, 279; trans. 215. Between the letter from Julie and Saint-Preux's answer, there is another letter from Saint-Preux in which he "paints" the women of Paris for her: the long description he gives of them functions as an antitype of Julie's portrait. In letter 23, he will give Claire a (similar) account of the Opera. The composition of the text thus emphasizes the dangers that weigh upon the portrait, the social artifices that threaten to distort the image.

again, that Rousseau should have preferred to leave this last piece of information encoded exclusively in allusion).[22] But this apparition of Julie receives its certification in language—in the ruptures of a "fragmentary style" which, if it connotes the emotion of the subject affected by the near presence of the loved object, also hints at the extraordinary specter of a mimology, through the liberation of the sequence, "vois" [I see], as a perfect homonym of those "voix" [voices] ("simples sons", "cris", "gémissements", "sons inarticulés" ["simple sounds, cries, groaning, inarticulate sounds]), that is those vowels which predominate in passionate languages, the languages of the south (*Essai*, 70, 112), especially Italian, whose cause is championed by Saint-Preux.[23] At this moment, once there is complete confusion between the physiognomical "traits" of the model and the graphic traits of the portrait, the "magical effect of these dear traits" (*Julie*, part two, Letter 22, 280; 215) is instantly communicated by sight to Saint-Preux, whose adoration of the cherished image, adored in the same way as its model, instills magic into the *iconodulie* and so skirts idolatry. At the very moment in which the first (empathetic) property of the portrait-talisman is verified, the third (telepathic) finds its confirmation:

> Pourquoi des *impressions* que l'ame porte avec tant d'activité n'iroient-elles pas aussi loin qu'elle? . . . Ne sens-tu pas tes yeux, tes joues, ta bouche, ton sein, *pressés, comprimés*, accablés de mes ardens baisers? [My emphasis]

> Why should the *impressions* which my soul carries so energetically not reach out to yours? . . . Do you not feel your eyes, your lips, your bosom caressed, *pressed*, overwhelmed by my ardent kisses?

In her response, Julie, for whom the "banter" of the talisman will have become a reality, will say that she too feels "something of the charming effects" it exercises upon her at a distance,[24] that are always thematized in this same register of the *impression:*

> Oui, mon ami, le sort a beau nous séparer, *pressons* nos coeurs l'un contre l'autre. . . . Je m'imagine que tu tiens mon portrait, et suis si

---

22. Op. cit., 62. On the theory of unveiling that can be deduced from the *Morceau allégorique* and from *Pygmalion*, cf., Starobinksi, op. cit., 84–101, and on the veil in *La Nouvelle Héloise*, 102–10.

23. Part one, letter 48, 131–35; trans. 111–12). The letter should, of course, be read in the context of the "Querelle des Bouffons," in which Rousseau took an active part.

24. Letter 24, 289; trans. 216. The same contact at a distance is arranged, in the scene with Madame Basile, through the mediation of a mirror (*Confessions*, Book 1, op.

folle que je crois sentir l'*impression* des caresses que tu lui fais et des baisers que tu lui donnes. [My emphasis]

Yes, my friend, fate separates us in vain. Let us *press* our hearts together . . . I imagine that you are holding my portrait, and I am so carried away that I think I can feel the *pressure* of the caresses you give it and the kisses you bestow on it.

Nevertheless, as this last sentence already suggests ("je m'imagine," "je crois" [I imagine, I believe]), the magical virtues of the portrait-talisman exist in the order of belief—the effect not of some "electrical virtue" à la Mesmer, but of the imagination: "sweet illusions," "chimeras." Saint-Preux had also had the same experience. Once past the moment of revelation (the unveiling of the portrait), his joy was quickly mixed with bitterness; he too had entered into the system of disabused credulity, of illusion that is self-conscious, of delusion, oscillating henceforth between "I believe even though" and "I know very well but nonetheless":

Je crois en te voyant te revoir encore; je crois me retrouver à ces momens délicieux dont le souvenir fait maintenant le malheur de ma vie, et que le Ciel m'a donnés et ravis dans sa colere! Hélas, un instant me desabuse.   [Letter 22, 290]

Seeing it, I think I see you again; I imagine I am back in those delightful times again, which I remember now with the greatest sorrow, the times which Heaven gave me and took from me in its anger. Alas, the next instant undeceives me.   [Letter 22, 215]

The only possible compensation for the "pain of absence" would be effective telepathy with the absent one: "Oh Julie, if only it were true that it might transmit to your senses the delirium and the illusion of mine." But, as we have seen, the "impression" that Julie thinks she feels is itself merely the result of belief.

For the passion of the model along with that of the spectator can never make up for this initial lack: indifferent to the truth of his model, the painter has never made anything but art. Given that he is not Saint-Preux, in painting Julie's portrait he painted only his own, putting, as they say, a bit of himself in it. Julie, moreover, will notice this when,

---

cit., 75). A propos of this episode, Starobinski notes that magic, which "establishes both distance and contact, effects the miracle of contact at a distance." Cf. "Jean-JacquesRousseau et le péril de la rélexion," *L'Oeil vivant* (Paris: Gallimard, 1961), 111. On recourse to magic, cf. *La Transparence et l'obstacle*, 77 ff.

immediately after presenting the consequences of an imperfect resemblance, she will justify herself for not appearing "more carefully dressed":

> Je te prie, au moins, de croire qu'excepté la coëffure, cet ajustement n'a point été pris sur le mien, que le peintre a tout fait de sa grace, et qu'il a orné ma personne des ouvrages de son imagination.
>
> [Letter 24, 290]

> I beg you at least to believe that except for the head-dress, this attire was not drawn from mine, that the painter did all as he pleased, and that he adorned my person with works of his imagination.
>
> [Letter 24, 217]

Such indeed is the grievance that Saint-Preux later articulates against the painter, once the "first enchantment" has worn off (ibid, 290), And further, to do so he makes a distinction that allows the responsibility of the artist to be circumscribed very precisely. In this way, the artist would not be considered responsible for things related to the "insufficiency of art" (ibid, 291), which will, as such, always leave the mark of a constitutive defect on every painted image. Saint-Preux reproaches the portrait for "resembling" Julie without "being" Julie, for having her "face" while remaining *insensible:* the painter has "rendered" the eyes and the traits, but not "that sweet sentiment which gives them life." He has not *rendered* that which *gives* life and which cannot be rendered; he has rendered Julie's face, but not the "fard" [make-up] of her face: "The make-up of your face is to be found, my Julie, in your heart, and your heart cannot be imitated."

The notion of make-up [*fard*], its localization (in the heart), and the inimitability attributed to it, are curious enough to justify a moment's pause. A series of paradoxes obtain which frustrate all semantic projections. As a cosmetic artifice lavished upon the face to supplement [*suppléer*] its natural color, for Rousseau, make-up can only be the object of the most emphatic condemnation. Hence, in his letter on Parisian women, noting that "their complexion is a mediocre white" (Letter 21, 266), Saint-Preux draws attention both to the cosmetic artifice to which they resort and to the linguistic artifice designed to disguise it:

> Elles ont vû que le peuple avoit en horreur le rouge, qu'il s'obstine à nommer grossiérement du fard; elles se sont appliqué quatre doigts, non de fard, mais de rouge; car le mot changé, la chose n'est plus la même. [Ibid., 267; cf. n. 1.]

They had observed that the people were horrified by *rouge,* which they insist on crudely naming "make-up"; they had applied two inches worth of rouge, not make-up; for, once the word has been changed, the thing is no longer the same.

The double *suppléance,* "en abyme," in which are implicated both the thing and the word, designates make-up as the very prototype of the "bad" supplement, that which in order to "bring out" [*relever*] the natural rosy tone of the flesh (to enliven or emphasize it) in fact supplements it by counterfeiting it, by painting its aspect. It is a veneer, a mask stretched over the skin's medium white reserve [*réserve médiocrement blanche*], and in this way seeks to pass for the real color of that for which it has been substituted. We know, moreover, that the notion of make-up was, for apologetic [*apologétique*] or polemical reasons, very early assimilated to the figures of discourse (the *colores rhetorici*) and to pictoral coloring, and that it has since antiquity come to fuel the many debates concerning both sets of figures. There is no doubt that in either case Rousseau would have sided with Plato against the Sophists, with Atticism against Asianism or, in the quarrel between Rubenists and Poussinists, with LeBrun and Champaigne against Blanchard and de Piles.[25] In this respect, it is worth pointing out that his resolutely antimaterialist and antisensualist positions on the status of sensation, as attested to among other things by his project for a *Morale sensitive,* caused him to espouse arguments very close to those upheld in the previous century by the strictest academic orthodoxy, and that, from this point of view, the way in which he opposes drawing and color is reminiscent of the doctrine which dominated the Royal Academy of painting under LeBrun.[26] Rousseau therefore cut

25. On the rhetorical and pictorial stakes of make-up, cf., J. Lichtenstein, *La Couleur éloquente* (Paris: Flammarion, 1989), and my article "Les Lectures de Platon," Po&sie 52, (March 1990): 112–20. On Rousseau and color see the following note. As to his rejection of sophistry and the rhetorical artifices that support it, it can be teased out of various texts: see in particular the opposition between Socrates and the virtuous Romans, on the one hand and the "artificial and subtle Greeks" on the other, in the first *Discourse* op. cit., 13–14, the brief fragment "Sur l'éloquence," *O.C.,* vol. 2, 1241, the passage from the *Essai* on the decline of music and of poetry in favor of sophistry, op. cit., 138–39), etc.

26. The essential texts can be found in A. Fontaine, *Conférences inédites de l'Académie royale de peinture et de sculpture* (Paris: Albert Fontemoing, 1903), "La Querelle du dessin et de la couleur," 3–68. Cf., *Essai,* op. cit., n. 2., 118, 225. References to painters are rare in the work of Rousseau. Revealing in this respect is the laudatory allusion to Le Brun, in the *Confessions* à propos of the "vaste salon peint d'une excellente main" of the château de Montmorency, Book 10, op. cit., 517—the same Le Brun whose

himself off from the painting of the great colorists, his contemporaries (Chardin and Fragonard), those very artists for whom Diderot came to develop his moralism and his sensualism. But did Rousseau ever *see* painting?

In this perspective, we would have to re-read those passages dealing with color as opposed to drawing, in their respective relations to harmony and melody, and with the "great advantages" of the musician's art over that of the painter (*Essai*, ch. 13, 118–21, and 16, 129–33). Here it will suffice to remember that drawing, for Rousseau, derives its privileged status from its imitative virtue, when color turns into "pure" sensation:

> De belles couleurs nuancées plaisent à la vüe, mais ce plaisir est purement de sensation. C'est le dessein, c'est l'imitation qui donne à ces couleurs de la vie et de l'ame, ce sont les passions qu'elles expriment qui viennent émouvoir les nôtres, ce sont les objets qu'elles représentent qui viennent nous affecter.

> Beautiful nuanced colors are pleasing to the eye, but this pleasure is purely sensual. It is drawing, it is imitation that gives these colors life and soul, it is the passions they express that move our own, it is the objects they represent that come to affect us.   [Ibid., 118.]

And in fact what follows will demonstrate, with an ironic verve rather rare for Rousseau, that color without drawing could not constitute painting as an art of imitation. As a print (drawing without color) can hardly touch its spectator, so too a tableau deprived of its lines [*traits*] (something like the chaos of Frenhofer's painting) would be nothing but a smear offering to the spectator only that pleasure which is strictly confined to the "physique" of art (ibid., 120).

Thus we are obliged to understand that if the make-up of Julie's face has its real place (its *milieu*) in her heart, it is insofar as color can receive its determination as tactile imitation only from the heart where the image (the drawing) of Julie is *imprinted*: the heart of the model is in some way the depositary of the transcendental drawing whose spacing would structure, from the bottom up, the color-make-

---

style a detractor of Rousseau's compared to "l'effroyable peinture des maux que l'état civil a enfantés" the second *Discourse*, op. cit., n. 1, 230, 1384). By the same token it is revealing, as the editors of the *Confessions*, op. cit., n. 2, 313, 1398–99) emphasize, that with reference to Rousseau's stay in Venice no mention is made of the painters who became famous there. On the other hand, when he invokes the help of painters to describe the loves of Emile and Sophie, Rousseau turns to Raphaël and Albani, *Emile*, 1. V., op. cit., 790, two of the masters who inspired the academic adherents of drawing.

up that shrines upon the surface. The only real imitation of Julie, then, should go through an "imitation"—in the quasi-Christian sense of the term—of her essential being, which for Rousseau is the only real model on which the portrait should be made—what he names, in the first drafts of the *Confessions*, precisely the "modelle intérieur."[27] In other words, the painted image is *"insensible"* because the feeling which produces the face as make-up is absent. And in this respect, the painter is helpless to change this, he whose entire art is to supplement the make-up with coloring, to spread pigments onto the canvas like make-up onto the skin, whose sufficiency as an artist blind to the insufficiency of his art depends on his belief that he has *rendered* the inimitable make-up by imitating the color that shines on Julie's face, whereas this make-up is in her heart. At least then we can suppose that Saint-Preux as passionate spectator will be able to draw this feeling from the depths of the portrait as though from himself, to recall it from the past in order to project it onto the portrait, or better, to impregnate or imprint the portrait with it. The passion of the spectator thus makes the two inimitable "images" of Julie conflate and coincide in the painted image: the image that is in Julie's heart, as her truth, and the image in his own, as an impression of this feeling. It is in this possibility of the portrait as screen and support, that those magical virtues of the talisman, as we have pointed out, its empathetic and telepathic properties, could take root—since no subsequent verification of the sympathetic property has thus far been produced. In sum, the portrait would be entirely justified, saved, so to speak, from art, if it were simply a moment in the effusive communion of *"belles âmes,"* the hypostasis through which the communication of feelings passes in transit, a mediation instantaneously consumed by the fire of sentiment, pure transparency, *"in-différant"* relay, "immediate sign." Beyond this, it must also still resemble; resemble the model and not the painter, not the idea which the painter fabricates of the model in the name of art, that is of the painting, and thus of art. This is what the theoretician and the autobiographer hold to be impossible, as soon as it is not the subject painting *himself,* but what Saint-Preux, in his lover's fervor, believes to be possible. Saint-Preux who, having allowed for the "insufficiency of art," patiently corrects the artist where he has not been "exact en tout ce qui dépendoit de lui" [exact in everything that depended on him alone].

In order to take full measure of the trust or the credulity of Saint-

27. *O.C.*, vol. 1, 1149. In the same text, he opposes *"se peindre"* and *"se farder,"* 1154.

Preux, we would need to follow in detail the minute list he gives of all the details which, together, create a resemblance—those anatomical particularities that make up Julie's charm and beauty: the distance between her hair and the base of her temples, the veinlets under the skin, the coloring of her cheeks, the dimples at the corners of her mouth. Defects, too, that authenticate Julie's identity, making her like no other and thus inexchangeable: the spots under her right eye and on her neck, the small scar underneath her lip, the nuanced colors of her hair and eyebrows, the slightly irregular contour of her cheeks, and in general that *caractéristique* which governs her particular system of attire [*ajustements*], headdress, clothing. . . . Saint-Preux becomes here the exemplary exegete of a theory of the portrait which is, in the very choice of such detail, the one defended by Diderot, some ten years later, in *Les Deux Amis de Bourbonne:*

> Un peintre exécute sur la toile une tête. Toutes les formes en sont fortes, grandes et régulières; c'est l'ensemble le plus parfait et le plus rare. J'éprouve, en le considérant, du respect, de l'admiration, de l'effroi; j'en cherche le modèle dans la nature, et ne l'y trouve pas; en comparaison, tout y est faible, petit et mesquin; c'est une tête idéale; je le sens, je me le dis. Mais que l'artiste me fasse apercevoir au front de cette tête une cicatrice légère, une verrue à l'une de ses tempes, une coupure imperceptible à la lèvre inférieure; et, d'idéale qu'elle était, à l'instant la tête devient un portrait; une marque de petite vérole au coin de l'oeil ou à côté du nez, et ce visage de femme n'est plus celui de Vénus; c'est le portrait de quelqu'une de mes voisines.

> A painter paints a head on the canvas. All of its forms are strong, large and regular; it is the rarest, most perfect ensemble. In considering it, I experience respect, admiration, fear. I seek its model in nature, and do not find it; in comparison, everything there is weak, small and mean. I feel, I tell myself that it is an ideal head. But should the artist allow me to see on the forehead of this head a light scar, a wart on the temple, an imperceptible cut on the bottom lip, immediately the head passes from ideal head to portrait. A chicken pox mark at the corner of the eye or next to the nose, and this woman's face is no longer that of Venus; it is the portrait of one of my neighbors.[28]

Yes, it is the portrait of someone, someone near. A bit like the salon-going Diderot who in those years begins to correct the paintings on

28. *Oeuvres complètes*, ed. J. Assézat and M. Tourneux (Paris: Garnier, 1875), vol. 5, 277.

exhibit, Saint-Preux will also undertake to "reform" Julie's portrait accordingly. The term is not trivial: it is the same term used by Rousseau in the *Confessions* to designate the changes he adopts in his dress, then in his life, when he decides to break off his commerce with others (Confession, Book 8, 363–64). The pictorial asceticism, however, is more cautious, and in line with the rule that one must not damage the "original" (which is perhaps itself, we should remember, merely a copy), calls for the printing of a new copy. The transformations are tried out on it before being applied, once approved, to the original, in such a way that the original, without resembling the two other portraits (two copies or an original and a copy), should resemble the model more closely. And should resemble it more closely to the degree that passion governs this reform. The ultimate salvation for the portrait is to be corrected by the brush of a skilled painter appointed by the lover's passion.

The artist may be surprised by the "subtlety" of the observations put forward by Saint-Preux: "il ne comprend pas combien celui qui me les dicte est un maitre plus savant que lui" [he does not understand how the one who dictates them to me is a much more learned a master than he is] (ibid., 293). Nor does he understand the strange modesty that prompts Saint-Preux to insist that he disguise those charms which, in the lover's eyes, are never sufficiently exposed and which the first painter, presuming on his prerogatives, had tried to imagine in order to suggest them. For this modesty is itself the response to the attraction of Julie's charms, and to the [her] modesty that veils them. The charms imagined by the first painter are thus erased in favor of these retouches, such that henceforth "le spectateur *ému* les supposera tels qu'ils sont" [the *moved* spectator will suppose them to be such as they are] (my emphasis). Such as they are, no more: veiled, and thus with no existence apart from the one imagined by the emotion of him that sees and animates them. Saint-Preux's final words on the portrait pronounce an impossible wish:

> Ah! que ton portrait seroit bien plus touchant, si je pouvais inventer des moyens d'y montrer ton ame avec ton visage, et d'y peindre à la fois ta modestie et tes attraits!

> Ah! how much more touching your portrait would be, if I could find a way of showing your soul with your face, and paint in it both your modesty and your charms.

The retouched portrait can only bring Saint-Preux back to what he at the outset called the "insufficiency of art": the portrait lacks the power to reproduce [Julie's] modesty with her charms, her soul with her face, which are required in order to "touch," to arouse emotion—her face, and the make-up [*fard*] that is in her heart. These are his last words on the portrait, but not the last words of the letter: Saint-Preux goes back to the model and to what must be considered, in light of the portrait, as its magical action, its radiance:

> Je ne sais quel enchantement secret regne dans ta personne; mais tout ce qui la *touche* semble y participer; il ne faut qu'appercevoir un coin de ta robe pour adorer celle qui la porte. On *sent*, en regardant ton ajustement, que c'est par tout le *voile* des graces qui couvre la beauté: et le goût de ta modeste personne semble annoncer au *coeur* tous les charmes qu'elle récele. [My emphasis]

> I do not know what secret enchantment governs your person; but everything that *touches* it seems to participate in it; one need only see the corner of your dress to adore its wearer. One *feels*, in looking at your dress, that everywhere the *veil* of grace covers your beauty, and the tact [*goût*] of your modest person seems to announce to the heart all the charms it conceals.

Saint-Preux has passed without transition from the reformed portrait, which will always lack something in order to be more "touching," to the way in which things participate in Julie's person merely by touching it. Substitution of one vocabulary and sensorial register for another, in the mode of *suppléance:* the sense of touch is added to and substituted for sight ("il ne faut qu'appercevoir," "en regardant" [one need only catch a glimpse of, by looking]) at the moment when touch transcends sight in adoration, the feeling of sentiment and of sensation, the heart: there alone can Julie *make an impression,* from a distance, free from the mediation of any painting, even a portrait-talisman, free from the mediation of any sign, except perhaps for the clothing which, in touching her, remains as close as possible to the thing, and draws its contours [*indiciellement*] (4).

Failure of the portrait: of the three properties Julie associated with it, the portrait will have developed only two. And those two are subtly marked as illusion. As for the third, the "prophylactic" property, one hardly need wait to discover its entirely illusory efficacy. In the letter which immediately follows the one in which Saint-Preux summons Julie's magical presence against the portrait, comes the confession of the crime committed in the land of galantry: fooled by the substitution of "images" made possible by wine, Saint-Preux betrays Julie with a "*créature*": "Hélas! ne pouvant écarter de mon coeur une trop chere image, je m'efforçois de la voiler" [Alas! unable to cast forth from my heart a too-cherished image, I attempted to veil it] (ibid., 297). A painted portrait is erased itself, is corrected itself, and multiplies into copies. The image in the heart, by contrast, is never erased and even less is it corrected or multiplied; but one can veil it, keep it without looking at it, no longer "see" it. And in veiling it one not only fools oneself, taking the creature for the image, one *betrays oneself:* cut off from oneself as from the other, opaque to oneself as to the other: absolutely unhappy [*malheureux*].

—Translated by Christine Cano and Peter Hallward

MICHEL THÉVOZ

Dubuffet: The Nutcracker*

> Casser une noix n'est vraiment pas un art, aussi personne n'osera-t-il
> jamais convoquer un public pour le distraire en cassant des noix. S'il
> le fait cependant, et que son intention se voie couronnée de succès,
> c'est qu'il s'agit au fond d'autre chose que d'un simple cassement de
> noix. Ou bien s'il ne s'agit que d'un cassement de noix, c'est qu'il est
> apparu que nous n'avions jamais pensé à cet art parce que nous le
> possédions à fond, et que le nouveau casseur de noix nous en a révélé
> la véritable essence, et pour cela il peut être nécessaire qu'il soit un
> peu moins adroit que nous.
> —Kafka, *Joséphine la Cantatrice, ou le Peuple des Souris*

There probably is at the source of any literary vocation a problematic
relationship to one's maternal language, or rather, to one's paternal
language, in the case of Jean Dubuffet. His father, he tells us in his
Biographie au pas de course (unpublished), was an authoritarian man
who, given any opportunity, would lapse into terrifying fits of anger. He
had a passion for books and constantly bought them and piled them up
everywhere. He had a chauvinist's exclusive and purist reverence for
French classical language. In his *salon,* he loved to bring together brilliant conversationalists, Parisian ones if possible. This was so near to
his heart, notes Jean Dubuffet, that "l'existence auprès de lui d'une
épouse et d'un fils avait peu de consistance. Ma mère n'avait guère la
parole, il lui était enjoint de se taire comminatoirement, j'en ressentais
indignation. De moi, on exigeait que je sois au lycée le premier de ma
classe en toutes matières et si j'y manquais éclataient les effrayantes
colères" [the existence of a wife and a son at his side had little substance for him. My mother was never allowed to speak; she was told
unceremoniously to be silent; I felt indignant. As for me, it was required that in school I be the first in my class in all subjects, and if I
failed to do so, frightening fits of anger followed].

In brief, everything was done to correct* both the child and the

---

*"Dubuffet le casseur de noix," *Détournement d'écriture* (Editions de Minuit, 1989).
All illustrations courtesy of the Dubuffet Foundation.

*châtier: To correct, or purify is used in French for both the child and the language.—
Translator's note.

YFS 84, *Boundaries: Writing & Drawing,* ed. M. Reid, © 1994 by Yale University.

language at the same time, and to assimilate the latter to paternal tyranny. It is thus understandable that painting became feminine, or maternal:

> Au cours d'un séjour au Mont-Dore, je rencontrai dans la campagne une femme devant un chevalet et qui peignait le paysage avec des pastels, dont elle avait une boîte pleine auprès d'elle. Les coloris de cette boîte me frappèrent fortement et son tableau aussi. On n'y distinguait pas grand chose que des taches de différents verts, justement ce que les moqueurs nomment "un plat d'épinards." Ce m'incita dans la suite à faire de petites peintures semblablement absconses. Je les thésaurisais dans un porte-document que je me plaisais vivement à compulser. J'éprouvais vif désir, mais aussi grande hésitation, à les montrer à une fillette de mon âge que j'affectionnais (j'avais sept ou huit ans) dans la crainte de me leurrer sur le bien-fondé de l'émerveillement que je leur portais. Je n'ai, pour finir, pas osé le faire, je les ai cachées puis détruites.

> During a stay at the Mont-Dore, I encountered in the fields a woman in front of an easel who was painting the countryside with pastels, of which she had a full box next to her. The colors of this box struck me and her painting too. In it one could not make out much more than spots of different greens, exactly what is mockingly called "a plate of spinach." Later this prompted me to make some small, similarly abstruse paintings. I collected them in a briefcase which I took vivid pleasure in consulting. I had a great desire, but an equally great hesitation, to show them to a little girl my age whom I liked (I was seven or eight) for fear that I was deluding myself as to the justified wonder that I derived from them. I did not, in the end, dare do it; I hid them and then destroyed them.

Thus the Oedipal triangulation is determined in this case with reference to language: the man proffers the arrogant discourse of power, and the woman paints silently, in spinach style, the real, in other words, the unnameable.[1] Jean Dubuffet, the child, also paints secretly, and with guilt. But come the time, the time of adolescence and revolt, painting would take the upper hand, conceived of as a weapon against words, against culture, and against the enslavement of the mind (they are all one):

> Mon dispositif (la peinture) fonctionne comme une machine à abolir les noms des choses, à faire tomber les cloisons que l'esprit dresse

---

1. Cf. Michel Thévoz, *Dubuffet* (Geneva: Skira, 1986).

entre les divers objets, entre les divers systèmes d'objets, entre les
différents registres de faits et de choses et les différents plans de la
pensée, une machine à brouiller tout l'ordre institué par l'esprit dans
le mur des phénomènes et effacer d'un coup tous les chemins qu'il y
a tracées, une machine à mettre en échec toute raison et à replacer
toutes les choses dans l'équivoque et la confusion.[2]

My weapon (painting) functions as a machine to abolish the
names of things, to knock down the partitions that the mind erects
between different objects, between different systems of objects,
between different registers of facts and objects and different levels of
thought, a machine to blur the entire order instituted by the mind in
the wall of phenomena and to erase with one fell swoop all the paths
that it had mapped out, a machine to foil all reason and return all
things to ambiguity and confusion.[2]

But a child cannot settle his Oedipal relationships by falling back
on the maternal register and leaving the father to occupy center stage.
Painting, as offensive as it may be to cultural stereotypes, could not
exempt the budding artist from having to take on verbal language.
After meals that were endured like sessions of sempiternal repri-
mands, Jean would rush to the garden to execute Indian ceremonies in
a redskin language of his own invention, whose lexicon he had carefully established in a school notebook, a childish way of signifying
through linguistic aberration that he was not duped by paternal
loutishness—the *"non-dupe erre,"** wrote Lacan, taking apart precisely that forbidden name . . .

At the origin of Dubuffet's literary activity there is therefore a uto-
pia, or "uglossia" as the linguists call it, or in other words the belief in a
first language, pre-Babel, phylogenetically anterior to the law of the
Father, and consequently untouched by any sollicitation of power, a
primitive language, childish in the etymological sense of the word, a
language, if we can risk this paradox, hallucinated at times by para-
noiacs or mediums. The logophobia manifested toward the languages
so improperly called "natural" is always the other face of a passionate
logophilia, polarized by an intrauterine fantasy of interpersonal fusion,
of immediacy, of unity, of totality, of ineffable communion. During his

---

*Play on words between *nom du père*, that is, "the name of the father," and the
homophonous *non-dupe erre*, meaning "the one who is not a dupe wanders"—
Translator's note.
  2. "Empreintes," in *Prospectus et tous écrits suivants* (Paris: Gallimard, 1967),
vol. 2, 148–49.

entire life Dubuffet will remain fascinated by the inventors of languages who take on the tyranny of the instituted word and who radicalize in their adult strength his own childish rebellions. Certainly, the freedom is illusory, and the possibilities delirious. In the end, they enclose these authors to another prison, that of incommunicability. It remains that the acceptance of the socially necessary "idols of the tribe" [mots de la tribu], constitutes for Dubuffet a capitulation and a mutilation of the mind:

> Communiquer c'est une bonne chose, pas si grave. Mais il y a que nos mots, nos langues, ne servent pas seulement à communiquer la pensée; elles la font. . . . Le monde regorge de gens devenus inaptes à toute appréhension directe des choses. Ils ne peuvent les appréhender qu'au travers de la grille des mots. Rien ne leur est perceptible qu'après transcription sur la grille. Ils ne sont plus branchés sur les faits et les choses, mais sur leur formulation. Ce n'est plus de vin qu'ils sont gourmands, c'est maintenant seulement d'étiquettes.[3]

> To communicate is a good thing, not so serious. But the issue is that our words, our languages, do not serve simply to communicate thought; they make it. . . . The world is overrun with people who have become inept at all direct apprehension of things. They can only perceive them through the grid of language. Nothing is perceptible to them except after transcription on the grid. They are no longer tuned into facts and objects, but into the formulation of these. It is no longer wine that they have a taste for, only labels (Fig. 1).

As a result, an individual in love with the living word is confronted with the dilemma of autism and stereotypy, between which there is certainly no middle course. Dubuffet shares with Nietzsche the feeling that all roads lead to Rome, except that of compromise. He chooses on all occasions that of inflation and parody. Thus, if verbalization petrifies thought, and if we must use it nonetheless, we might as well go directly to the ultimate stage of fossilization, as the only way to bypass the logos and to confront, once again, the concrete. In his period of Parisian dilettantism, Dubuffet applied himself to learning languages that are preferably dead ones, frozen in clay, marble, parchment, or papyrus, sedimented in their own epigraphy, and if possible enigmatic

---

3. "Un grand salut très déférent au Martelandre," reproduced in Michel Thévoz, Ecrits Bruts (Paris: P. U. F. "Perspectives critiques," 1979), 230–235.

1. Jean Dubuffet, "La Botte à Nique," pages 2 and 3 of the manuscript.

in meaning, like Egyptian hieroglyphs. Ultimately he undertook a search for those ultrasecret and hyperindividualistic hieroglyphs that are exhumed from the archives of psychiatric institutes and which he will call "l'art brut dans l'écrire"[4] [raw art in writing] (Fig. 2).

However, Dubuffet knows well that, once initiated into the culture of the educated, he is inexorably immersed in instituted language, and that "on ne sort pas de l'arbre par les moyens de l'arbre" [one does not get out of the tree by means of the tree], as his friend Francis Ponge put it.[5] He does not even make the paranoiac pretence of circumventing the logosphere or of dominating it from above. As for him he will proceed by a sort of internal swaggering aimed at a disruption of the representational function of language, seeking to stress its articulations, its mechanisms, its constraints. He will therefore, as a writer, attempt a balance between the genealogical and structural extremes of verbalization, between primitive vociferation and the learned turn of phrase, between glossolalia and literature, between the graphic instinct and the alphabetical code, between the substance of the sign and the ideality of the meaning. From one pole to the other we find the

4. "Projet pour un petit texte liminaire introduisant les publications de *L'art dans l'écrire*," ibid., 229–30.

5. Francis Ponge, *Le Parti pris des choses* (Paris: Gallimard, 1942), 25.

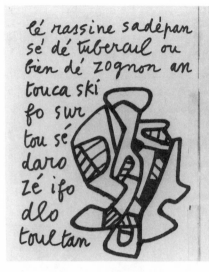

lé nassine sadépan
sé dé tuberaul ou
bien dé zognon an
touca ski
fo sur
tou sé
daro
zé ifo
dlo
toultan

pour la cemance on
peul lachté chéle
grennetié 3 ru du
Bēque i restouvère
jusca uitewre ivan
oci dépodfleure ila
tousquifo ivandtou
skifo surtou sédlo
ian na quifopaque
sagèle fo lé bichoné
danlewrpo pourpa

2. Jean Dubuffet, "La Botte à Nique," pages 4 and 5 of the manuscript.

essays on aesthetic and philosophical themes, the calligraphic essays (*La Fleur de Barbe, Oriflammes*) (Fig. 3), the texts in "jargon relatif" [*relative jargon*], in other words a free phonetic rendition of popular speech which defies spelling (*An vouaiaje, Oukiva trèné sèbot*, etc.), the texts in "jargon absolu" [absolute jargon], in other words formed by invented words which cannot be found in any lexicon (*Couinque, l'Hourloupe*, etc.), the engraved or lithographed calligraphies in which the substance of the sign tends to overcome the meaning (*Ler dla canpane, La bonfam abeber*), the paintings which (re)present inscriptions (the series of *Messages*, of *Murs*, of *Paris Circus*, of *Tables Paysagées*), and the final series of *Mires* and of *Non-Lieux* which cipher the real according to an unpublished script. One comes to realize that Dubuffet has spread out, so to speak, the spectrum which goes from legibility to visibility. He evolves in all its registers, from childish babble to the preciousness of erudite language, like an insane linguist who has cast off all moorings and allows be borne by the trials of morphological and syntactical variation and commutation, oscillating from side to side in the verbal field.

Given this, would it be possible to identify a Dubuffet "style"? This extraordinary *fading** of expressiveness verifies by default the Laca-

*In English in the original.—Translator's note.

3. Jean Dubuffet, *Paysage jaseur.*

nian assertion that the subject constitutes itself only as a linguistic effect. Dubuffet uses, or rather misuses verbalization as a jubilant disintegration of self that should cause an earthquake to spread throughout the entire literary field. He always obstinately denied that he was a writer, against the protestations of his critics who took this for modesty, whereas in fact it was a challenge: "Qu'ai-je à faire avec ces colonels des Lettres, hauts dignitaires du Bel-écrire, commissaires aux Syntaxes, moi qui ne hisse de pavillon que noir, noir comme du cirage, votre échotier ne le sait-il pas?" [What have I to do with the colonels of Letters, the high dignitaries of Beautiful Prose, the commissaries of Syntax, I who raise only a black flag, black as shoe polish, doesn't your hack know that?], he writes in a letter to the *Figaro littéraire* (*Prospectus*, vol. 2, 513). Far from experiencing with regard to language that sentiment of mastery, of familiarity, or of property felt by officially patented writers, Dubuffet has instead the impression that he is an undesirable addressee or tenant. He therefore might as well precipitate the conflict, make the worst of the situation, hoist the black flag, and instigate linguistic catastrophes that would disqualify the distinguished idioms and tics of expression that are supposed to qualify the style of an author: "Le mythe du Bel-écrire est une pièce capitale de la défense bourgeoise. Si vous voulez frapper au coeur de la caste sévissante, frappez-la à ses subjonctifs, à son cérémonial de beau langage creux, à ses minauderies d'esthète" [The myth of Beautiful Prose is an essential piece of bourgeois defense. If you want a direct hit at the caste in power, hit it in the subjunctives, in the ceremonial of beautiful shallow language, in its effete mannerisms], he writes of Céline (*Prospectus*, vol. 2, 52).

To be sure, the majority of Dubuffet's writings defer to lexical and grammatical rules, and even show what one must call quirks of style, which Raymond Queneau takes perverse pleasure in recording:[6] the shift of the adverb to the end of the sentence, the suppression of the article, the inversion of the noun and its attributive adjective, the position of the verb at the beginning of the sentence, certain archaisms or neologisms, and even, occasionally, the proscription of the subjunctive, deemed to be a superfluous mood. Is there any reason other than the customary infatuation of an author for these peculiarities? Undoubtedly, as Queneau notes, one reason might be the pragmatic use of

6. "Quelques citations choisies dans le corpus des écrits de Jean Dubuffet," in *Jean Dubuffet*, special issue of *L'Herne*, (1973): 372–76.

language, a determination to go directly to the essential without niceties, even if it is at the expense of syntax. But Dubuffet also seems maliciously to search out with Machiavellian malice moments of friction between the order of ideas and the order of words. And it is all the better if he gives the impression of struggling with an excessively heavy apparatus of language, too-rigid concepts and excessively procedural grammatical rules! If the expression seems laborious and language is strained at the seams, it is precisely so that we may understand that there are seams, that is, a linguistic conditioning of thought. Dubuffet the writer can be compared in this respect to the nutcracker in Kafka's short story, who, through a heuristic clumsiness, informs us about his art much better than would a virtuoso.

Consider the antecedence of the adjective, even when it has more syllables than the noun, transgressing the rule called "du second lourd" [of the heavier second] (for example, "la fallacieuse image" [the image fallacious], "une frappante marque" [a sign striking]).* It is certainly an expressive turn of phrase, which indicates the quality before the thing, and consequently corresponds to the synthetic movement of sensation, whereas the succession of the noun and its attribute follows the analytical-rational order of intellection. The same can be said about the position of the verb at the beginning of the sentence, which gives the movement before the identification of the agent ("cessera alors la réfraction . . ." [thus will end refraction . . .], "Frappe dans ces dessins . . . " [Strikes in these designs . . .]). There is thus an inversion, but with respect to what norm? Is there an order of words that is *naturally* related to objects? Perhaps logic commands us to say: "le sang est rouge" [blood is red] and sensation: "rouge est le sang" [red is the blood]. In any case, the experience is all-encompassing, sensation and intellection intermingle, and it would not be possible to prescribe an order of succession limiting verbal expression. In fact, Dubuffet prefers the less canonical order, not because it is more faithful to the real or to the sequence of ideas, but because it betrays the ideolinguistic *double bind*† from which verbalization proceeds. (Thévoz, *Le Langage de la rupture,* op. cit.) If it is true that thought is not independent of the words which formulate it, the irregularity will at least have the effect of emphasizing this subjugation. Generally, the order of words is never innocent, and it is when it is the most "natural," in other words

*Unlike in English, in French the adjective generally comes after the noun. The reversal of normal order is as noticeable in French as it is in English.—Translator's note.
†In English in the original.—Translator's note.

the most transparent to meaning, that it is the most ideological, since it naturalizes precisely the significations which it induces. The natural in writing has no ontological value, but is only a lubricant of which, speaking of the movement of the pen and the linking of the alphabetical characters, the encyclopedist Paillasson gives the composition: "Sans recourir à des observations anatomiques, l'expérience, d'accord avec la raison, me fait reconnaître une liqueur onctueuse appelée par les anatomistes synoviale qui, se filtrant par les glandes qui portent son nom, arrose, pénètre, humecte les ligaments des nerfs et leur donne le jeu, le ressort que demande l'articulation la plus facile et la plus complète"[7] [Without recourse to anatomical observations, experience, in tune with reason, makes me recognize an unctuous liquid called "synovial" by anatomists that, filtering though the glands that have its name, waters, penetrates, and moistens the ligaments of the nerves and gives them the play, the tensile strength required by the easiest and most complete articulation].

Dubuffet does not like discourses that are bathed in synovial liquid. He prefers the machinery of language to grate, like Ratier's cranks,[8] betraying its inertia, its bone structure, and its friction. He takes pleasure in stressing the limits of the speakable, in other words, he likes to "friser le code" [brush up against the code]. The neologisms which he fashions out of suffixes, prefixes, derivation and analogy still proceed from linguistic rules, certainly, but in an application at once extensive and excessive (Oedipal, one would be tempted to say, recalling his authoritarian father) which demonstratively accelerates that which could be an imperceptible process of evolution of the language ("notionneuse est capitalement la culture . . . " [notionous is culture capitally . . .], "il fait mêmement de l'inutilitaire son site . . . " [he does likewise with the uselessitarian his site . . .]). These singularities are at once motivated and striking, they underline the workings of language, they propagate their own opacity in words that have already passed into common usage by reactivating their etymology, they consequently elude the opposition between lexical legality and infraction by showing that all of *language is a neologism*—even though, as they age, words assume the affectation of "naturalness".

7. Paillasson, in the article "L'Art d'écrire" of the *Encyclopédie* of Diderot and d'Alembert, quoted in Jérôme Peignot, "De La Calligraphie latine," in *Signes et Ecritures*, catalog of the exhibition at the *Centre d'art contemporain*, Brussels (1984): 25.
8. Cf. A. Wolff, "Les Manivelles d'Emile Ratier," in *L'Art Brut*, fascicule 9 (1973): 69–78.

The same can be said of the syntactical initiatives, such as the proscription of the subjunctive or the famous "une personne ria si volontiers" [a person laughed so willingly] that so amused Paulhan (*Prospectus*, vol. 2, 500). Dubuffet knows full well that he will not start a school. One cannot make language evolve voluntarily. The will in language, which proceeds from consciousness, thus from language itself, is tautological, and thus is incapable of innovation. Just like the genetic code, the code of language resists premeditated intervention. If it is nevertheless modified, it is unbeknownst to the agents of that change. The paradox requires that it is enough merely to question language for language to reinforce its system, and, conversely, that one must lose oneself in language to the point of losing consciousness in order to have a chance of modifying it. Thus Dubuffet does not claim to be either an inventor or a reformer. He merely wants to experience the body of signs which he inhabits and in which he thinks as a living, autonomous organism, with its chance conversions, its own initiatives, and especially its *assertive* character, proper to our logocentric culture. Words do not adjust themselves to reality, nor do they represent it; they fashion it and order it according to their own devices. In other words, the real that they pretend to describe is apocryphal. Dubuffet does not intend to stop language from reinventing the world, but only to expose this construction by preventing it from disappearing into the objective evidence which it creates. Thus he will readily proceed by outbidding or provoking, speculating on the referential power of discourse, in order to accredit the most paradoxical and the most contradictory opinions. When it is pointed out to him that his writings contain contradictions, he answers that he reproaches himself for not having been contradictory enough, given the fact that any affirmation maintained for too long a time turns into absurdity.[9]

The greatest contradiction is already evident in the disparity of his writings: while the commentaries of the painter on his own work aim toward elucidation and intelligibility, and thus toward the transparency of language, the jargons and the *fatrasies* wordplay dismiss reasoned meaning and deliberately obfuscate linguistic sign. In other words, Dubuffet the writer behaves alternatively as a virtuoso and as an agitator. He is even both simultaneously, and thus more contradictory than ever, in the texts said to be in "jargon relatif" [relative jargon], which expressly emerge out of a desire for reform, and yet precipitate

9. Jean Dubuffet, *Bâtons rompus* (Paris: Minuit, 1986), 66.

the catastrophe. For the Oedipal reasons that we have mentioned, Dubuffet is sensitive more than anyone else to the disparity between current French and the classical language such as it is taught in school, a disparity further aggravated by writing, which preserves only the words, not the intonations, the accents and the idiosyncrasies of elocution which play a major role in verbal messages: "Une certaine manière de prononcer un mot ou de souligner une syllabe, ou d'élever la voix un tout petit peu autrement qu'il n'est d'usage, donne subtilement le sens exact, comme le donne aussi à l'écriture le tracé d'un jambage, au dessin celui d'une hachure" (*Prospectus*, vol. 1, 82) [A certain way of pronouncing a word or stressing a syllable, of raising one's voice just a little differently than the norm, subtly gives the exact meaning, just as the tracing of the downstrokes in handwriting and a streak in drawing]. Evidently, Dubuffet takes the side of orality against what he calls the "langue-éteinte" [burnt-out language] and its sedimented spelling: "C'est inconcevable que les gens faisant profession de poésie—Breton ou autres—fassent usage de la même langue écrite que les secrétariats commerciaux ou les journaux—qui est à peu de chose près la même langue que celle des actes notariés ou traités de médecine. Ils n'ont aucune chance de nous émouvoir dans cette langue-là" (*Prospectus*, vol 1, 480) [It is inconceivable that people making a profession of poetry—Breton or others—use the same written language as commercial establishments or newspapers—which is with few exceptions that same language found in notary acts or medical treatises. They stand no chance of moving us in that language].

In 1937 already—although Dubuffet was not aware of it—Raymond Queneau had proposed and put into practice a form of writing that was "photographically" traced from current spoken language.[10] Nonetheless, at the conclusion of the experiment, Queneau agreed that once the first moment of surprise and amusement was past, the phonetic transcription ended up substituting a new orthodoxy with respect to the spelling that it was rejecting. Dubuffet's proposal differs markedly in its inspiration. During a stay in the Sahara in 1947, seeking initiation to an Arab dialect spoken by the Bedouins, he had been led to write this language phonetically in Latin characters. The unusual aspect of these transcriptions had given him the idea of doing the same thing with spoken French, as if he were a foreigner ignorant of all the terms

10. Raymond Queneau, *Bâtons, chiffres et lettres* (Paris: Gallimard, "Idées," 1965), 22.

and their separation from one another: (Prospectus (vol. 1, 481–82)
"SQON NAPELE LEPE ISAJE SAVEDIR LA CANPANE IARIIN QI MANBETE
COMSA LACANPANE LACAMPANE SEPLIN DLEGUME ONDIRE UNE SOUPE
MINESTRON, etc." [WATSCALD AVIU MEEN SDH QUNTRY NUHTHINGBA
THERSME MORTHANDHE QUNRTY ITSFULO VEGTA BLE SLAIKA MIN-
ESTRONEE, etc.]. Dubuffet ironically presents his little book entitled
LER DLA CANPANE [QUNTRY EYER] as "le premier texte publié en langue
française vivante depuis les Serments de Strasbourg" [the first text
published in French as a living language since the Oaths of Strasbourg].
In the end, it was certainly not a question of rejuvenating or reviving
the language, but of upsetting its functions.

Certainly the recourse to integral phonetics can lead to confusion,
especially after the precedent set by Queneau, by appearing to be a
reform of spelling and a renewed fidelity to the spoken word. The latter
is supposed to be a prelude to writing. All the more since we currently
define the phonogram, in other words alphabetical writing, by its opposition to the ideogram, by assigning to the latter the direct representation of meaning, and to the former the representation of the word.
But this is a simplistic opposition. As phonetic as it might claim to be,
alphabetical writing is never properly speaking, a graphic representation of voice: it does not reproduce the physical sounds as they were
proffered, but only their intelligible articulations. As Jacques Derrida
notes, "s'il n'y a pas d'écriture purement phonétique, c'est qu'il n'y a
pas de phonè purement phonétique"[11] [if there is no purely phonetic
writing, it is because there is no purely phonetic phonè]. Supposedly
phonetic writing aims, within the phonè, only at what pertains to
writing in a wide sense, in other words at a combination of discrimina-
tive units. This does not mean that for all that one should invert the
order of precession and consider writing to be originary. In the phono-
centrist system, spelling functions as the auxiliary of meaning, in the
manner of a well-groomed valet, both efficacious and self-effacing at
once, worn out from the effort of never allowing himself to be distinguished as the object of attention. To make a fetish of voice or handwriting and to invest the second with the repressive instinct of Western metaphysics, would constitute two symmetrical errors. One
should consider instead that graphemes and phonemes mutually correspond to one another, form a system and stand against each other as

---

11. Jacques Derrida, "La Différance," in *Théorie d'ensemble* (Paris: Le Seuil, 1968), 43.

representative idealities, through reciprocal alibis, as it were: oral expression refers to writing as to its norm, and writing presents itself as a phonographic representation of the word, like two mirrors which face one another. In other words, the written and the oral are disincarnated through a specular effect that bounces the presumption of an objective referent back and forth. As brash as it might appear, the living word evolves at the limits of writing, in a freedom on probation. As a corollary, the written message tends to claim its innocence against its spelling by putting on the fluidity of oral expression: "Il y a lieu d'observer au passage que cette conception de l'écrire réduit à une simple notation de l'oral, outre qu'elle a pour effet de faire oublier toutes les ressources visuelles des graphies, a par ailleurs aussi celui de faire oublier de même toutes les ressources du parler qui ne peuvent être transcrites dans le sytème adopté" (*Prospectus*, vol. 1, 293) [One should observe in passing that this conception of writing reduced to a simple notation of the oral, beyond the fact that it has the effect of making us forget all the visual resources of calligraphy, also makes us forget the resources of speech which cannot be transcribed in the adopted system]. One must have recourse to irregular writing in order to elude the mirage effect, that is, the ideality of discourse, and to redirect our attention to the substance of the sign, that is, respectively, on the vocal aspect as an inscription of sound, and on written speech as a trace.

This is why the attempt to create a phonetic transcription faithful to empirical discourse, or the "textualisation de la diglossie" [textualization of diglossia] as linguists call it, results not in a transparent writing that ultimately vanishes in its representative function, but instead and paradoxically in a disintegration of the oral-written system and in a blurring of the signified. The oral and graphic signifiers become opaque and consubstantially meet each other as fragments in a play of mirrors that thereafter is dislocated. This is why Dubuffet, initially thinking perhaps, like Queneau, that he would readjust written language to oral language thereby regenerating writing, realizes that he has behaved like a sorcerer's apprentice and has triggered off a chain of semantic catastrophes which eventually take him under their spell.

Having set out to reestablish the representational function of writing with respect to the spoken word, he ends up with the realization that he has unhinged the overall system of linguistic representation.

Wild phonetic transcription does not restore naturalness to language, since for the literate, its only users, it is precisely correct spelling that constitutes language's naturalness. One would obviously lose the essential in the jargon texts by listening to them being read, since there would be nothing left but the drivel of *Monsieur-Tout-le-monde* or the wild imaginings of a senile gardener. Dubuffet's populism is not socially vindictive, rather it is anarchist or nihilist; it is not a question of reestablishing popular genius against the jargon of intellectuals. Rather, the silliness of the discourse should make us turn our attention toward a *contre-écriture* [anti-writing] that does not respect the phono-centrist game and thwarts the specular recourse of writing and voice. The fact is that reading the texts in relative jargon is initially discon-certing: they have to be read aloud to be understood, as was apparently done until the Renaissance. Various accounts, including Augustine's, indicate that reading, even solitary, was oral: one read by mumbling. The printed book has since imposed silence by sustaining sight exclu-sively. In other words typography has provided a powerful contribution to spiritualizing one's relation to the book by inhibiting the pulmo-nary, glottal, and lingual elements of reading. With his uncanny pho-netic transcription, Dubuffet compels meaning to pass through ut-terance once again, in other words through the body. By thwarting and delaying the intelligibility of the text, by forcing the reader to take this somatic detour, the writer of jargon reactivates the libidinal genealogy of verbal expression and the excremental origin of concepts.

Childish babble is not originally determined by an intention to communicate, but, as psychoanalysts say, by the convergence of the first undifferentiated instincts towards the buccal area.[12] The pulmo-nary contractions, the occlusion of the glottal sphincter, the friction of the air against the palate, salivary lubrication, cranial vibrations, the touches of the tongue, the suction of the lips, the anal investment of sound substances, represent the various elements of this primitive oral eroticism. It is only in a second phase that an articulated word hurls forth in this libidinal sound magma, and gradually converts phonatory elements to signification. (We find the same phenomena of *fortuitous semantic* meaningfulness in the graphic register when the initial scrib-ble suddenly turns into figuration.) By delaying the precipitation of meaning, Dubuffet awakens for a suspended moment this primitive erogeneity of the word.

There is no regression in this. Words are never completely objects, even if they recover their body—indeed, especially if they recover it. What point would there be in depriving the word of its meaning if it

12. Cf. Fonagy, *La Vive voix. Essai de psycho-phonétique* (Paris: Payot, 1983).

then simply took up the vacant place of the referent and proposed itself as a substitute substantial being? Thus one must conversely avoid an ontological valorization of the vocal or graphic substance which, following Bachelard's psychoanalysis of the materials of painting, would send us back to an intuitive wholeness. Even the infant who is not initiated to lexical signification of words senses their symbolic value, as Freud showed regarding the game with the spinning top. Conversely, in the adult, although latent, the muscular and tactile sensations related to articulated language will remain a source of pleasure even and especially in the most sophisticated discourse. Syllabic mastication, wet or liquid sounds, erectile, fricative, constrictive or nasal consonants: the technical metaphors of phonetics already indicate the subconscious sexualization of the gestures of phonation. Erudite language never frees itself in full from primitive magic; meaning is not able to steal away sound completely. The university chair, the bar, or the political pulpit open the way for an honorable derivation of the initial oral sadism.

In short, language always evolves between the poles of the sonorous body and of ideality. Dubuffet takes a perverse pleasure in accelerating this oscillation, in order to prevent the resolution of the harmony between sound and meaning. The vocal or graphic materiality that we would be tempted to savor for itself nonetheless continues to be articulated in phonemes and letters and to call for a meaning upon which, conversely, we cannot concentrate without becoming distracted by its unusual incarnation—hence the deliberate ineptitude of speech. The same game of mirrors which in the practice of writing with proper spelling functioned in an illusionist manner reverses itself to rob us indefinitely of the idea that would resolve the reading.

There is more: words in general have multiple meanings, at times proceeding from different etymologies, or from a semantic evolution that allows the coexistence of successive meanings, or from metaphorical usages that do not exclude the primary meaning, or from homonymy, aggravated by oral expression and its ambiguities regarding the separation of words (once again the *non-dupe erre* in all the meanings authorized by orality awaiting the intervention of paternal spelling—*orthographe*—a noun that French alas puts in the feminine . . .).* Far from hindering the use of language, polysemy contributes to its *generative potential:* it entails semantic slippages, associations of ideas, metonymical displacements, metaphorical conversions,

---

*Orthographe, or spelling, is a feminine noun in French—Translator's note.

in brief, an openness toward invention. If language were a code rigorously systematized by bi-univocal relationships between signifiers and signifieds, as in computer science, it would remain protected from the original and subject to the field that was already verbalized. It is the indecision of the signs, their constitutive ambiguity, their internal play, that exposes them to the attraction of virtual signifieds in search of formulation. This passage from latency to expression which allows an unconscious or potential thought suddenly to take over homologous signifiers, converting them to an unexpected usage follows what psychoanalysts call the primary process; it is manifested in the *witz* [pun], the slip of the tongue, or poetic invention; it makes us laugh or feel anguish, and in any case disrupts the working of the code in a process similar to genetic mutation in the animal realm.[13]

Of course, in normal communication, words restrict their semantic spectrum to a precise acceptation by joint interdependent determination. It is said that context reduces meaning. This takes place just as in those graphic games that theoretically allow us to interpret motifs that are in relief or hollowed out, but that in fact force us to choose a perceptive option from which it becomes difficult to escape. The clarity required by communication, reinforced by redundancy, thus constrains words to a univocal meaning. And spelling, we have noted, powerfully contributes to the reduction of polysemy, by thwarting oral ambiguities, by making the syntax precise, by rooting words in etymology, in grammatical legality, etc. Any discourse—and especially the discourse of power—refers to its potential transcription as to its canonical version and its guarantee of ideality. Hence the ideological over-determination of spelling in the specular relationship of writing and speech: the master is one who speaks the way we write. Claude Hagège gives the example of the *liaison* without linking ("il avait un plan" [he had a plan] pronounced "il avète . . . un plan,")* the orally inadequate hypercorrection of one for whom spelling is self-evident and who wants to make this fact known.[14] The flights of oratory paradoxically have as their condition this mooring to writing, just like the kite that would rush downwards without its string. This is illustrated *a contrario* by the intellectual coquetry of giving orthographic precision

---

*Although the consonant at the end of *avait* is not normally pronounced, because the next word begins with a vowel the *liaison* causes this consonant to be pronounced as if followed by that vowel in the same word.—Translator's note.

13. Cf. Octave Mannoni, *Clefs pour l'imaginaire, ou L'Autre Scène* (Paris: Le Seuil, 1969), 34 ff.

14. Claude Hagège, *L'Homme de paroles* (Paris: Fayard, 1985), 282.

in order to dispel ambiguity, whereas the purpose is really to bring attention to its existence (thus as it happens I would say that I am analyzing—with a *y*—the writings of Dubuffet, even when we are dealing with the excremental nature of concepts). As a general rule, spelling intervenes like a censor, by imposing a despotic meaning and exacerbating the libidinal character of the significations that it represses—and inevitably take on a sexual or obscene coloring. The corrected writing does not oppose itself to speech as its antithesis but as its superego.

Hence the reason why Dubuffet's practice of *désécriture* [unwriting] has the effect of freeing us from that sort of semantic cramp that subjugates us to a despotic meaning; thus it makes us more sensitive to uncontrolled transverse significations. Within obvious (and pointless) speech, it awakens a latent polysemy which is of concern to psychoanalysts, particularly when they attempt to break the intentional sequence of their patients' discourse in order to submit its fragments to the play of free association. Like them, Dubuffet cuts the "points of anchorage" that secure the signifier to an exclusive signified, and reestablishes the indefinite and uncontrollable movement of a universal "logology." If it is true that the order of words is the order of the world, the accrued fragility of the system of language is a prefiguration of the mental cataclysm initiated by a different ordering of signs and a redistribution of their elements.

The texts in "jargon absolu" [absolute jargon], which is characterized by the disappearance of any explicit meaning and by an integral formalism, are presented as a radicalization of the experience of phoneticization. This does indeed prove that the latter did not aim to reward the fault of writing nor to reinforce its ties to the living word, but on the contrary to focus the substance of the sign to the point of abandoning any narrative alibi: "Qualle pesse! Qualle pesse d'argule! Amin d'ingander l'anquet rijoube à l'argule! Podissons l'anctuaire! J'ombile au jude. Les merisseaux fasculent! Anjandés! Rambochent! J'enduquais l'omboque, j'arduchais gravant—bovant la turluque en rabellant crovoche un dermi d'entourle. L'ouve aux racharles! Bancarles! Pas d'avermis d'ongular l'anque! J'ardonnais canut la pinousse. Fripaillais le richot dans tous les cachards du magrole: à sige, à sonagre" ("Couinque," in *Prospectus*, vol. 1, 145).*

---

*The words used are all nonsense words that do not exist in French, except for prepositions, articles and pronouns; the grammatical forms (like conjugation) are derived from French—Translator's note.

Absolute jargon is certainly not a phonetic or grammatological creation *ex nihilo.* It remains dependent on the French language, of which it respects the general morphology, the grammatical forms, and the punctuation. It would even appear to follow the rules of spelling more than the relative jargon. But the meaning emphatically refuses to surrender. Language is functioning correctly, but for no purpose, a little like the machines of Tinguely that have no other purpose than to move on their own through the nonsensical or tautological multiplication of their mechanism. The phonemes follow upon one another anarchically, as if the language, struck with a generalized cancer, had exhausted itself in interminable metastases that emptied it of meaning—this could be academic confinement and logorrhoea in their parodic degree.

It would therefore be an error to equate Dubuffet with the inventors of languages like Hélène Smith and her ultramartian idiom,[15] like Louis Wolfson and his system of conversion of the maternal word,[16] or like so many other authors of raw writings who withdraw into inaccessible idiolects. We have said that the repudiation of maternal language is always illusory; in wanting to encode language or make it cryptic at his pleasure, the speaker rarely heightens with a simulacrum the prison of signs in which he is condemned to think. In his analysis of Hélène Smith's ultramartian language, Ferdinand de Saussure noted that it was conceived in order to appear as exotic as possible, and that it thus emerged from the most fantastic morphological principles, with only one constraint, but a sizeable one: not to resemble French— which evidently put it in counterdependency with the repudiated language, thus in a dependency aggravated by its semiotic conditioning.[17] Saussure also stresses the infantile origin of this cryptographic impulse: "Les enfants sont très souvent *onomatopoioi* et, chez les malades, les névrosés, cette faculté persiste dans l'âge adulte. Mon frère, dans sa première enfance, s'était composé ainsi tout un langage à lui. Ma grand-mère, qui était remarquablement intelligente, pouvait encore réciter *verbo tenus* dans son extrême vieillesse un petit jargon d'une dizaine de lignes qu'elle s'était composé dans son enfance" (ibid., 182) [Children are very often *onomatopoioi* and, in the case of the sick, the neurotic, this faculty persists into adulthood. My brother, in his

15. Théodore Flournoy, *Des Indes à la planète Mars* (Paris: Le Seuil, 1983).

16. Cf. Louis Wolfson, *Le Schizo et les langues* (Paris: Gallimard, 1970).

17. Cf. Olivier Flournoy, *Théodore et Léopold* (Neuchâtel, à la Baconnière, 1986), 193–94. The author has reproduced the correspondence between Saussure and his grandfather, Thèodore Flournoy, concerning the problem of invented languages.

early childhood, had thus invented a language that was all his own. My grandmother, who was remarkably intelligent, could still recite *verbo tenus* in her extreme old age a little jargon of ten lines or so that she had composed in her childhood]. We should note that Théodore Flournoy had already quoted this observation by Saussure in his book on Hélène Smith, but that he had omitted the reference to the sick and the neurotic (a reference which would probably have frustrated the relationship of transference . . . and countertransference with his seductive patient before its time) [Théodore Flournoy, op. cit., 269]. We should also note that we cannot hold Saussure, who was writing in 1896, responsible for speaking of neurosis instead of perversion, whereas in fact it was a case of regression to an infantile position—in this case, ludic glossolalia and the practice of an idiolect as a resistance to parental discourse.

Of course, it is true that Dubuffet's invented redskin language illustrates what Saussure says about infantile *onomatopoiesis.* Yet, the jargons and the delirium cannot simply be attributed to the persistence of this obsession—and we need not take the same precautions with Dubuffet as Flournoy took with his medium. Certainly, by semantically unmooring French words and communicating with the reader only with blank morphemes, Dubuffet brings into play what could be considered a psychotic potentiality. Roman Jakobson notes cases of "semantic aphasia," in other words the incapacity of certain patients to communicate anything at all even though they express themselves with apparent ease by respecting the morpho-syntactical rules of the language.[18] Their discourse still has an architecture, but the meaning is lost. But Dubuffet remains bilingual, and he plays parodically with the alternatives without becoming their tool. If we were to speak of perversion in his case, it would not be in the pathological or infantile sense, but in a subversive or nihilist one: his texts in absolute jargon, which present all the superficial forms of French (as opposed to those of Hélène Smith) announce a conceptual meaning that they do not honor, since the words finally do not express anything that transcends their own linguistic substance. The movement of reading suddenly comes to an impasse and flows back upon itself like the thrust of a battering ram that dislocates the whole system. This is a manner of *semiological epochè* which leads us to experience language as the mold of thought and to sense its infused innate ideology.

18. Roman Jakobson, *Langage enfantin et aphasie* (Paris: Minuit, 1969).

As opposed to the paranoid cryptographies which still guarantee the signs of a semantic recuperation, be it hidden, Dubuffet's jargons lead to a heuristic disappointment. The vacuousness that is produced is unstable, like certain chemical compounds: at any moment an uncertain signified can *stabilize* and turn the graphic substance into a message. Writing resists semantic void and, rather than remaining a dead letter, it will lend itself to any and all conjectures (preferably sexual or obscene) without confirming any of them. Absolute jargon exacerbates polysemy, and with it, our need for meaning, identity, univocity, security, objectivity, being or *en-soi* [being-in-oneself]. Or, to say the same thing in a different way, the ablation of meaning functions like zero in numbers, multiplying its effects. We feel in it the vertigo of a limitless language, which effectively finds its pictorial equivalent, especially in the cycle of the *Hourloupe,* and even more spectacularly in the aptly named *Cabinet logologique.*

Concerning this, we can affirm that the hiatus between writing and figural motif has never been so close to being stitched up. Words that follow upon one another independent from any intelligible signification can constitute only a simulacrum of writing, or a text in a figural representation, like written pages depicted in painting, for example on the table of the figure, for instance, pages which the painter has wanted to make identifiable as writing, but at the same time indecipherable, for fear of converting the visible to the legible. We can understand why Dubuffet would have felt the need to consign his jargons to a script that was as laborious as possible, by engraving them in linoleum for example, in wood planks, or even in the bottoms of Camembert boxes, all materials appropriate to render the sign opaque and create a meaning decipherable only through paleography, as in the dead languages that he had been so passionately interested in deciphering:

> LER DLA CANPANE fut tiré par moi à l'aide de ma femme, page après page, sur la table de la salle à manger débarrassée après les repas, à un nombre d'exemplaires dont je ne me souviens pas au juste, deux cents je crois (cela nous occupa bon nombre de soirées), sans autre machine que le plat de la main pour les gravures, et, pour les pages de texte, un rudimentaire stencil (fine grille de soie tendue dans un petit cadre) sur lequel j'écrivais avec une pointe. D'où une impression, comme on peut penser, assez barbare, et que venait aggraver l'emploi d'un papier mince qui laisse transparaître le verso et brouille par là quelque peu les caractères maigres du texte. Mais j'aimais l'effet qui en résultait. J'aimais que fût difficultueuse la

lecture des mots comme l'est le déchiffrement des vieilles inscriptions en langues mal connues et à demi effacées par les intempéries. C'est dans le même esprit que j'avais omis de mettre les accents aux *e*, ce qui cause, je le sais bien, un surcroît de couci à la lecture, les *e* accentués ne se distinguant pas des muets. Obscurcir un peu est parfois efficace. Encore l'édition comporta-t-elle une dizaine d'exemplaires favorisés, spécialement ténébreux, toutes les pages adornées de maculatures, imprimées au rouleau, qui rendaient le texte à peine visible   [*Prospectus*, vol. 1, 477–78]

LER DLA CANPANE was printed by me with the help of my wife, page after page, on the dining room table, quickly cleared after meals; it was printed in a number of copies that I do not remember exactly, two hundred I think (this occupied us for quite a number of evenings), without any instrument but the flat part of our hands for the engravings, and, for the pages of text, a rudimentary stencil (a fine silk grid stretched in a little frame) which I wrote on with a spike. Hence an impression, as one might expect, that was rather barbarous, and was aggravated by the use of thin paper that let the other side of the page show through, blurring the meager characters of the text. But I liked the effect that resulted. But I liked the resultant effect that the reading of the words was difficult like the deciphering of old inscriptions in languages that are little known and half-erased by bad weather. It was in the same spirit that I had omitted the accents on the *e*, which causes, I am well aware, a further difficulty in reading, since the accented *e* become confused with the silent ones. To darken is sometimes effective. Furthermore the edition included ten favored copies, particularly dark, all the pages being decorated with stains, printed with a roller, which rendered the text barely visible (Fig. 4).

Dubuffet the writer likes to fight fiercely with a resistant material, using a tool that he is unfamiliar with, once again like the nutcracker. Typographical characters? The term, for him, is contradictory: he is fond of characters that earn their name, resisting normalization, at once threatening the authority of voice, in other words, of breath, of meaning, of spirit, and reactivating its corporal premises, its physiological machinery, its work of vociferation. The phonetism of jargons is the polar opposite of phonology, obstinately restoring the repressed element of the chain of equations that oppose phoneme to word, meaning to sound, typography to tracing, intelligibility to the graphic instinct, semantic value to the work of writing, etc. All things considered, Dubuffet's *contre-écritures* do not dismiss meaning but instead

4. Jean Dubuffet, *Le Courrier.*

only frustrate its functioning, reactivate its genesis through a set of perturbations, spatialize sound, temporalize the letter, visualize meaning, spiritualize the graphic evidence; they invert the poles of the legible and the visible, unglue their relations, and provoke oscillations that carry the mind to the limits of the Gutenberg galaxy.

—Translated by Laura Harwood Wittman

JAN BAETENS

Latent Violence (Escher, Franc, Vaughn-James)

In recent discussions concerning the relationship between text and image, the decompartmentalization of the two semiotic systems has gradually eclipsed attempts to define their respective specificity. Rather than analyzing the ways in which the verbal and the iconic are inexorably opposed,[1] the task has increasingly become one of contesting the watertightness of the line that supposedly separates them. Even if the antinomy between them has become more and more nuanced, the image is usually studied as a spatial sign whose parts are *simultaneously* visible, whereas writing, confined to linearity, lends itself to an essentially *temporal* reading. For example, influenced by deconstruction, many theorists currently delight in exposing the impossibility of completely preserving the frontier between words and visible representations.[2]

Although interest in the encounter between text and image takes many divergent forms, there are two whose significance is worth emphasizing here.

The first involves the actual fusion of the two systems: numerous analyses are organized around the more or less gradual, more or less realized, thorough reconciliation of word and image (In literature,

---

1. This was, one may recall, the structuralist objective, of which certain works by Jean Ricardou bear exemplary evidence. See, for instance, the chapters entitled "Plume et caméra" and "Page, film, récit" in the collection *Problèmes du nouveau roman* (Paris: Seuil, 1967), as well as the fourth part of *Le Théâtre des métamorphoses* (Paris: Seuil, 1982).

2. A good example of such an approach is the work of W. J. T. Mitchell, the success and rapid dissemination of which are symptomatic of the present strength of the trend toward "antispecificity." See *Iconology* (Chicago: University of Chicago Press, 1985).

YFS 84, *Boundaries: Writing & Drawing*, ed. M. Reid, © 1994 by Yale University.

these could be situated on the side of grammatextuality initiated by Jean Lapacherie.)[3] The logograms of Christian Dotrement[4] or Henri Michaux[5] (purely "visible" scripts) and the visual puns of someone like Martin Vaughn-James[6] (images that function remarkably like rebuses) aptly illustrate an exchange that may be characterized as *direct*.

The second form, repeatedly embodied in the essays in this volume, concerns *indirect* exchange. The latter envisages the merging of text and iconic signs not on the ontological plane, but rather on the spatiotemporal axis, the joining of the two codes being carried out by way of alternation, or relay.

The present essay will attempt to combine these different points of view (a penchant for specificity and an awareness of its relative nature; a blending of codes and the necessary separation of the written and the graphic). But before examining the case of an apparently peaceful or unresisting alliance of verb and drawing, I want to consider two examples that are antagonistic at first glance, having in common only a departure from the conventional relationships governing the two intersecting classes of signs.

Upon closer examination, it becomes evident that in the case of semiotic productions where words and images come into contact, numerous prohibitions weigh on their union. Two such taboos, whose concrete forms obviously vary according to the work being considered, seem to play a dominant role: on the one hand, there is the taboo concerning the respective *places* occupied by words and images; on the other, the taboo governing their *contents*. In each case, however, the same logic prevails: the middle way, so to speak, which tries to prevent relationships from being either too close or too lax.

3. Such analyses could be placed alongside the research on grammatextuality initiated by Jean Gérard Lapacherie. See his seminal article "De la grammatextualité," in *Poétique* 59 (1984): 283–94.

4. See especially the volume entitled *Traces* (Brussels: Jacques Antoine, 1980). A good synthesis of the problematics of the logogram is furnished by two recent articles by Ana Gonzalez Salvador: "Irrégularité et catastrophe," in *Correspondance* 2 (1991): 89–99, and "Ecriture automatique et écriture désautomatisée," in *Textyles* 8 (1991): 207–20.

5. Until the publication of the philological dossier promised for the Pléiade edition directed by Raymond Bellour, readers should consult the reedition of Michaux's famous *Mouvements* (1951) in the volume *Face aux verrous* (Paris: Gallimard/ Collection Poésie, 1992).

6. A good example of this is provided by the short graphic narrative called *Le Parc. Un Mystère*, published in *Conséquences* 4 (1984): 7–22. The narrative is followed by a reading by Daniel Fleury, "L'Antireprésentation minutieuse" (ibid., 23–27). Fleury examines these puns in detail.

Let us first examine relationships of place. The double pitfall to be avoided, according to the traditional view of the problem, is of course the pure and simple superimposition (which brings about inevitable effects of censorship of one of the two classes of signs, the words hiding the images or vice versa) and excessive distance (which tends to preclude any perception of relationship). When the link between text and corresponding image lacks precision, tradition advocates recourse to all sorts of auxiliaries. (In the comic strip, for example, a genre that is clearly strategic for the purposes of this essay, the articulation of the "balloon" with the figures or actors is often carried out by means of arrows attributing the words to the characters supposedly uttering them.) And when an overlapping of occupied zones occurs, a compromise is usually hoped for. Although the comic strip can readily infuse an image with text, it is careful either to forge a zone of demarcation between the two, or to place the script in a zone divested of image: if a balloon is not properly circumscribed, the verbal information surfaces at a place in the square where the image seems empty. Any conflict of precedence is thus avoided. The script does not hide the image, and the image does not hinder the deciphering of the script. Should a character's head run into the balloon containing his or her discourse, the script adeptly skirts this pitfall. And if, inversely, the color of the image risks merging with the black of the printed characters, the latter promptly turn white.

Turning next to relationships of content, one sees that what is frequently condemned is both total incoherence and strict repetition. The stakes of this symmetrical depreciation are in fact less technical than ideological. In each case (absence of immediately perceptible relationships and/or flagrant redundancy), readers-spectators find themselves insidiously forced into resolving a conflict of domination: they either have to decide that the image eludes the words accompanying it or, inversely, that its suggestive force is quelled by the text—or they must conclude that the text simply echoes the image or that the image restates the information provided by the text. The classic division of labor, in which words and images jointly collaborate to forge a message of a higher level,[7] evidently evades such choices, which prove to be anything but neutral. This aspect is of capital importance, since it

7. Here one may recognize the function of the *relay* [relais] described by Barthes in his article "Rhétorique de l'image," reprinted in *L'Obvie et l'obtus* (Paris: Seuil, 1982). See especially 32–33.

foregrounds the conflict of codes whose union, it should be repeated, is hardly self-evident. It is this violence underlying the problem of the relationship between text and image that I would like to unearth in the following pages.

Permitting the analysis of certain borderline cases (although they are at first glance completely innocent), my first two examples—a drawing by M. C. Escher and a comic strip by Régis Franc—are both paradoxical. In Escher, in fact, one finds at once an extremely prudent spatial separation of the two types of signs and an aggressive repetition on the level of content. With Franc, on the other hand, content is not at all restated, and the weaving together of word and design suggests splitting rather than association. In each case, my analysis will attempt to expose the layering of conflicts and, especially, the reciprocal resistance of the types of signs involved. My third and final example, a book cover by Martin Vaughn-James, provides an occasion to track down, within an apparently unified space, previously muted zones and modes of tension.

THE PEDALTERNOROTANDOMOVENS CENTROLCULATUS ARTICULOSUS OR PRODUCTIVE REDUNDANCY

As I have already pointed out, critics not only reject the redundancy of connections between the iconic and the verbal, but they also warn against the submission of one system (usually that of the image, which is considered weaker or more fragile) to the other (that of words). Thus, as they approach their object, studies of the encounter between the two modes of representation are regularly accompanied by a caveat against the privileges, or even the imperialism, of discourse, which is perhaps a bit hastily believed to be in a position to stifle the intrinsic polysemy of the iconic code.

This suspicion of discourse, in the realm of the comic strip for example, needs to be critically interrogated. It is in fact possible to see in such mistrust the effect, not of a theoretical reflection on the status of and relationship between writing and image, but of an excessive amount of attention granted to the current production of the genre, which freely parades the redundancy of codes and the submission of the visible to its accompanying discourse. At a time when the most stimulating contemporary efforts either abandon altogether or enfran-

De Pedalternorotandomovens centroculatus articulosus ontstond, (generatio spontanea!) uit onbevredigdheid over het in de natuur ontbreken van wielvormige, levende schepselen met het vermogen zich rollend voort te bewegen. Het hierbij afgebeelde diertje, in de volksmond genaamd "wentelteefje" of "rolpens", tracht dus in een diepgevoelde behoefte te voorzien. Biologische bijzonderheden zijn nog schaars: is het een zoogdier, een reptiel, of een insekt? Het heeft een langgerekt, uit verhoornde geledingen gevormd lichaam en drie paren poten, waarvan de uiteinden gelijkenis vertonen met de menselijke voet. In het midden van de dikke, ronde kop, die voorzien is van een sterk gebogen papagaaiensnavel, bevinden zich de bolvormige ogen, die, op stelen geplaatst, ter weerszijden van de kop ver uitsteken. In gestrekte positie kan het dier zich, traag en bedachtzaam, door middel van zijn zes poten, voort bewegen over een willekeurig substraat (het kan eventueel steile trappen opklimmen of afdalen, door struikgewas heendringen of over rotsblokken klauteren). Zodra het echter een lange weg moet afleggen en daartoe een betrekkelijk vlakke baan tot zijn beschikking heeft, drukt het zijn kop op de grond en rolt zich bliksemsnel op, waarbij het zich afduwt met zijn poten voor zoveel deze dan nog de grond raken. In opgerolde toestand vertoont het de gedaante van een discus-schijf, waarvan de centrale as gevormd wordt door de ogen-op-stelen. Door zich beurtelings af te zetten met één van zijn drie paren poten, kan het een grote snelheid bereiken. Ook trekt het naar believen tijdens het rollen (b.v. bij het afdalen van een helling, of om zijn vaart uit te lopen) de poten in en gaat "freewheelende" verder. Wanneer het er aanleiding toe heeft, kan het op twee wijzen weer in wandel-positie overgaan: ten eerste abrupt, door zijn lichaam plotseling te strekken, maar dan ligt het op zijn rug, met zijn poten in de lucht en ten tweede door geleidelijke snelheidsvermindering (remming met de poten) en langzame achterwaartse ontrolling in stilstaande toestand.

XI-'51

1. M. C. Escher, *le Roulenboule*.

chise verbal narrative,[8] as in the work of Patrice Hamel and José Calvelo, or bring the materiality of scriptural signifiers into line with the density [*épaisseur*] of icons, as Guy Lelong does,[9] it hardly seems illogical to propose that, more than anything else, the condemnation of pleonastic connections between script and image, as well as the mistrust of discourse's supposed ascendancy, reflect (and reflect nothing but) the genre's recent commercial developments.

Although relative in practice and ontologically open to criticism, the two codes' alterity is in fact a guarantee of the possibility they offer of generating analogous meanings [*significations*] without, however, this union being doomed to mere tautology. An engraving by M. C. Escher called *Le Roulenboule** (affiliated to the universe of the comic strip in that it could be perfectly transposed into its register), an engaging pastiche of encyclopedia articles, will allow me to sketch out a few details of one such nonredundant convergence.

In this work, which is moreover rather marginal in the artist's *oeuvre*, as much for its emphasis on words as for the apparent absence of the paradoxical architectures that have established Escher's reputation, modern stereotypes about redundancy are, at least at an initial level, violently taken to task (see Fig. 1). On the one hand, the image initially presents itself as a simple illustration of the commentary surrounding it. On the other, departure from the spatial code of the image and the temporal code of writing is neither rejected nor celebrated here. On the contrary, Escher attempts to effect a generalized exchange of their specific features, not through the iconization of writing or the verbalization of the image, but rather by way of their confrontation within a bifurcated structure that is capable of transcending their intrinsic differences. Here is a translation of that commentary:

> The pedalternorotandomovens centroculatus articulosus was born (generatio spontanea!) from the dissatisfaction produced by the absence, in nature, of living creatures who are wheel-shaped, endowed with the capacity for movement by rolling. Commonly called "roll-in-a-ball" or "stuffed belly," the little creature

---

*The imaginary animal giving this work its title will henceforth be referred to in the text as "the roll-in-a-ball."—Translator's note.

8. See especially *Contrebande*, an arrangement of sixteen plates inserted in the leading article of *Conséquences* 13–14 (1990).

9. See "Un plan tramé," in *Conséquences* 9 (1986): 5–16. This work, closer to *Un coup de dés* than the conventional comic strip, is followed by the author's commentary, "La Place de la réflexion," ibid., 17–27.

reproduced here is thus striving to respond to a deeply felt need. Its biological features are not yet well-known: is it a mammal, a reptile, or an insect? The animal has a drawn-out body composed of hardened segments, and three pairs of paws whose extremities slightly resemble human feet. In the middle of its head, fat and round and equipped with a curved parrot's beak, are spherical eyes which, placed at the top of a stem, widely overhang the head on both sides. When its body is tense, the animal, slowly and warily, is able to move along, using its six paws, on any given substratum (thus it can go up or down steep flights of stairs, move through undergrowth, or climb up rocks). When it has to undertake a long journey /// /// and finds a relatively even path at its disposal, it presses its head against the ground and quickly rolls itself up into a ball, while it propels itself along with the help of its paws, insofar as they are still in contact with the ground. When its body is rolled up, it looks like a disk whose central axis is constituted by the eyes perched on stems. Pushing itself forward alternately with one of its three pairs of paws, it is able to attain a very high speed. When rolling, it can draw in its paws at will (to go downhill, for example, or simply to forge ahead) and thus continue, coasting. When obliged to readopt a walking position, it can do so in two ways: either abruptly, by suddenly bracing its body, in which case it finds itself lying supine, paws in the air; or else by a gradual deceleration (it brakes with its feet), and by slowly unrolling itself backwards in an immobile position.

Although every rectangle, as we normally conceive of it in space, is necessarily positioned in a certain way, the relationships between top and bottom, between left and right, are distributed differently depending on whether the surface is invested with an image or with a text. In the first case, the support or ground may, as a rule, be scanned in every direction. But in the second, the interpretive process is often unidirectional: the eye follows the signs from left to right and from top to bottom. In Escher's engraving, however, the arrangement of the handwritten characters, because of the geometrical properties of the zones in which they are situated, immediately privileges the diagonal. And the image ceases to be a visual whole that is turned in on itself; it is distributed along an oblique line, thus becoming narration. Both script and image therefore take an initial step toward each other: the image becomes linear; the script is transformed into space.

The gaze, growing more attentive, easily discovers that the image's metamorphosis into script, and hence into an emblem of the scriptural code, is not limited to the passage from the animal's representation to that of the course it follows. No less revealing in this respect is the morphology of the *pedalternorotandomovens centroculatos articulosus*, a kind of millipede whose identical segments strikingly recall the division of a written chain into grammatical units. Similarly, and necessarily because of context, the shift from the roll-in-a-ball's horizontal position to its circular state evokes, relatively speaking, the way in which sentences end with periods.

Even more spectacular is the range of measures taken to emphasize the iconic properties of the duplicated text. The addition of an orientating element, in this case the diagonal, to the direction reading usually takes, is indeed hardly sufficient, if only because of its proximity to the itinerary of a cursory reading, to buttress the analogy between script and image. In order to achieve this correspondence, Escher has recourse to at least five different techniques.

To begin with, the vocabulary of the inscription, which at the outset features long neologisms in Latin, deliberately precludes immediate comprehension, imposing a rather careful spelling-out of the letters. Such scrutiny makes it possible to see affinities between the roll-in-a-ball's shell and its scientific denomination, which is also divided into segments. The text's relative overpunctuation, with its countless hyphens, dashes, and parentheses, points in a similar direction.

In the second place, Escher also manipulates interlineation, the drastic reduction of which has the effect of visually crushing the line's division into words. What results is a complication of the reading process,[10] which consequently supplements the figure of the triangles.

Thirdly, the lettered blocks are inscribed according to the same laws of perspective to which the figure of the roll-in-a-ball adheres. If the white band in the middle is able to grow wider toward the bottom of the page and actualize its lines of flight in the image, it's because the hypothenuses of the grammatical blocks progressively separate as the roll-in-a-ball follows its course. Not unlike the little animal, the text surrounding it is thus shown and focused on from a certain point of view and becomes the transposition of an already existing discourse, as if the artist had had in front of him an open book upon which the roll-

10. The same sort of complication led Hergé, during the elaboration of his album *Le Temple du soleil* (1948), to revise his lettering system, changing from capital to lower case letters. See Benoît Peeters's preface to the new edition of the album's original version (Paris and Tournai: Editions Casterman, 1989).

in-a-ball was shifting and developing. The suture of the text and the image becomes even more striking if one considers the unequal irregularity of the two oblique sides. Rather than playing with the typographical model of feathered composition, their jagged edges hug the contours of the imaginary animal. It is therefore normal that they should be less smooth on the right side than on the left.

The script's mutation into design also appears, and this is my fourth point, in its participation in the engraving's title. For "roll-in-a-ball," without being an inexact translation of the Dutch *wentelteefje*, nevertheless constitutes a highly truncated version of it. The literal sense of the term, lost in translation, in fact designates a sort of French toast, which must be turned over in the pan and cooked on both sides, a bit in the way the scriptural triangle turns over on the page.[11]

A final procedure, facilitated by the overall spatialization of the discourse, consists in the ordered investment of its strategic sites (essentially the points where the script starts up and fades out). The symmetrically inverse inlaying of the perigraphic apparatus, with the artist's logo to the right of the roll-in-a-ball's caudal appendix and the printer's imprint to the left of the animal's final mutation, also functions as a powerful instigator for the extraction of the topologically determined zones constituted by the script's opposite angles. A comparison of the words and letters situated at the tips of the triangles, makes it immediately apparent that in the spots where the commentary breaks off and then continues, the same series of graphemes, "EN," is encountered. "EN," which is the Dutch equivalent of the coordinating conjunction "and," conveys the idea of union and reconciliation. The text is moreover very rich in a self-reflexive way, since at the end of the first block one reads: "When [the roll-in-a-ball] has to undertake a long journey," and then discovers, having gone back up to the top of the page: "and finds a relatively even path at its disposal. . . ." Furthermore, because of the reiteration of the letter *D*, beginning and end converge, which signifies that after having located its internal division, the flow of the interminable script, exceeds its linearity.

It obviously won't do to explain the close enmeshment of linguistic and iconic codes in detail. But what is at stake in such an involvement, and what reinforces it, needs to be defined.

11. Certain other characteristics of the word *wentelteefje* will not be discussed here because they are irrelevant to my analysis. One example would be the fact that the seme *teefje* signifies "little bitch" [petite chienne].

At the root of the two systems' convergence could lie their subsumption by a third code: lithography (if verbal signs and visual units are *produced* in the same way, their formal differences can lose their distinctness). Moreover, the engraving's very subject (the animal passing over a printed surface) can be read as a *mise-en-abyme* of the process of creation: the fantastic animal is similar to the ink roller whose pressure assures the transmission of the material onto paper.

At the same time, it must be recognized that the fusion of codes is anything but complete. The script is not radically converted into design, nor the design into script. Even in the case of Escher's script, which can be taken up again infinitely, the words continue to be read linearly when, for example, the commentary informs us that the image also allows for a retrograde movement (to resume its initial position, the roll-in-a-ball must move backwards, lest it wind up on its back). Concurrently, we learn that, unlike the image, the verbal discourse cannot roll itself up without becoming unreadable. Observing such discrepancies, however, is not in the least incompatible with the possibility of a partial overlapping of codes. Every material object is in fact composed of two inextricably linked dimensions: the *object* dimension, which concerns the internal constitution of the object's formal aspects; and the *interpretive* dimension, which involves the reception of such parameters. Now the fact that script and image are produced in an identical way does not by any means suggest that their reception or decoding follows equally identical paths. It is therefore logical that Escher installs a muted tension between the two. This ubiquitous discord finds in the drastic spatial separation of the two codes its most flagrant symptom. Beyond this segregation, one's attention is especially drawn to a series of paradoxes arising from an association with the two regimes.

On the one hand, even if the script visually resembles the traces left by the tracked vehicle embodied by the roll-in-a-ball, it is no less true that this mark is *displaced*, since it only appears on either side of the path followed by the little animal. The relationship between script and image thus presents itself as an impossible articulation. Even though the script is modelled on the image, it can only emerge in the places from which the image is excluded. The trace's spatial displacement, invisible beneath the roll-in-a-ball's feet, thus becomes a metaphor for the modification of the code that simultaneouly occurs. In other words: banished, the trace is transformed and the iconic order is abandoned for the order of discourse.

On the other hand, because of the blank strip dividing the written zones, the image almost automatically discloses its resemblance to an eraser, that is, to an anti-image or a nonimage. Nevertheless this impression is false: since the trail in question is already empty (the groove separating the two scriptural blocks could be at issue), the censoring activity is thoroughly transformed. It empties itself, so to speak, of its substance, since the roll-in-a-ball conceals nothing as it moves along except itself, one part of which, continually growing, is hidden from view. Forced to withdraw, for fear of censorship, from the operational field of the image, the script therefore upsets the internal functioning of the visual code, which simultaneously reveals itself to be at once origin and result of its own screenlike function.

Through the patient exploration of these maneuvers, Escher teaches us that the most overwhelming redundancies can foment, to the delight of the partisans of specificity, the most ruthless "*differends.*"*

HONG KONG, TERRE DE CONTRASTES OR THE INTEGRATION OF DIVISION

Although the early comic strips of Régis Franc bring an analogous problematic into play, they do so from a completely different angle. Far from playing up the false redundancy of two compartmentalized registers, the narratives in question aggravate the discrepancy between the scriptural and graphic codes, while aggressively superimposing them one on the other so as to create interpretive disruptions. What gets lost in such an accomplishment is the quantitative and qualitative balance of design and language. In *Nouvelles histoires*,[12] for example, the script is often overdeveloped, whereas the image is relatively impoverished (occasionally, the dialogues and commentaries are all that seem to change from one vignette to the next). Furthermore, the peculiarities of the lettering consistently hinder readability, while the confusion and stacking-up of countless balloons set up serious obstacles to the reconstruction of word chains. Finally, the rift between the immobility of

---

*The word "differend" is a simple Anglicization of the French *différend*, which I have chosen not to translate here both in deference to Jean-François Lyotard, thanks to whom the term has gained currency in contemporary critical thought, and because of the range of meanings it encompasses. A *différend* can be an argument, a difference of opinion, or a state of open conflict. It indicates both a slight difference or nuance (of opinion), and a radical opposition.—Translator's note.

12. *Nouvelles histoires* (Paris: Dargaud, 1979).

the images and the proliferation of the texts is hardly favorable to the elaboration of a shuttle movement between text and image: reading tends to concentrate on the problems of interpretation posed by the script alone.

A more detailed examination, however, fails to confirm these impressions. Rather, it illuminates numerous ways of fusing, at perhaps less obvious levels, words and visual fragments that seem incompatible at first glance. In order to illustrate this new role played by script and image, I would like to reconsider, from an angle rarely explored previously, Franc's most famous story: *Hong Kong, Terre de contrastes).* [13]

As in the majority of the stories that make up *Nouvelles histoires,* the narration of *Hong Kong* consists above all in the interweaving of several plots which seem independent upon a cursory reading. At the top of each vignette, whose characters and decor remain constant, a scheming broker manages to rent a dilapidated villa to a couple of naïve tourists. In the middle of the squares, but at the back of the image, two characters in Chinese dress run up and down a staircase. They blithely indulge in all sorts of gossip about the sexual rivalry between two revolutionary leaders. At the bottom of the vignettes, in the foreground, a gangster calls out to one of his subordinates. But the death threats he issues remain fruitless, provoking hilarity: the mafioso doesn't realize that he has "parrot shit" in his hair. Only the reader who manages to connect the three stories, on the one hand, and the links between the texts and images, on the other, will be able to discern the rigorous composition of the whole (see Fig. 2).

An initial key is provided by the title, which in fact combines sameness and otherness, analogy and paronomasis ("Hong Kong"), and the dissimilarity indicated by the attribute ("land of contrasts"). From the very beginning of the narrative, the title invites the reader to become attentive to the play of variants, and to mistrust apparent redundancies.

The first vignette contains, toward the middle, two balloons and the beginning of a dialogue: "... Bien sûr, à partir de ce moment-là, il est devenu insupportable! ... / ... Ah bon! ... " [... Of course, from that moment on, he became intolerable! ... / ... You don't say! ...]. But only one of the interlocutors, far off, minuscule, appears

13. For an interesting reading of the other major aspects of this work, see Benoît Peeters's *Case, planche, récit* (Paris and Tournai: Casterman, 1991), 50–52.

2. Régis Franc, *Hong Kong, Terre des contrastes,* three plates.

234

in the image. The second speaker is completely hidden by the first. An identical duplicity surfaces on the level of the spelling, with the belated addition of a *p* to the word "insup*p*ortable." This "correction," which a simple rewriting could have erased is echoed by the curious segmentation of the words, some of which are scarcely detached from others, even though there is certainly ample room for them in the balloons. Such idiosyncrasies, which tend *potentially to duplicate* each of the units featured in the story, urge the reader to scrutinize the manipulation of language carefully.

The second vignette does much in the way of elucidating this functioning. In the first place, one finds the rest of the dialogue: " . . . Oui, moi, par exemple, j'étais de tendance Chou, . . . **il** ne me l'a pas pardonné . . . / . . . Pensez! . . . " . . . Yeah, for instance, I was leaning toward Chou. . . . he never forgave me. . . . / . . . Imagine! . . . "]. Next, at the bottom of the vignette in the foreground a new exchange gets under way: "Alors Chang tu **les** as? . . . " [. . . So Chang, you have them? . . .]. (Throughout this banter, the character named Chang remains outside of the visual field.) If one now looks closely at the articulation of these fragments, which seem insignificant at first glance, one detects the narrative's principal strong points. One way of connecting the two dialogues—two zones that are as a rule separated from the square—consists in setting off, using bold type, data whose functions are comparable. In this case, the letters are boldest when they are displaying pronouns or, more precisely, since everything proliferates here, the false censor of names—implicit but capable of being reconstructed—to which they are cataphorically related: "il" [he] is, probably, Mao Tse-tung (for the *long march,* on the steps [*marches*] of an interminable staircase, is what the characters in the background are discussing); "les" [them] is, doubtlessly, a heap of green bills (for it is indeed in dollars that the negotiation at the top of the page is carried out, and it is the absence of this money that perhaps signifies the invisible Chang's death sentence.

The other plates thematically develop this first wave of analogies between the various zones of the square: each of the three superimposed fictions thematizes the revenge of the meek on the strong. In the center of the page, the rivalry between Chou and Mao quickly takes an erotic turn: rumor has it that the former was the lover of the latter's wife. On the bottom of the page, the gangster's threats elicit only Chang's mirth: he has seen the parrot's *caca* [shit] fall on the garrulous villain's head. Lastly, at the top of this plate, the shifty broker who rents a ramshackle villa to the naïve pair of lovers has been cunning enough to exploit, in his clients, the "weakness" of the supposedly "strong" sex, vulnerable to the caresses of the "weak" sex.

Alongside these thematic convergences, far subtler but wider-ranging relationships emerge. Thus the opposition of pronouns and proper names ("il" and "Chou," for example) makes it easier to understand the arrival of a culinary interlude and the sexual connotations that promptly pervade it. If it is true that the term "il" ends up changing into another, namely "Mao," it is not so difficult to imagine the same thing happening with the name "Chou," which in French signifies a well-known vegetable (cabbage).[14] If one is also willing to hear in the repetition of the adjective "insupportable" [intolerable] a supplementary allusion to "table," one will have no trouble grasping why the mention of Chou is attached to an incident of culinary etiquette: " . . . je me souviens de ce jour à table, . . . il y avait des beignets de crevettes, c'est gluant, difficile à attraper avec des baguettes . . . /Ça, c'est vrai / Eh bien, Chou les mangeait avec une élégance naturelle qui **lui** était insupportable, **lui** n'arrivait pas à les attraper . . . /Et alors?/Eh bien **il** a demandé un couteau et une fourchette comme les occidentaux!!! . . . . " [. . . I remember that day at table, . . . there were shrimp rolls, they're sticky, hard to pick up with chopsticks . . . / . . . Yes, that's true . . . / . . . Well, Chou ate them with a natural elegance that was intolerable to **him,** he couldn't pick them up . . . / . . . So? . . . / . . . So **he** asked for a knife and fork, like a westerner!!! . . . /!!! . . .]. At the bottom of the page, the pronominal structures are brought into play a second time with the uninterrupted ternary repetition of the syntagm "les avoir": "Alors Chang tu **les** as? . . . /Non Eddie je **les** ai pas! . . . /Tu **les** as pas! . . . " [So Chang, you have **them?** . . . /No Eddie I don't have them! . . . You don't have **them!** . . .] The insistence on this expression is so straightforward, the detachment of the pronoun "les" is so strong, that only a slightly different expression comes inexorably to mind: **en avoir*** (and Chou "en a"). It now becomes clear that the handling of chopsticks (*baguettes*) is hardly innocent, and that the technique of suppressing or adding a letter (compare the additional grapheme encountered in "insup*P*ortable" or, inversely, the broker's

---

*"En avoir" is a vulgar expression roughly signifying "to have guts."—Translator's note.

14. Suspicious readers are strongly advised to go back to the isolated balloon on the book's cover, which comprises a symmetrically inverse maneuver (one must go through the common noun in order to find the proper name): "Marcel, encore une *madeleine!*"

faulty pronunciation, which causes him to say "ma'ame" when he is trying to fool his client, coaxing her with a pastry) manages to work the word *braguette*† into the word *baguette,* and then insinuates, into the circulation of forks, knives, and other *b(r)aguettes,* desire or the anxiety of castration.

Hong Kong is teeming with these sorts of microscopic operations. Just after the mention of the word "beignets" [fritters], the crafty broker points out an extraordinary "baie" [picture window] to the two tourists, whom the reader cannot help but name, even though the word does not physically appear on the page, as *bénêts* (dolts). Similarly, it is only after the introduction of the theme of *death* that the visitors to the exotic pavillion enter the "living" [living room], and that the crowning of the narrative of adultery by the word "cocu" [cuckold] introduces the motif of *caca.*

But Franc takes things even further. Thus he diverts the rhetoric of his lettering in order to present a veritable reading lesson. The sugary exclamation: "Oh! Diiiiiiiick! ! ! ! ! ! ! ! " and the variants coating the words uttered by his "chérie" become a literal mirror, through the inversion of the small *i*s and the dense exclamation points, of the shuttle movement between the base and the apex of the plates and of the vignettes whose stories join forces at every level. Thus the letters, but also the punctuation, say as much about the architecture of the page as the characters who climb up the staircase they have just come down—a fitting emblem of the multidirectional reading that the contemporary comic strip demands.

LA CAGE OR TREMBLING PRECISION

The cover of Martin Vaughn-James's book *La Cage,* one of the most renowned avant-garde comic strips,[15] seems to confront readers with a classic, indeed academic, solution that may seem surprising in the work of this artist (see Fig. 3). What could be more conventional, one might ask, than the assembly, in this particular place and form, of a title, an illustration, an author's name, and the publisher's logo? And what could be more traditional, one might add, than the studied con-

---

†The French *braguette* indicates the fly on a pair of trousers as well as, metonymically, what lies beneath it.—Translator's note.

15. For the purposes of this article, I will be referring to the French version of Vaughn-James's book (Paris: Les Impressions Nouvelles, 1986). The first edition, published in Toronto by the Coach House Press in 1975, is currently out of print.

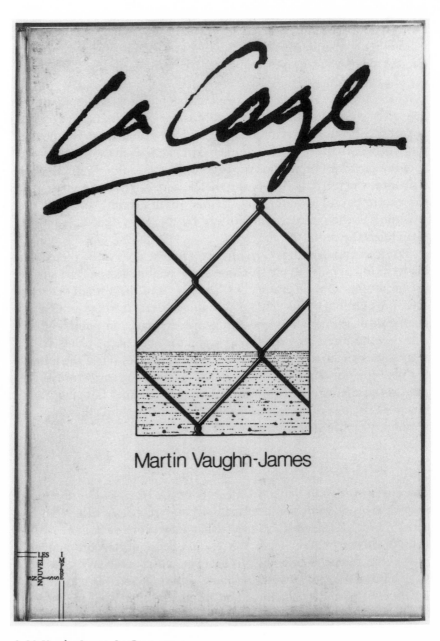

3. M. Vaughn-James, *La Cage*, cover.

238

trast between a rigorously designed image and a script that is relatively free of constraints, which the seemingly "spontaneous" writing of the title neatly illustrates? But in fact, this calm montage of the volume's first page betrays vivid tensions that require careful scrutiny.

There is no longer any cause, here, either for *opposing* text and image, or for contrasting *particular* texts and images, since the two codes at once reveal their underlying analogies and manifest an irreducible plurality.

I would like, first of all, to bring the relationships of homology to light. Each of the three linguistic data is in fact modelled, from the bottom up, on a particular aspect of an image that is obviously a reduced, and therefore privileged, model of the page as a whole. The prolonged downstroke of the *g* in the title almost perfectly continues the meshwork traced by the artist. The typographic justification of the author's name coincides with the width of the image. And like the illustration in the middle of the page, the *Impressions Nouvelles* logo in the lower left-hand corner combines the interwoven geometric motifs of the square and rectangle. The image, for its part, strongly emphasizes those properties which are also common to writing: the *segmented line* (the curiously horizontal arrangement of the rows of rocks and of various sand formations evokes a chain of words, letters, blanks, and punctuation marks as much as it evokes some fictional desert; the immaculate whiteness of the sky perfectly merges with the whiteness of the ground that the image is supposed to cover up) and the *reticulated* line (the display of the net's interweaving is a plausible metaphor for the transformation of a single line into text, that is, into an articulated network).

The shuttle movements between an extremely "written" image and a very "visual" text do not exhaust, however, the relationships for which this page sets the stage. Just as important as this exhange of codes is in fact the heterogeneity of each of them. The textual elements, then, follow systematic changes in the following three domains: the *nature of the script* (the title is handwritten, the author's name is photocomposed with sanserif characters, the units of the logo feature serifs), *size* (decreasing as they move from the apex to the base), and the *positioning on the page* (aligning itself to the left and to the right in the cover's margins, the title is completely justified relative to the page; the author's name is left- and right-justified, but relative to the main design; and the logo is left-justified).

The logo's displacement, which violently offsets the dextroascen-

```
        LES    I
         L     M
         E     P
         V     R
         U     E
     S N O - S S I O N S
         N
```

4. M. Vaughn-James, *La Cage,* logo of the publisher, Les Impressions Nouvelles.

sional dynamics of the line underscoring the title, in fact throws off balance, through the leftward extension of the two lines continuing the letters, the cover as a whole, which opens onto the *back* of the book. Readers of *La Cage,* instead of being invited to turn the page to begin the reading of the work proper, are forced to *turn the volume* in order to examine the paratextual diptych formed by the cover's front and back sides. This far from benign gesture disturbs the normal orientation of reading. Proceeding not from left to right (from the cover to the interior of the volume), but from right to left (from the cover to the back of the book), the reading process performs a double *dépassement.* On the one hand it subverts linear conceptions of writing, privileging the translinear model provided by the logo,[16] which can be read in every direction first from left to right, then from top to bottom, and finally from the top to the bottom (see Fig. 4). On the other hand, it no less destabilizes the dominant role previously accorded to the illustration, which benefited as much from its central position as from its homological relationship to the surface of the page. The privileged link between the rectangle encompassing the page and the rectangle encompassed by the design in the middle disappears as soon as the joining of the cover's front and back causes a new structure to emerge, whose logo, with its hollows and excesses, is much closer than the illustration imprisoned within its frame.

The substitution of translinear logic for simple linearity not only affects the image, stripped of its preeminence, but also assails writing, even in its most spectacular occurrence: the title. Unusually positioned here, the handwriting used to form *La Cage* in fact irresistibly recalls the author's signature, which normally appears in a completely different place: at the end of a text, in a double gesture of appropriation and closure. In this case, the work's *abutment* finds itself transferred to an antithetical position. It is as if, at the origin of the work, the very

16. The logo was designed by Patrice Hamel. For more details about this innovative artist, see my "Une Revue à mesure: *Conséquences*" in *Communication et langages* 85 (1990): 72–82, and "Une réédition peu banale: *La Bibliothèque de Villiers,*" in *Communication et langages* 89 (1991): 73–82.

distinction of origin and end were emptied of pertinence, making way for the infinite circuits embodied first by the logo, and then by the adventures of the book itself.

An exploration of its own properties (manifested here though the ordered occupation of the front and back covers), *La Cage* ultimately reveals its affinities with the most recent trends in *in situ* artistic productions, where a given work evolves through its contact with the medium and place accommodating it, which it in turn transforms by way of this very dialogue.[17]

—Translated by Caren Litherland

17. On the various practices of *in situ* art, see Guy Lelong's essay *Des Relations édifiantes* (Paris: Les Impressions Nouvelles, 1992).

RENÉE RIESE HUBERT

Derrida, Dupin, Adami: "Il faut être plusieurs pour écrire"[1]

"LE TRAIT, LA LIGNE"

These two words are frequently used by Jacques Derrida in texts which, more often than not, translate or adapt intertexts—allusions as well as quotations without quotation marks. The texts consist of lines, sounds, words which are borrowed or appropriated, transformed, multiplied or fragmented. Since "Le trait, la ligne" simultaneously refer to the acts of drawing and of writing, their implications remain both verbal and visual. *La Vérité en peinture* comprises a variety of texts, notably "+ R+," which oppose conventional and programmatic criticism and make frequent use of polysemic language. Naturally, the philosopher deliberately refrains from providing a straightforward argument concerning the confrontation or collusion of writing and drawing. His strategies amount nonetheless to the deliberate transgressions of borderlines, margins, and frames. If we were to choose the obvious example of Antonin Artaud—on whose career as man of the theater Derrida wrote two chapters, ("La Parole soufflée" and "Le Théâtre de la cruauté," in *L'Ecriture et la différence*) and to whose drawings he has recently devoted, in collaboration with Paule Thévenin, a lengthy essay—it would be erroneous to claim that he separates the draftsman from the writer, all the more so because he quite frequently returns to his previous texts and their problematics while pursuing a

---

1. Jacques Derrida, "+ R (par dessus le marché)," *Derrière le Miroir*, no. 214, May 1978, reprinted in *La Vérité en peinture*, (Paris: Flammarion, 1979), 175. "One must be several in order to write," *The Truth in Painting*, trans. Geoff Bennington and Ian McLeod (Chicago: Chicago University Press, 1987), 152.

YFS 84, *Boundaries: Writing & Drawing*, ed. M. Reid, © 1994 by Yale University.

new line of thought.[2] In "+R+," Derrida looks at Valerio Adami, a painter who, like Artaud the writer, comes close to displaying a double talent, for instance when he mercilessly entraps his reader/viewer in a delightful double bind. Adami "portrays" many writers, notably Walter Benjamin, August Strindberg, and Sigmund Freud, while introducing into his canvasses and drawings words, titles, and signatures that need to be deciphered. Since Derrida focuses on a painter who transgresses the boundaries of two languages or two arts, he makes use of their dual inscription as a springboard for his own sometimes parallel inquiries. He thus continues the experimentation of his own *Glas* and *Marges de la philosophie* in substituting for the standard format of the page spatial columns, cylinders, bifurcations, and other means of subdivision.[3] These writings consistently overdetermine concepts of framing. By thus interrelating and interweaving drawing and writing, Derrida adapts in his own way a not uncommon practice among twentieth-century artists, including, of course, book designers. In fact, some artists often rely on an invented form of writing in such a way that their figures, representational or not, lose their autonomy, imbedded as they are in an illegible text. In many instances, however, the letters are assembled into constellations capable of enhancing rather than eliminating the figurative element.

Cy Twombly's works are exemplary in this regard since they consist essentially of undecipherable scribbles. These handwritten lines which willfully refuse to follow the linear organization of the page would seem to belong to both writing and drawing, perhaps mainly for the purpose of undermining both systems of representation. His gestural art relies on and indeed invokes the movements of an invisible hand, movements that establish unmediated communication with the viewers/readers, provided they consent to bypass recognizable alphabets and abandon conventional mind-sets. Without relying on always already established patterns, Twombly succeeds in producing his own pulsational language which shows affinities with graffiti, that is with anonymously produced signs defying single authorship so as to propose immediate reactions to an event.

2. Derrida, *L'Ecriture et la différence*, (Paris: Seuil, 1967); *Dessins et portraits*, (Paris: Gallimard, 1986).

3. ————, *Glas* (Paris: Galilée, 1974); *Marges de la philosophie*, (Paris: Editions de Minuit, 1972). Claudette Sartiliot's article "Telepathy and Writing in Jacques Derrida's *Glas*," *Paragraph* 12, (1989): 214–28, has been particularly useful to me.

Henry Michaux, a truly major double talent, can provide us with equally telling examples. His imaginary creatures transcend the usual categories of human, animal, and vegetable. His distorted vocal articulations produce a nondiscourse, his gestural lines waver between absence and presence; and his haunting creatures, often reduced to a single line, evolve outside space while defying the laws of gravity. His visual and verbal subversions undercut the sequential unfolding of material or, for that matter, immaterial events. Moving further and further away from mimesis, representation, and narration, Henry Michaux's languages, seemingly stemming from the same body, finally merge or at least collapse. No less than Twombly's, Michaux's audience is asked to perceive, read, decipher lines—"le trait, la ligne"—pertaining neither to a familiar alphabet nor to a recognizable outline and defying the principles of repetition and analysis. The bifold discourse thus generated by Twombly's and Michaux's graphic practice can also be derived from the confrontation between Jacques Dupin and Valerio Adami, as well as from Jacques Derrida's dialogue with the painter.

Adami's art, which maintains close ties with the verbal, has elicited searching commentaries from several prominent critics, poets, and philosophers. The Pompidou catalogue includes texts by Hubert Damisch, Jacques Derrida, Jacques Dupin, and Jean-Francois Lyotard.[4] The painter, an Italian by birth, lives in Paris where he can engage in frequent discussions with them. Rather than scrutinize the various types of criticism that Adami has generated, whether philosophical, psychoanalytic, deconstructive, or sociopolitical, I prefer to focus on the reciprocal relationships that have somehow bridged the gap between writing and drawing not only in Adami's œuvre, but in the writings of Dupin and Derrida.[5] We owe much of the interchange among them to the Galerie Maeght, which not only organizes exhibits accompanied by exhaustive catalogues, but publishes *livres de peintre*, including two by Adami, and, in *Derrière le miroir*, features encounters between graphic artists and poets. Four issues of this illustrated journal have been devoted to Adami so far.

---

4. *Adami* (Paris: Centre Georges Pompidou, 1985). Damisch in collaboration with Henri Martin also published a study entitled *Adami* (Paris: Maeght, 1974), which includes a lengthy commentary on *Viaggio verso Londra* comparing the writing in this painting to so many flies (12ff).

5. Jacques Dupin, "Valerio Adami," *Derrière le Miroir*, no. 188, Nov. 1970; *L'Espace autrement dit* (Paris: Galilée, 1982).

The Italian artist favors fairly bright but never glaring tones which can hardly be confused with primary or natural colors. His use of color is defined by Derrida as a second thrust, if not an aftermath: "Color is never anticipated in it, it never arrives before the complete halt of the motor *trait*" (172). Drawing would thus function as the primary force, shaping and framing figures by means of black lines. Such painterly devices as brushstrokes never appear on Adami's posterlike surfaces. The engraving entitled *Crisis* displays in exemplary fashion the key characteristics of Adami's art and its commitment to both drawing and writing (Fig. 1). Clearly calligraphic letters stand out, while the signature, far more prominently displayed than a mere sign of recognition would warrant, is apparently inscribed as a potent source of energy. By the impact given to and by each of its five letters, the signature simultaneously asserts continuity and discontinuity. The title of the work of art, also "handwritten," inscribed not so much within the pictorial surface as in a pictorial no-man's-land, participates in the structure instead of functioning as a mere label mediating between artist and viewer. The title and the date, 1927, neither of which occupies a central position, serve as a minimal narrative substitute for an absent text that the viewer, reduced to whatever clues s/he can assemble, feels compelled to piece together and embroider. The written word "Crisis" not only adds to the constellation of lines, but somehow takes the place of the scene that the viewer would normally expect to contemplate. It abstracts or, better still, usurps continuity, discursive dominance, representation. Telescoped writing replaces the pictorial and anecdotal spectacle of conventional art. The visually absent scene is paraphrased by means of a single word whose etymology suggests separation.

Three small red rectangular zones reveal the structural pattern of the engraving consisting of dividing frames and windows, which, like Harold Lloyd's glasses, do not contain or open onto anything. The red zones suggest magnified fingerprints of which one, marked with a black cross, points to the futile identification of another absent event or person, another change of perspective, or still another signature. The fingerprints, perhaps bloodstained, can be linked to a barely recognizable index finger drawn in the same red ink. The finger could belong to the artist, the actor and/or a possible criminal who may have left the prints, one of them marked with a black cross suggestive of murder, but nonetheless far too ambiguous to provide a meaningful clue. It might indeed induce the reader to pursue one red herring after another! Unlike the red zones and lines, the unrelieved green areas provide no more

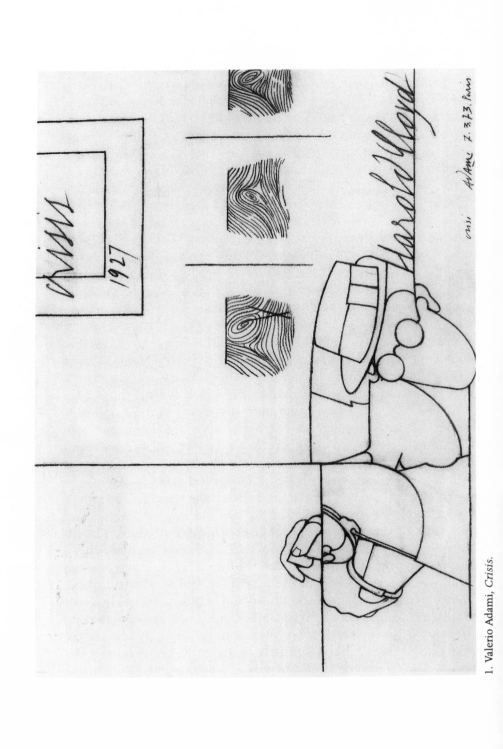

1. Valerio Adami, Crisis.

and no less than a pleated paper surface which neither seduces nor repulses the viewer. A folded page is both double and incomplete, for it also comprises an absent, hidden part. Emotional reactions might deter any scrutinizer less concerned with meaning as such than intent on confronting and perhaps objectively defining what is there. Red ink, possible blood stains, and the suggestion of a police record combine the signifying process with the signified act, purportedly translated. The hand, so often present in Adami, compounds the energy of the actions of writing and drawing. Here, it situates us at the crossroads of identity and anonymity.

In addition to the artist's signature and the title, the name of Harold Lloyd appears in the engraving. Lloyd joins the ranks of portraits good and bad—as Derrida labels them—of artists and politicians who have provided both matter and titles for Adami's art. *Crisis,* for Harold Lloyd, is a suppressed or absent movie recalling the star's reduced mobility and flexibility following an accident that damaged his right hand in 1919. Analogies relating the fingerprints, the hands, and the double portrait of the star, present only in the familiar hat and glasses tantamount to his signature, produces a mise en abyme, a subversion of reality culminating in the facelessness of the actor whose eyes have been obliterated. And these variegated signs, some of which evoke the actor's serious accident, irresistibly converge on writing and drawing. The date, 1927, can be considered critical for the movie industry, for it marked the end of the silent film.

The 1980 "livre de peintre" entitled *Sang,* a poem by Jacques Dupin lithographed by Adami in his inimitable script, provides quite a different type of collusion between alphabetical inscriptions and poetic words (Fig. 2). Harshness and multiple fragmentation predominate in this ascetic and triturated text, close in many respects to Adami's decapitated imagery.[6] Both the painter and the poet seem to shy away from transitions and digressions. Comparable again are the effects of suffocation, lack of movement, lack of an engaging opening. Indeed, lack—the inevitability of doing without some vital necessity—rivals in importance the idea of blood, and for that reason the title may well contain a pun: "sang" and "sans." In most of his long poem Dupin also shares with Adami a preoccupation with anonymity, because speaker, figure, voice, and narratee tend to remain undefined and unnamed. The poet's struggle is marked by suffering, wounds, and of course blood-

6. Dupin, *Sang,* lithographies originales d'Adami, (Paris: Maeght, 1980).

2. Valerio Adami, page from *Sang*.

shed. Any contact is painful. Far from suggesting a warm erotic embrace, the expression "faire corps avec" expresses a painful curtailing of distances. And conversely, blood also provides the pulsation of life overcoming immobility, inertia, and nothingness. This disturbing outpouring from a faceless struggle can have a salutary and almost baptismal effect by providing a writing fluid for the poet and transforming the clotted earth into a palimpsest. The wound, the fundamental contact between the poet and the world, is transmitted to the reader through a multiplicity of gestures, signs, and inscriptions. Instead of dwelling on his usual devices, Adami shows how carefully he has read *Sang*. In his characteristic calligraphy he has lithographed, in mostly red lettering, the poetic text. He thus points out that writing is not merely instrumental, but generates the main thrust of the poem; for it makes visible the poet's links to his wounds which will not heal as long as he pursues his quest, as long as writing fails to lead to self-definition, however limited that may be. Adami's paintings, as I have argued, include words penned in his undisguised handwriting, show a displacement of his signature, or give a name to a faceless persona. By maintaining his own handwriting in *Sang*, Adami only marginally appropriates the poem and thus stresses collaboration. As the metaphor of blood endows the poem with both a corporal and a symbolic dimension the handwritten letters in themselves provide far more than routine textuality: a living body.

Adami has forsaken, however, the regularity he usually bestows on his lines and letters. Their unwanted irregularity suggests that several warring forces may be at play, impelling individual letters to move upward or downward. It is also possible that these letters have a will of their own, or that the surface of the paper has the power to displace them. We can assume in any case that the regularity of a page of poetry, printed or lithographed, has lost some, if not all, of its relevance, and also that it is futile to apply conventional typographical standards. Indeed, the downward swoop of some of the letters never comes to a halt in conformity with prescribed patterns. These unpredictable and unexpected leaps of letters or extensions of lines may of course reverberate poetic pulsations, throbbing from a flow of blood, disturbed in, or deviated from, its organic course in reaction to threats and obstacles. All of this goes to show that in spite of the inexorable linearity of most of his paintings, Adami has left some room for organic movements.

Movies, however, appear to be more in keeping with his approach to art than lie's inexorable pulsations. In "Les Règles du montage," autobiography, esthetics, and cultural critique crossfertilize each other.[7] The title reveals an inherent paradox, which is one of the rhetorical traits he shares with Derrida. In selecting the acrobatic but immobilized Harold Lloyd for an essentially still engraving, Adami uses the cinema to play with the notion of immobility versus motion. The montage, initially a cinematographic technique made famous by Eisenstein, may in spite of its codification apply to Adami's work. The title "Les Règles" seems to belie the fact that Adami always remains open to random solicitations as he works: "I have my rules about professionalism yet I only know how to draw according to chance" (22). Before formulating this paradoxical credo, he had repeatedly alluded to conversations and interviews with Derrida. These and other autobiographical notations recount his progress in relating textually and graphically to *Glas*. Adami's heterogenous text, moving from reductive stylized telegraphic notations about everyday experiences to aphorisms about artistic creation, accompanied by visual quotations in the margins, simultaneously orders and disrupts his as well as our progression. These strategies are not unlike those to which Derrida resorts in his own texts, although the various substrata are more consistently interwoven and directed in the latter's writings.

Adami the painter textualizes himself in "Les Règles du montage" by dint of multiplying quotations. He mentions several of his works, both finished and unfinished, arising from experience and critical thinking as well as from historical principles adhered to or deconstructed. He not only expresses verbally the process that put his hands in motion, but also reproduces earlier drawings, photographs, and paintings (Fig. 3). The visual quotations are more than a still replica, more than memories made present, for Adami develops thoughts which encompass drawing and painting together with the act of writing the present text. He claims that each work of art offers all elements required for interpretation and, like Derrida, that each work of art is open-ended. Adami states that whenever he finishes a painting, he ends with ellipses, thus equating graphic art with an incomplete sentence.

The painter enumerates the multiple stimuli that activate a drawing or painting: miniexperiences, pulsational thrusts, aggressive incidents, personal memories, readings of words and images. We may not know when a work of art begins, and during the process of its produc-

7. "Les Règles du montage," *Derrière le Miroir*, no. 220, Oct., 1976.

En descendant du taxi, à New York, le chauffeur se tourne vers moi et s'écrie :"eh, peintre! Ne te coupe pas l'oreille !"
Le magistrat est venu, il a saisi deux vieux fusils et les photos de mes amis barbus.
Entre Paris et Bruxelles nous parlions du Chili sur des banquettes recouvertes d'azur. / Le vieux retraité attendait la mort, assis dans le jardin.

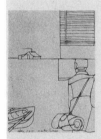

19.12.75.
Au magnétophone je réécoute une conversation avec Carlos Franqui enregistrée à Arona en 1969 ; nous parlions des hôtels, du thème des latrines, des massacres privés...
C'étaient d'autres façons de vivre, un autre système nerveux, je ne sortais qu'avec un appareil photo...
Dîner à la Coupole avec Arakawa, nous parlons de Chirico. Pourquoi je n'aime pas ses derniers tableaux ? A cause de la cuisine. Il n'ébauche que des théories techniques et ses tableaux ne sèchent pas. Je raconte l'histoire du cuirassé américain qui s'est volatilisé dans le port de Naples. Entièrement démonté et escamoté en une nuit pendant l'absence de l'équipage. J'aimerais en tirer un film.
Je termine "Un matin d'hiver". / Un système de signes...

20.12.
En travaillant au "Récit sur Virginia Woolf", j'écoute la seconde bande de la conversation avec Franqui ; contre la guerre au Vietnam, les manifestations de Chicago, le massacre à Mexico, etc.

21.12.
La lecture est le travail du lecteur. / Un tableau donne toutes informations sur lui-même.

3. Valerio Adami, page from *Derrière le miroir.*

tion unaccountable surprises might emerge. Deviations and substitutions frequently recur. Since drawing for him is essentially an activity in which the border between the self and the other is repeatedly infringed, it definitely shows affinities with modern poetry. Indeed, Adami advocates transgressive techniques, practices, and concepts borrowed from both art and literature. He explicitly argues against generic separation, against standard clarifications. It is therefore hardly surprising that the word should reach into his paintings and drawings. The "written" word not only replaces the narrative, but encompasses it within, rather than outside, the frame. His signature, included within the frame, builds an indestructible bridge between the word and the image. Not only does he strive toward, but he even pleads for, the integration of literary discourse within his work: "I would like to use in painting the terms prose and poetry and define my work as prose painting" (8). Adami wishes to emulate the prose poem, the kind of text that defies homogeneity, that unites contrasting elements, and that features verbal experimentation with space and time. He keys into narrativity, no longer definable as a story arising from events, but as a profile unexpectedly traced in the pursuit of form.

"To draw color" (8): the color does not enjoy the same autonomy as drawing. "You use everything in drawing: your own life, the life of others, last night's films seen on television, reflections on water, paradox, popular art, uncertainties, allusions, the nervous system, the left hand" (8). It would seem that Adami refuses to reduce drawing to a mere technique or even to a medium in the visual arts. Although he regrets to a certain extent the order and rigor of the classical tradition, he accepts the necessity of its irretrievable loss in present times. Just like writing, drawing encompasses personal and cultural stimuli, inner and outer impulses, abstract and concrete figments, above all paradoxes and reversals which circumvent repetition. Adami presents a text about progressive conceptualization, rather than a discussion of works reproduced in the text. In spite of the bridges he builds he never completely obliterates the borders: "Drawing, imitation of the object. Writing, imitation of the spoken word" (23). He insists on the analogy of the process, while arguing elsewhere that such imitation has little to do with mirrors and mimesis.

"Les Règles du montage" introduces undercut and subverted narratives. An orderly time sequence heads toward entanglement. Adami's telegraphic style, his drastic reductions, his repeated dispersions make us lose the thread of his thwarted attempts at *affabulation*. The painter who draws with an eraser, who abolishes words and lines, attracts our attention to absence and negation. As in Mallarmé's poetry, his negations are potently evocative. When a contemporary writer such as René Char or a draftsman such as Joseph Sima deliberately refrains from providing a full-fledged narration, s/he often entices the readers to plug the holes by enmeshing the most suitable corollaries and intertexts. When Adami as visual artist translates the problematics of his production into verbal fragments, he simultaneously transposes into linear shapes the works of the writer he portrays, for instance Freud and Benjamin. But the essence of their works can hardly accede to representability in Adami's paintings. Freud is on his way to London to die; Benjamin crosses still another frontier only to commit suicide. Adami's reductive system of lines, his sectionalizations, which eclipse content, narative, and depth, entrap in, and reduce these thinkers' lifelong meditations to a single, philosophically negligible, incident. They are on their way and caught on the move, so to speak, at an insuperable remove from the ineffable graphic pattern that might encapsulate their writings—in both senses of the term. In *Freud's Voyage to London*, illegible scribbles point perhaps to the writing process at some subconscious stage. As a text, it provides an imaginary semiotic or symbolic stage, before writing and drawing had become differentiated. Harold Lloyd, Sigmund Freud, Walter Benjamin, and many other famous people remain absent. Their eyeless glasses point to a "dehumanization," as Derrida calls it in (par-dessus le marché). Portraiture and identity become paradoxical. Lines are added and subtracted but never to be arrested in accordance with a conventional mode. Adami strives toward a commitment, an "art poétique," a conceptualization constantly weighted against, and at odds with, gestural equivalents of the movement of the hand.

By insisting on montage in his title, Adami not only reasserts his allegiance to film, but he situates his text in relation to his own *Potemkin* and *Crisis*. A movie is motion, and Adami often refers to voyages, even to the extent of entitling the exhibit discussed here "Le Voyage du dessin," a show chronicled by Derrida. In many of Adami's works, motion becomes at once a still, a simultaneity, and a sort of "happening," thanks to the device of "folding" pages and subdividing sections. "Montage" suggests not only film but "photomontage," an assemblage of photographic fragments similar to the collage techniques that characterize much of his graphic work and play so prominent a part in Derrida's *Glas*. A comparison that Adami makes between his art on the one hand, the close-up and the unfocused on the other, may help us define the place of the irrational while acounting for the impossibility of centralization and even pointing to the (en)closure of the "systems" he attempts to define.

Since the title "Les Règles du montage" is in the artist's handwriting, it marks still another collision or collusion of writing and drawing. Because it is somehow reminiscent of a crossed-out signature, the still recognizable lettering multiplies paradoxes and analogies. While these incompletely cancelled signs tamper with convention, the straight double line crossing them has the advantage of translating writing into a musical score, thus into yet another language and another medium. It so happens that the French word "partition" and the Italian "partitura" derive etymologically from a division into parts, akin to the idea of separation inherent in "crisis." In any case, both divisions and sounds, consistent with frames and soundtracks in movies, also play a significant role in Derrida's "+R+."

Adami entitles a sequence of three drawings *Etudes pour un dessin d'après Glas*. In the exhibit "Voyage du dessin," they may not have been assigned a prominent place, for the show stressed the importance of drawing rather than of concepts in Adami's work. The drawings *d'après Glas* highlight the interaction between the philosopher and the artist by revealing the crucial importance of interpretation, of reading and writing for both creators (Figs. 4, 5). The same exhibit also refers to "Elegy for young lovers" by Auden, includes a drawing called *Autobiografia* as well as one entitled *The Portrait of Walter Benjamin*" (Fig. 6). *Autobiografia* resembles the drawings *d'après Glas* because of the use of a divided page, the refusal of any kind of centralization or marginalization, and the presence of similar handwriting. It has in common with "Les Règles du montage" a rejection of the kind of full-fledged narrative which attempts to give meaning to assorted words and dates by setting them in arbitrarily coherent sentences. While alluding to political violence, it draws parallels with *The Portrait of Benjamin*. *Autobiografia* portrays an unrecognizable self somehow related to the "Ich" that Derrida will stress in "+R+." More important still, Adami has designated this portrait by means of a purely literary term.

The painter refrains from giving his drawings *d'après Glas* a definitive status. He asserts that the sequence is no more than a study: tentative, spontaneous, in keeping with his theories in "Les Règles du montage," and Derrida's perspectives in *Glas*. Adami replaces the dou-

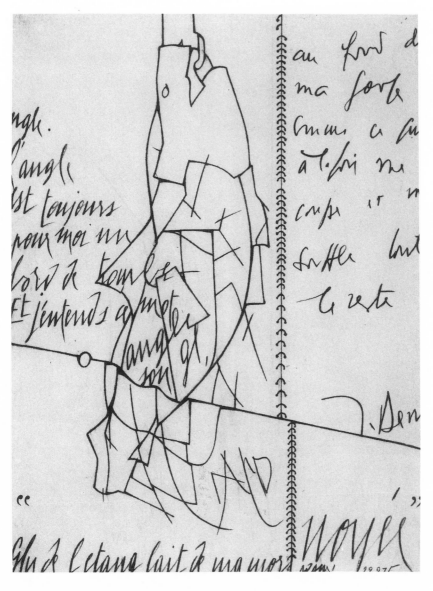

4. Valerio Adami, *Etude pour un dessin d'après "Glas,"* page from *Derrière le miroir,* no. 214.

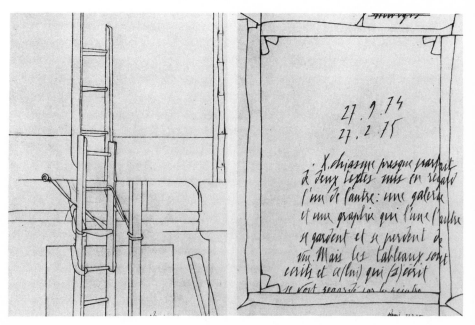

5. Valerio Adami, *Etude pour un dessin d'après "Glas,"* page from *Derrière le miroir,* no. 214.

6. Valerio Adami, *Ritratto di Walter Benjamin*

ble columned page by a double-faced drawing. By means of subdivisions, connections, and ruptures the front functions as a modified page, a translation, a transposition, a summary of lengthy texts by Derrida, Hegel, and Genet that include a multiplicity of quotations from, and references to, a wide variety of texts. Adami emphasizes Derrida's radical undercutting of writing conventions, his challenging of the single-minded page, and the new kind of readable visibility that his experiment has produced. Nor has the painter in any way disguised his handwriting or hidden his personal involvement. He suggests both verbally and graphically that in his reading of *Glas*, margins, ruptures, chiasmas, and frames, must upstage all other aspects of the work. But this substitution of graphic for discursive means has not prevented him from distorting the frame or crossing out of the word "margins," already exiled from the frame. Graphic if not verbal paradoxes are thus multiplied; enclosure and transgression are made to challenge one another other while raising all along the conjoined problematics of the canvas and the page. By such devices, the painter addresses the problematics of *Glas*, in which two texts, separated but sharing the same page and deconstructing each other from within, induce the reader to search, even if in vain, for the main discursive thrust. Thus summarized by Adami, Derrida's textualization appears to transgress margins, personify writing, treat texts as though they were writers forced alternatively to observe and lose sight of one another. By moving from text to graphics and back again, the artist has made drawing and writing interchangeable: "Mais les tableaux sont écrits et ce(lui) qui (s)'écrit se voit regardé par le peintre" (173). [But the paintings are written and the one who writes (or gets written) sees himself (or itself) looked at by the painter.] It is Derrida's turn to decipher Adami who had already (mis)quoted and decrypted other texts by the philosopher. Since Derrida in "+R+" comments on the drawings, a mise en abyme becomes inevitable. The drawing on the back of the page provides a counterpart to the front, insofar as it excludes written, curved, and rounded lines, showing instead assembled ladders as well as geometrical, horizontal, and vertical divisions moving reversibly in an upward and downward direction. And it continues to multiply frames and windows without suggesting where any of them might lead.

First published in *Derrière le miroir,* "+R+" introduces Adami's drawing exhibit "Le Voyage du dessin." The full title as it appears in the illustrated journal reads: *Le Voyage du dessin, accompagné par + R (par-dessus le marché).* Derrida's text thus functions as part of the show, metaphorically providing a musical accompaniment for the displacement of the drawings together with an ambiguous remark in (pardessus le marché) on the commercial underpinnings of all art exhibits and on the supplemental function of all critical commentary. The presence within the title of three-pronged allusiveness problematizes the margins supposedly separating art from commerce and discourse, while giving an ironic twist to the idea of a musical accompaniment. The title thus performs in the manner of many of Derrida's texts. By repeated erasure, Derrida circumscribes the field of esthetics, then transports the reader to political, historical, economic, and philosophical situations seen as indispensable supplements in written works. Adami's drawings are exposed in a double sense of the word as visible language and production. Such doubleness leads to increased plurality and makes the presence of a third partner in the association almost indispensable: that of Walter Benjamin, who wrote a key essay on the work of art in the age of mechanical reproduction. In any case, Benjamin has provided indispensable intertexts for "+R+," besides functioning as a translator in the multiple sense that Derrida gives this word. It is ultimately through Adami's *Portrait of Benjamin* that the meaning of drawing and writing comes quite literally to a head. Yet everything remains of course open-ended. Reproduced with Derrida's text, Adami's drawing of Benjamin becomes somehow verbalized. It shows in telescoped outlines the man threatened by military power crossing a border and going into exile. But this drawing that Derrida appropriates into his own problematics also reiterates "le Voyage du dessin." Adami's portrayals of writers and thinkers dwell on spatial transitions, political displacements, violence, and imminence of death. However, these allusions, these minimal outlines, these ambiguities involving absence are not primarily thematic. Derrida's simultaneously descriptive and theoretical appropriations accompany in addition a verbal voyage, generated by sounds, letters, syllables, and words. Derrida moves toward a language where meaning is never fixed, where semantics is to a large extent subverted. Sounds and syllables travel autonomously or by means of newly discovered analogies. The spatial expanse on the printed page shows recurring verbal reflections of written clusters in a constant process of modification, whereas in the drawings, the black outlines reduce almost to sign language the portrait of an author, compounding a biographical and a textual event. The inevitable link between Derrida's writing a text, ultimately including *La Vérité en peinture,* and Adami exposing his drawings partially based on his reading of *Glas* and including *The portrait of Ben-*

jamin, retranslated by Derrida, links authorships, identities, names, and signatures. "One must be several in order to write" (152), states Derrida. The presence of "da" in Derrida and Adami, of "mi" in Benjamin and Adami is stressed in Derrida's efforts to supplant logical categories and linear causalities. These syllables, these fragmentary repetitions serve to generate affinities that can be extended, echoed, silenced, or amplified at will.

"+R+" has no beginning and no end, since it neither begins with a capital letter nor ends with a period (Fig. 7). In the original edition there are no margins, so that beginning and end are denied in the layout of the page. The general subversion of meaning in language would undermine Cartesian step-by-step reasoning, leading from one certainty to the next. But the path toward doubt or, better still, toward undecidability, that Derrida's readers may follow if so inclined, does not reveal the need for a new system, for it is apt to turn back on itself in an endless pattern of reversibility: no beginning, no end. Written as if dictated by stimuli, the text, printed with seeming homogeneity and unity, features multiple interruptions and gaps which do not require to be filled or even overtaken. It forms a web without traceable patterns, so that what might have appeared to be a loose end resurfaces at a later stage of the text. Inquiry into, or play with, language can thus lead to partial collusions followed by dispersions if not by disseminations. But it would be wrong to claim that, for Derrida, in the beginning was the word. Here as elsewhere, he enters by the activity of writing into an existing world of pulsations, lines and anecdotes which will form new associations and groupings, unsuspected knots opening onto new enmeshments. The drawing, entitled "Ich" in "+ R+," combining as it does the image of a hooked fish with fragments of texts in Adami's and Derrida's handwriting, provides a response to the latter's two-columned writing in *Glas* which, again and again, subdivides into a many zones page.[8] In Derrida's response to Adami's double-columned drawing we are treated not to, let us say, a confrontation between texts by Genet and Hegel, but an up-to-the-minute handwritten exchange between Derrida and Adami. It would thus seem that (par-dessus le

8. "Among a hundred or so other drawings, it is worth recalling here two studies for a drawing 'after Glas'. They were preparations for the two works which received their titles, ICH and CHI (CHIMERES for the whole) from the following text. This text was printed in 18 point type, without margin, border or passe-partout of any kind. And is primarily concerned to explain this fact." (Note from the translators of *The Truth in Painting*, 150).

et si, le résonnement dans cette autre langue vous égarant encore, j'aimais les mots *pour trahir* (pour traiter, triturer, traîner, tramer, traquer).

Par exemple, *pour trahir* Adami, être traître à son travail, je me laisserais donner un cadre.

L'exhiberai-je sans reste ? Comment évaluer l'économie des moyens, les contraintes d'une échéance (tant de jours, mais c'est plus retors, je procède à partir d'une accumulation difficile à mesurer), d'un format (tant de signes, mais je plie et multiplie les tropes, surdétermine les codes, engrosse les langues et les marges, capitalise l'ellipse, jusqu'à un certain point qui me regarde mais que je vois mal), et puis ce qu'ils appellent les conditions-de-la-reproduction, le marché-de-la-peinture : mais aussi de la signature, de l'écriture et même, ici prise en compte, de la rature.

Il dessinait à la gomme, le voici qui rature.

Que fait-il, lui, du marché, des cadres et des marges?
En parler de toute évidence ne lui suffit pas. Ni l'énoncé de thèses *à ce sujet*. Benjamin, ici portraituré, enjoint à *L'auteur comme producteur* : qu'il ne se contente pas de prendre position, par des discours, *au sujet* de la société et que jamais, fût-ce de thèses ou de produits révolutionnaires, il n'approvisionne un appareil de production sans transformer la structure même de l'appareil, sans le tordre, le trahir, l'attirer hors de son élément. Après l'avoir piégé, l'ayant d'un mauvais coup pris au mot ou au mors.
Ici même, voyez, il a forcé un cadre. Il l'a mis à nu et retourné, s'acharnant à disloquer les angles, fouillant les encoignures. *A tergo,* laissant croire qu'on pouvait tourner autour, faire un tour de propriété, passer derrière la reproduction spéculaire.
Mais où le dos fait face, le texte était déjà : lettres initiales *déjà* écrites de ce que vous croyez être *sa* main par quelqu'un qui écrit ici *moi*, disant (quoi? lisez, regardez) ici maintenant, mais depuis toujours entraînées dans *Glas* par une incroyable scène de séduction entre Rembrandt et Genet. Avec passage à l'acte, bien sûr, comme on entend la séduction dans la psychanalyse.
Mettant le cadre en avant, le poussant sur la scène, maltraité, sous les projecteurs, il a barré *marges*, il a écrit, donc raturé, ce qu'il faisait; il a dessiné, trait pour trait, ce qu'il écrivait, ce qu'il raturait plutôt : ces *Marges* que je tenterais en vain de me réapproprier comme une rente ou un titre.
Pour ce double geste, et ce mobile d'une citation, déjà, de la double gravure (disque et dessin), *Concerto per un quadro di Adami*, il lui fallait deux fois deux mains. Il compose, il

7. Jacques Derrida, first page of "+R+" from *Derrière le miroir,* no. 214.

marché) was actually generated by their double signature on the drawing, which necessarily combines sectionalized writing and graphics, as well as by the more complete image of the fish. "Ich" becomes imbricated or implicated in the net in which it was caught. Origin does not matter since thematically, philosophically, and strategically, Derrida has reached back to *Glas* and, further still, to Genet's concern about mortal treason. The text becomes intricately interwoven with the drawing whose own ingredients have been borrowed from *Glas*, insofar as it has brought to the surface from the depth of the sea the shadows and illuminations of fragments capable of providing further progress in the "voyage du dessin" toward parts unknown. Derrida's words create a trajectory abounding in surprises and complications by alternatively focusing on a single drawing or on a sequence. One can no more isolate a drawing from the exhibition than Derrida's accompanying text from the show. The latter's network of quotations is "schemed" and "caught," "in order to take it from him in turn and hold it at the end of my line" (157) in the same manner that "Freud et la scène de l'écriture,"[9] *Concerto a quattro mani, Marges de la philosophie,* and *Freud in viaggio verso Londra* crossfertilize one another, not as framed separate works, but as atoms of life or pulsating memories. There is no beginning or end, as there is no origin to Derrida's text. And language without quotation is no longer possible in "Les Règles du montage." Adami had also mentioned the impossibility of disregarding earlier art, of starting from scratch.

In looking at the spiral double page of the exercise book which allows the notion of "Etude" to become visible while referring to both writing and drawing, Derrida suggests the almost labyrinthian twists and turns that hold the authors together. By designating Adami as author, Derrida obliterates by still another device the line that separates drawing from writing. The philosopher comments on the double page which has been fractured and divided on the outer border. The spiral link occupying a central position once again raises the question of originality and, of course, origin. Indeed, Derrida's signature on the drawing is not original but reproduced. The reader thus faces the reproduction of a reproduction. This signature becomes almost as much Adami's as Derrida's, since it belongs to the drawing. This constant shift from one medium to another generates a double language by reciprocal appropriations of verbal and visual signs. The texts by Der-

9. Derrida, *L'Ecriture et la différence,* 293–340.

rida and Adami are so heavily sectionalized in the drawing that they cannot be deciphered according to content. As a result, their narrative continuity or coherence is completely undermined. These fragmented pieces of writing come very close to drawing. In Derrida's handwritten passage, only a few words are highlighted: "Ma gorge," "coupe," "souffle." Nonetheless, they can provide a minimal narrative concerning the hooked fish outlined in the middle of the page. The words "à la fois" and "comme" corroborate the validity of this analogy which establishes the relations between the two handwritten texts, reflects the two columns of *Glas,* and shows the impossibility of deriving a unidirectional meaning. Whereas Derrida's key words point to death and violence, relevant to the hanging fish, Adami's "tomber" and "noyé" pursue the allusions to death, programmed in the title, so central to *Glas.* It would, however, be misleading to consider the outlines of the fish as pure drawing or the texts as pure writing, since the reader's eye moves down the page or even plunges until it drowns, thus repeating in a sense the downward direction, the fall of Genet's presence in *Glas.* The outlines of the fish become loose, ultimately to be transformed into a scribble. And even this apparent order is subverted by a horizontal fold. As in other works by Adami, the folded-over page proves to be double, since parts are necessarily hidden by folding. As a result, displacement, collusion, and duplication are shifted onto another level. It is therefore hardly surprising that Adami has included *Concerto a quattro mani* in his exhibition, and that it is reproduced with Derrida's text (Fig. 8).[1] This drawing returns in multiple ways to the problematics of *Glas.* As the concerto is played by four hands, or two players, the drawing implicitly represents the relationship between Derrida and Adami who work together without collaborating in a conventional sense, who accompany each other through counterpoint. Adami provided not only the drawing but its mirror image, one more double, looking and being looked at, the self and the other.

If in *Glas* the reader has to generate meaningful relationships by moving from one text to another, or to a word in the other text, or by reading between the two texts, in (par-dessus le marché) the reader moves, while often addressing the same problematics, between drawing and writing, in this instance, much more closely interwoven. Indeed, the seemingly arbitrary juxtaposition of texts in *Glas* no longer applies here. Interpreters have mentioned the patriarchal and matriarchal opposition between Hegel and Genet, but such considerations would hardly explain the pages of *Derrière le miroir.* Derrida points out

8. Valerio Adami, *Concerto a quattro mani.*

that Adami's drawings, which do not relate to specific sections in *Glas*, cannot be treated as illustrations. In (par-dessus le marché) they function to a certain extent in the manner of documentation for a critical text. Derrida's refutation of the idea of illustration seems crucial, all the more so because the drawings function in his text as just another accompaniment. Moreover, these drawings, which do not provide embellishments or interpretations of the text, cannot be and should not be related to specific passages. Actually, they provide new stimulations more intense than other intertexts to which category in many respects they belong. They transfer the book's problematics; they accomplish what Derrida claims to have done in (par-dessus le marché): "traîter, triturer, traîner, tramer, tracer, traquer," (171) [to treat, triturate, trail, in-trigue, trace, track] (151), a complex set of operations which condenses and disperses the uniqueness of *Glas*. Derrida functions as the painter's translator, a painter beset with multilingual associations to which the translator cannot remain faithful. In such "infidelity" lies a deep complicity between the painter and the philosopher, a complicity that may also provide a clue to Derrida's affinities with Genet.

As we have seen throughout Derrida's text, the double plays a significant role. He significantly translates "the double bind" as "la double bande." To begin with, the issue of translation refers to a double in language, to the same as well as the other. Neither one is fixed, and Derrida concentrates on language in transition rather than on discourse leading to solutions. As I have already suggested, *Concerto a quattro mani* reveals the overlapping hands of absent players. The performing hands recurring in Adami's art, just as the scene, the event, and the scenario, are part of Derrida's vocabulary. In his (par-dessus le marché), the gestures of writing emerge within the space of the margin-less text. Derrida accompanies Adami's drawings on their trip. His accompaniment is neither muted nor subordinated, for all traces require the same undivided attention on the part of the reader.

Contributors

Jan Baetens teaches French at the Antwerp Business School (Belgium) and is the author of four books. His most recent work, *Les Mesures de l'excès* (1992), is a study of the avant-garde novels of Renaud Camus. He has recently completed two book-length manuscripts on the photographic novel and on contemporary French poetry. He is currently writing a series of photographic fictions with the Czechoslovakian artist Milan Chlumsky.

Yves Bonnefoy, France's great lyric poet, holds a chair at the Collège de France and has been a visiting professor at Yale University many times. Among his many recent volumes of poetry is *Ce qui fut sans lumière* (1987). He is a renowned verse translator and has produced French versions of works by Shakespeare and Yeats. He is particularly interested in painting and is the author of a monumental work on Giacometti, *Alberto Giacometti, biographie d'une œuvre* (1991).

Serge Bourjea is Director of the Centre d'études valéryennes at the Université de Montpellier and editor of its review, the *Bulletin des études valéryennes*. He is a member of the Institute of Modern Texts and Manuscripts and of the C.N.R.S. Last spring he was a visiting professor at U.C.L.A. in the department of French.

Alain Buisine is Professor of Modern and Contemporary French Literature at the Université Charles de Gaulle, Lille III. He is the author of numerous essays and has edited several anthologies, including *La Lettre d'écrivain*, *L'Exotisme*, and *Le Biographique*. His current work is directed specifically at the relationship between literature and photography, literature and painting. His new volume, *Atget ou la mélancolie en photographie* is forthcoming.

YFS 84, *Boundaries: Writing & Drawing*, ed. M. Reid, © 1994 by Yale University.

MICHEL BUTOR began his literary career in the wake of the *Nouveau Roman* movement with the publication of *Passage de Milan* in 1954. With *Mobile, Etude pour une représentation des Etats-Unis* (1962), he began to distance himself little by little from "traditional" literature in order to work more closely with contemporary artists and painters (including Dotremont and Alechinsky), about whom and with whom he has published many volumes.

CHRISTINE CANO is a Ph.D. candidate in the department of French at Yale University.

MARY ANN CAWS is Distinguished Professor of English, French, and Comparative Literature at the Graduate School, City University of New York. She is the author of many books on art, poetics, and literature, including *The Eye in the Text: Essays on Perception, Mannerist to Modern; The Art of Interference, Women of Bloomsbury;* and *Robert Motherwell: What Art Holds.* She is the Chief Editor of the Harper Collins *World Reader.*

JACQUES DERRIDA has for some time shown an active interest in the plastic arts. He published *La Vérité en peinture* in 1978, and since then he has been particularly interested in the graphic works of Antonin Artaud which he commented with Paule Thévenin. He has organized an exhibition at the Musée du Louvre on blindness in painting, accompanied by his *Mémoires d'aveugle* (1990). He currently is Directeur d'Etudes at the Ecole des Hautes Etudes en Sciences Sociales (Paris) and teaches at the University of California at Irvine.

MADELEINE DOBIE is a Ph.D. candidate in the French Department at Yale University and is completing a dissertation on figures of Oriental women in eighteenth- and nineteenth-century texts.

CLAUDE GANDELMAN was chairman of the French Department at the University of Haifa, Israel. He received his Ph.D. in Comparative Literature at the Sorbonne, Paris. His most recent books are: *Le Regard dans le texte: image et écriture du quattrocento au XXème siècle* (1986) and *Reading Pictures/Viewing Texts* (1991). He is co-editor of the Italian comparative literature journal *Athanor,* published at Bari University.

NOAH GUYNN is a Ph.D. candidate in the French department at Yale University and an editorial assistant at *Yale French Studies.*

PETER HALLWARD is a Ph.D. candidate in the French department at Yale University.

RENÉE RIESE HUBERT is Professor Emerita of Comparative Literature and French at the University of California. She has published six volumes of poetry in France as well as many articles on Surrealism, the Book Arts, Art and Literature and Women Artists. Her *Surrealism and the Book* appeared in 1988 and again in 1992, and her *Magnifying Mirrors: Women, Surrealism and Partnership* is forthcoming from the University of Nebraska Press.

JEAN-GÉRARD LAPACHERIE is Maître de Conférences at the Université Paul Valéry (Montpellier). He has published several articles on questions relating to writing as a "system of signs" and on artistic practice.

JACQUES LEENHARDT is currently Directeur du Groupe of Sociology and Literature at the Ecole des Hautes Etudes en Sciences Sociales (Paris) and President of the Association Internationale des Critiques d'Art. He has published several volumes, among which are *Lecture politique du roman* (1973); *Lire la lecture* (1982); *La Force des mots* (1982); *Existe-t-il un lecteur européen?* (1989); *Au Jardin des malentendus* (1990); and *Les Amériques latines en France* (1992).

ANNA LEHMANN is a Ph.D. candidate in the department of French at Yale University.

CAREN LITHERLAND is a Ph.D. candidate in the department of French at Yale University.

DIDIER MALEUVRE has recently completed a dissertation on French nineteenth-century literature in the department of French at Yale University. He is currently teaching French literature at the University of California at Santa Barbara.

JOHN T. NAUGHTON is Associate Professor of French literature at Colgate University. He has published widely in the area of modern French poetry and is the author of *The Poetics of Yves Bonnefoy*. He is the editor of *The Act and the Place of Poetry* and the translator of Bonnefoy's *Ce qui fut sans lumière*, which appears in English as *In the Shadow's Light*. All three books were published by the University of Chicago Press. A critical study of Louis-René des Forêts and a bilingual anthology of Bonnefoy's poetry which he edited are forthcoming.

MARTINE REID taught at Yale University for nine years before accepting the position of department chair of the French department at the University Antonio de Nebrija in Madrid. She published her *Stendhal en images* in 1991 and is currently preparing a volume on Flaubert's correspondence.

GEORGES ROQUE is a researcher at the C.N.R.S., Paris and is currently in residence at the Instituto de Investigaciones Estéticas de la

UNAM (Universidad National Autonoma de México). He has published several volumes including *Ceci n'est pas un Magritte* and is currently completing a work on the relationship between art and the science of color.

MICHEL THÉVOZ has been the curator of the Musée cantonal des beaux-arts de Lausanne and of the Collection de l'art brut since its creation in 1975. He is also a professor of Art history at the Université de Lausanne and has written many books relating aesthetics to psychoanalysis and sociology. One of these has been translated into English: *The Painted Body* (1984).

JOHN THOMPSON is a Ph.D. candidate in the department of French at Yale University and is currently completing a dissertation on translation and thirteenth-century French prose hagiography, particularly in the works of Wauchier of Denain.

SERGE TISSERON is a psychiatrist and psychoanalyst and also teaches at the Université de Paris VII. For some time he has been interested in the articulation of material images and psychical images and in the role of drawing in the construction of the psychological apparatus. He has published numerous articles and several volumes, notably: *Tintin chez le psychanalyste* (1985); *Psychanalyse de la bande dessinée* (1987); *Tintin et les secrets de famille* (1992); and *La Honte, psychanalyse d'un lien social* (1992).

NIGEL P. TURNER is Professeur Agrégé at the Université de Paris, Créteil.

BERNARD VOUILLOUX is Maître de Conférences at the Université Michel de Montaigne, Bordeaux III. After publishing several books and articles on the works of Julien Gracq, he dedicated himself to research on pictorial reference in literary texts and on the theoretical articulation of language and painting.

CARRIE WEBER is a Ph.D. candidate in the department of French at Yale University.

LAURA HARWOOD WITTMAN is a Ph.D. candidate in the Italian department at Yale University and specializes in medieval, nineteenth- and twentieth-century Italian, French, and English literature, especially poetry. She recently spent a year at the University of Bologna on a Fulbright scholarship.

The following issues are available through **Yale University Press,** Customer Service Department, 92A Yale Station, New Haven, CT 06520.

63 The Pedagogical Imperative: Teaching as a Literary Genre (1982) $17.00

64 Montaigne: Essays in Reading (1983) $17.00

65 The Language of Difference: Writing in QUEBEC(ois) (1983) $17.00

66 The Anxiety of Anticipation (1984) $17.00

67 Concepts of Closure (1984) $17.00

68 Sartre after Sartre (1985) $17.00

69 The Lesson of Paul de Man (1985) $17.00

70 Images of Power: Medieval History/Discourse/ Literature (1986) $17.00

71 Men/Women of Letters: Correspondence (1986) $17.00

72 Simone de Beauvoir: Witness to a Century (1987) $17.00

73 Everyday Life (1987) $17.00

74 Phantom Proxies (1988) $17.00

75 The Politics of Tradition: Placing Women in French Literature (1988) $17.00

Special Issue: After the Age of Suspicion: The French Novel Today (1989) $17.00

76 Autour de Racine: Studies in Intertextuality (1989) $17.00

77 Reading the Archive: On Texts and Institutions (1990) $17.00

78 On Bataille (1990) $17.00

79 Literature and the Ethical Question (1991) $17.00

Special Issue: Contexts: Style and Value in Medieval Art and Literature (1991) $17.00

80 Baroque Topographies: Literature/History/ Philosophy $17.00

81 On Leiris (1992) $17.00

82 Post/Colonial Conditions Vol. 1

83 Post/Colonial Conditions Vol. 2

Special subscription rates are available on a calendar year basis (2 issues per year):

Individual subscriptions $24.00   Institutional subscriptions $28.00

ORDER FORM   **Yale University Press,** 92A Yale Station, New Haven, CT 06520

I would like to purchase the following individual issues:

_____

_____

For individual issue, please add postage and handling:

Single issue, United States $2.75   Each additional issue $.50

Connecticut residents please add sales tax of 6%

Single issue, foreign countries $5.00   Each additional issue $1.00

Payment of $_____ is enclosed (including sales tax if applicable).

Mastercard no. _____

4-digit bank no._____Expiration date_____

VISA no._____Expiration date _____

Signature _____

SHIP TO _____

_____

_____

See the next page for ordering other back issues. Yale French Studies is also available through Xerox University Microfilms, 300 North Zeeb Road, Ann Arbor, MI 48106.

The following issues are still available through the **Yale French Studies Office,** 2504A Yale Station, New Haven, CT 06520.

19/20 Contemporary Art $3.50

33 Shakespeare $3.50

35 Sade $3.50

38 The Classical Line $3.50

39 Literature and Revolution $3.50

41 Game, Play, Literature $5.00

42 Zola $5.00

43 The Child's Part $5.00

44 Paul Valéry $5.00

45 Language as Action $5.00

46 From Stage to Street $3.50

47 Image & Symbol in the Renaissance $3.50

52 Graphesis $5.00

53 African Literature $3.50

54 Mallarmé $5.00

57 Locus in Modern French

Fiction: Space, Landscape, Decor $6.00

58 In Memory of Jacques Ehrmann $6.00

59 Rethinking History $6.00

61 Toward a Theory of Description $6.00

62 Feminist Readings: French Texts/American Contexts $6.00

Add for postage & handling

One-Two Issues, United States $2.90 (Priority Mail)   Each additional issue $.50

Single issue, United States $1.75 (Third Class)   Each additional issue $.50

Single issue, foreign countries $2.50   Each additional issue $1.50

YALE FRENCH STUDIES, 2504A Yale Station, New Haven, Connecticut 06520

A check made payable to YFS is enclosed. Please send me the following issue(s):

Issue no.   Title   Price

_____

_____

Postage & handling   _____

Total   _____

Name_____

Number/Street _____

City_____ State _____ Zip_____

The following issues are now available through Kraus Reprint Company, Route 100, Millwood, N. Y. 10546.

1 Critical Bibliography of Existentialism
2 Modern Poets
3 Criticism & Creation
4 Literature & Ideas
5 The Modern Theatre
6 France and World Literature
7 André Gide
8 What's Novel in the Novel
9 Symbolism
10 French-American Literature Relationships
11 Eros, Variations...
12 God & the Writer
13 Romanticism Revisited
14 Motley: Today's French Theater
15 Social & Political France
16 Foray through Existentialism

17 The Art of the Cinema
18 Passion & the Intellect, or Malraux
21 Poetry Since the Liberation
22 French Education
24 Midnight Novelists
25 Albert Camus
26 The Myth of Napoleon
27 Women Writers
28 Rousseau
29 The New Dramatists
30 Sartre
31 Surrealism
32 Paris in Literature
34 Proust
48 French Freud
51 Approaches to Medieval Romance

36/37 Structuralism has been reprinted by Doubleday as an Anchor Book.

55/56 Literature and Psychoanalysis has been reprinted by Johns Hopkins University Press, and can be ordered through Customer Service, Johns Hopkins University Press, Baltimore, MD 21218.